LIGHT IN THE DARK
LUZ EN LO OSCURO

LIGHT IN THE DARK
LUZ EN LO OSCURO

REWRITING IDENTITY, SPIRITUALITY, REALITY

GLORIA E. ANZALDÚA

EDITED BY
ANALOUISE KEATING

DUKE UNIVERSITY PRESS

DURHAM AND LONDON 2015

Library of Congress Cataloging-in-Publication Data
Anzaldúa, Gloria, author.
Light in the dark = Luz en lo oscuro : rewriting identity, spirituality,
reality / Gloria E. Anzaldúa ; edited by AnaLouise Keating.
pages cm—(Latin America otherwise : languages, empires, nations)
Includes bibliographical references and index.
ISBN 978-0-8223-5977-7 (hardcover : alk. paper)
ISBN 978-0-8223-6009-4 (pbk. : alk. paper)
ISBN 978-0-8223-7503-6 (e-book)
1. Anzaldúa, Gloria. 2. Creation (Literary, artistic, etc.) 3. Identity
(Psychology) 4. Mexican American women. I. Keating, AnaLouise,
1961– editor. II. Title. III. Title: Luz en lo oscuro. IV. Series: Latin
America otherwise.
PS3551.N95Z46 2015
818'.5409—dc23
[B]
2015014083

Cover art: Illustration by Natalie F. Smith using details of
Coyolxauhqui (figure FM.1)

DEDICO ESTE LIBRO A LAS MEMORIAS DE MIS ABUELAS Y
ESPECIALMENTE QUE TANTO SUFRIERON Y AGUANTARON Y ALIMENTARON
A HIJAS/OS, AMANTES Y AMIGAS

CONTENTS

‘

EDITOR'S INTRODUCTION

Re-envisioning Coyolxauhqui, Decolonizing Reality

Anzaldúa's Twenty-First-Century Imperative

AnaLouise Keating

For me, writing is a gesture of the body, a gesture of creativity, a working from the inside out. My feminism is grounded not on incorporeal abstraction but on corporeal realities. The material body is center, and central. The body is the ground of thought.

GLORIA ANZALDÚA, "PREFACE: GESTURES OF THE BODY"

What is the theme of my life's work? Is it accessing other realities?

GLORIA ANZALDÚA, WRITING NOTAS

In *Light in the Dark/Luz en lo oscuro—Rewriting Identity, Spirituality, Reality*, Gloria Anzaldúa excavates her creative process (her "gestures of the body") and uses this excavation to develop an aesthetics of transformation, grounded in her metaphysics of interconnectedness.[1] From the late 1980s, when she entered the doctoral program in literature at the University of California, Santa Cruz (UCSC), until her death in 2004, Anzaldúa aspired to write a book-length exploration of aesthetics and knowledge production as they are inflected through, and shaped by, issues of social justice, identity (trans)formation, and healing.[2] She viewed this project both as her dissertation and as a publishable monograph, although, as explained in more detail later, she did not follow a typical dissertation process. Thoroughly researched and repeatedly revised, this manuscript underwent numerous shifts in title, table of contents, and chapter organization; it exists in numerous partial iterations—handwritten notes, outlines, chapter drafts, e-mail communication, conversations with writing comadres, and computer files.[3] Because of her meticulous revision practices and various complicated life issues (including financial pressures, multiple simultaneous writing projects, philosophical changes in worldview, and diabetes-related health complications), Anzaldúa did not see this book through to publication. However, she was in the final stages of its completion at the time of her death.

Focusing closely on aesthetics, ontology, epistemology, and ethics, *Light in the Dark* investigates a number of intertwined issues, including the artist-activist's struggles; imagination as an embodied intellectual faculty that, with careful attention and specific strategies, can effect personal and social transformation; the creative process; decolonial alternatives to conventional nationalism; and more. *Light in the Dark* also contains important developments in Anzaldúa's theories of nepantla and nepantleras, spiritual activism, new tribalism, nos/otras, conocimiento, autohistoria, and autohistoria-teoría, as well as additional insights into her writing practice and her intellectual-physiological experiences with diabetes.[4] In this introduction, I showcase Anzaldúa as a multifaceted artist-scholar and offer background information about the complicated history of this book.[5] I summarize Anzaldúa's recursive writing and revision process and situate *Light in the Dark* within the context of her oeuvre; describe the state of the manuscript at the time of her passing; explore Anzaldúa's potential contributions to twenty-first-century continental philosophy and feminist thought (especially neo-materialisms, object-oriented ontology, and debates concerning the so-called linguistic turn); and speculate on some of the ways this book might affect Anzaldúan scholarship. I begin by summarizing Anzaldúa's complex recursive writing and revision process because this process is key to the history of her book.

Anzaldúa's writing process

Through a serendipitous series of events, I met Gloria Anzaldúa in 1991 and was fortunate to become one of her "writing comadres." I had known her only a few days when she gave me a draft of one of her Prieta stories to read and critique. She treated me not as an awestruck fan but, rather, as a colleague with valuable insights.[6] I was amazed by her gesture. There I was: an unknown, a nobody, stumbling through the very early stages of my career, and yet the creator of three ground-breaking books (*Borderlands/La Frontera*, *This Bridge Called My Back*, and *Making Face, Making Soul*) was giving *me* her manuscripts, asking *me* for feedback—for detailed, very specific commentary about her work. I was struck by Anzaldúa's intellectual-aesthetic humility, by her willingness to share her unfinished writings with others, and by the partial state of the manuscript itself. To be sure, it was a captivating story (good plot line, great characterization, interesting ideas, powerful metaphors, captivating dialogue, and so on); however, the draft was uneven and needed more work. (In fact, Anzaldúa had interspersed revision-related questions throughout the draft.) Because I had assumed that Anzaldúa's words flowed effortlessly and perfectly from her pen and keyboard, I was startled to realize the extent of her revision process. I am not alone in this type of Anzaldúan encounter. If you look through her archival materials, you'll see that she regularly shared work in progress with others.[7]

As this anecdote suggests, Anzaldúa's approach to writing was dialogic, recursive, democratic, spirit-inflected, and only partially within her conscious control. She relied extensively on intuition, imagination, and what she describes in this book as her "naguala." As she explains in the preface,

> I'm guided by the spirit of the image. My naguala (daimon or guiding spirit) is an inner sensibility that directs my life—an image, an action, or an internal experience.[8] My imagination and my naguala are connected—they are aspects of the same process, of creativity. Often my naguala draws to me things that are contrary to my will and purpose (compulsions, addictions, negativities), resulting in an anguished impasse. Overcoming these impasses becomes part of the process.

And what a process it was! Anzaldúa's writing process entailed multiple simultaneous projects; numerous drafts of each piece; extensive revisions of each draft; excruciatingly painful writing blocks; linkages and repetition among various writing projects; and peer critiques from her "writing comadres," editors, and others.[9]

Generally, Anzaldúa began a new project by meditating, visualizing, freewriting, and collecting diverse source materials; these materials were often hybrid and apparently random, including some or all of the following: dreams, meditations, journal entries, films she had seen, thoughts scribbled in notebooks and on pieces of paper, article clippings, scholarly books, observations from her interactions with human and nonhuman others, lecture notes, transcripts from previous lectures and interviews, and other "writing notas."[10] To create a first draft (or what she describes in chapter 5 as her first "pre-draft"), she would pull together various assemblages of these materials, following a few key headers or topic points as revealed through her free writes. This pre-draft was often quite rough, containing very short paragraphs and lacking transitions, logical organization, and other conventional writing elements. After completing several pre-drafts, Anzaldúa developed her first draft, which she would then begin to revise. She reread this draft multiple times, making extensive changes that involved some or all of the following acts: rearranging individual words, entire sentences, and paragraphs; adding or deleting large chunks of material; copying and repeating especially significant phrases; and inserting material from other works in progress.

Throughout this process, Anzaldúa focused simultaneously on content and form. She wanted the words to move in readers' bodies and transform them, from the inside out, and she revised repeatedly to achieve this impact. She revised for cadence, musicality, nuanced meaning, and metaphoric complexity. Anzaldúa repeated this revision step numerous times, at some point re-saving the draft under a new name and sharing it with one or more of her "writing comadres," requesting both specific and general comments, which she then selectively incorporated into future revisions. After revising multiple times, Anzaldúa moved on to proofreading and editing the draft. At some point, she would either send the draft out for publication or put it away, to be worked on at a later date.[11]

As this serpentine process suggests, for Anzaldúa, writing was epistemological, intuitive, and communal. Like many authors, she did not sit down at her keyboard with a fully developed idea and a logically organized outline. She generated her ideas as she wrote; the writing process was, itself, a co-creator of the theories—a co-author of sorts. As she explained in a 1991 interview, "I discover what I'm trying to say as the writing progresses."[12] She often began with a question, a personal experience, or a feeling; she worked through these seedling ideas as she wrote and revised, and she did so in ways only partially under her conscious control. The words took on lives of their own, morphing in ways that Anzaldúa didn't expect when she sat down to write. In short, she learned as she wrote; she developed her ideas as she revised. And for Anzaldúa, revision could be endless. One could argue that completion—final satisfaction—never exists in Anzaldúa's writing process. She has her own version of what Ralph Waldo Emerson calls "the Unattainable, the flying Perfect, around which the hands . . . can never meet, at once the inspirer and the condemner of every success." Even after publishing her work, she continued to revise it.[13]

Nowhere is this process more evident (and more confounding) than in Anzaldúa's creation of *Light in the Dark/Luz en lo oscuro*.

History of the Book(s)

Because Anzaldúa described *Light in the Dark* as her dissertation and viewed it as a continuation of her earlier dissertation work, I anchor this book's history in the story of her doctoral education. From 1974 to 1977, Anzaldúa was enrolled in the doctoral program in comparative literature at the University of Texas, Austin, where she focused on "Spanish literature, feminist theory, and Chicano literature."[14] Disappointed by the program's restrictions and determined to devote her life to her writing, she left before advancing to candidacy.[15] Fast-forward twelve years to 1988, when Anzaldúa, then living in San Francisco, decided to return to graduate school and complete her degree. She believed that enrolling in a doctoral program would enable her to prioritize her intellectual growth while offering protection from being overused as a resource (guest speaker, consultant, editor, and so on) for others. As she explained in an unpublished 1989 interview with Kate McCafferty, "Being back in school gives me access to more books, the latest theories and fellowship, while getting credit for it. I need this kind of environment to get a handle on my life. After *Borderlands* I was very much in demand in terms of attending a class or a reading. . . . Being too much out in the world was not balanced by my time at home."[16] Returning to graduate school—a location designed to foster the life of the mind—enabled Anzaldúa to prioritize her writing, obtain scholarly resources at a first-class university library, access a community of scholars who could give her critical feedback on her work, and hone her academic writing skills.[17] And so in 1988, Anzaldúa enrolled in the doctoral program in literature at the University of California, Santa Cruz.[18]

Even before she began taking classes, Anzaldúa had a sense of her dissertation topic, which would focus on literary representation, ethnic identity, and knowledge production. As she asserts in a 1990 interview with Hector Torres, "My goal was to put together this book on the mestiza and how she deals with space and identity."[19] Anzaldúa moved quickly through the program requirements and in fall 1991 began drafting her dissertation/book project. I describe this project as "dissertation/book" to underscore its liminality—its position "betwixt and between" conventional genres. Although Anzaldúa called it a dissertation and even selected a dissertation committee and chair, she did not follow conventional procedures, which typically include finalizing, submitting, and receiving faculty feedback on a prospectus; discussing the project with a dissertation committee; submitting chapter drafts to committee members and receiving feedback from them on these drafts; and revising drafts based on this feedback. In no point in her writing process did Anzaldúa interact with her dissertation committee in any of these ways.[20] Yet the fact that she viewed this project as both her dissertation and a publishable book subtly shaped her authorial decisions and voice.[21]

Anzaldúa viewed her dissertation/book project as an opportunity to return to and expand on several aesthetic-related themes from her previous work (especially *Borderlands/La Frontera* and "Speaking in Tongues: A Letter to Third World Women Writers"). As she explained in a 1995 interview with Ann Reuman:

> Chapter Six [of *Borderlands*], on writing and art, was put together really fast. . . . I felt like I was still regurgitating and sitting on some of the ideas and I hadn't done enough revisions and I didn't have enough time to unravel the ideas fully. Chapter Six . . . is an extension of "Speaking in Tongues" in *This Bridge*, and what I'm writing now in *Lloronas*, some of the concepts I'm working with, of which one is nepantla, is kind of a continuation of these other two. . . . [M]y writing is always in revision . . . The theoretical work in process, *Lloronas*, builds on all those that came before.[22]

Variously titled *Lloronas—Women Who Wail: (Self)Representation and the Production of Writing, Knowledge and Identity*; *Lloronas, mujeres que leen y escriben: Producing Writing, Knowledge, Cultures, and Identities*; and *Lloronas—Writing, Reading, Speaking, Dreaming*, Anzaldúa's projected dissertation/book focused on writing as personal and collective knowledge production by the "female post-colonial cultural Other (particularly the Chicana/mestiza)."[23] As these titles imply, la Llorona played a significant role in the 1990s versions. In chapter drafts, notes, conversations about the project, and public lectures from this time period, Anzaldúa explored diverse interpretations of Llorona's historical, mythic, and rhetorical manifestations. She aspired to include and go beyond the existing stories and analyses to offer both an archeology and a phenomenology of this multifaceted figure. As she writes in a chapter draft titled "Llorona, the Woman Who Wails: Chicana/Mestiza Transgressive Identities":

> As myth, the nocturnal site of [Llorona's] ghostly "body" is the place, el lugar, where myth, fantasy, utterance, and reality converge. It is the site of intersection, connection, and cultural transgression. Her "body" is comprised of all four bodies: the physical, psychic (which I explore in the chapter "*Las Pasiones de la Llorona*"), mythic/symbolic, and ghostly. La Llorona, the ghostly body, carries the nagual possessing la facultad, the capacity for shape-changing and shape-shifting of identity.[24]

Anzaldúa's shifting, mobile Llorona is especially significant as we consider her project's evolution from the twentieth-century to the twenty-first-century versions, where Llorona becomes partially eclipsed by Coyolxauhqui, Mexica lunar goddess and Coatlicue's eldest daughter.[25]

Anzaldúa worked intermittently throughout the 1990s on her "Lloronas book." Despite her extensive research, her passion for the project, and her commitment to completing her doctoral degree, she did not finish this manuscript—or even finalize her prospectus or meet with her dissertation committee. Instead, she has left us with a lengthy table of contents, lots of ideas, jotted notes, interview comments, and chapter drafts in various stages of completion.[26] As she observes in an e-mail from June 2002, "I finished all but dissertation in 3 years but then took a huge sabbatical & didn't return to [the] dissertation until last Oct."[27]

There are many reasons for this "huge sabbatical," including Anzaldúa's health, financial concerns, commitment to multiple writing projects (including some with fixed deadlines for completion), her complicated revision process, and her unrealistically high aesthetic standards. In 1992, Anzaldúa was diagnosed with type 1 diabetes.[28] This diagnosis altered her life on almost every level, forcing her to re-examine her self-definition, her relationship to her body, her writing process, and her worldview. Like many people diagnosed with a chronic illness, Anzaldúa first reacted with disbelief, denial, anger, and self-blame.[29] Gradually she shifted into a more complex understanding and pragmatic acceptance of the disease. However, processing the diagnosis, researching diabetes, learning treatment options, and securing adequate health insurance to pay for treatment and medicine consumed much of Anzaldúa's energy during the mid-1990s.

Indeed, managing the diabetes was an enormous drain on Anzaldúa for the remainder of her life. She often spent hours each day researching the latest treatments and diligently working to manage the disease. She kept up to date on medical and alternative health breakthroughs and recommendations; ate healthy food, exercised regularly, and monitored her blood glucose (sugar) levels repeatedly throughout the day; carefully coordinated her exercise and her food intake with her blood levels and insulin injections; and kept a detailed daily log of her blood sugar levels and necessary dosages, making minute adjustments as necessary. In addition to following a conventional treatment plan (insulin injections and regular medical visits), Anzaldúa explored a variety of alternative healing techniques, including meditation, herbs, acupuncture, affirmations, subliminal tapes, and visualizations. Despite these strenuous efforts, her blood sugar often careened out of control, leading to additional complications, including severe gastrointestinal reflux, charcoat foot, neuropathy, vision problems (blurred vision and burst capillaries requiring laser surgery), thyroid malfunction, and depression. Constant worry about her declining health put additional strains on Anzaldúa, intensifying the insomnia that had plagued her for much of her life. This insomnia clouded her thinking and interfered with her work, leading to even more delays.[30]

Anzaldúa's financial concerns—which were, themselves, made more challenging and dire by her costly medical needs—also contributed to her delayed completion of the Lloronas book.[31] As a full-time, self-employed author, Anzaldúa did not have a steady source of income but instead relied on publication royalties and speaking engagements to support herself. Because she did not have an agent or manager, Anzaldúa generally organized her own speaking engagements, which entailed booking the gigs, negotiating rates, making travel plans, and coordinating all related details with the conference organizers. This, too, took a lot of time.

Anzaldúa's complicated multitasking further contributed to her "huge sabbatical." Throughout the 1990s, Anzaldúa worked on multiple writing projects simultaneously, moving back and forth among manuscripts, often juggling more than a dozen projects. Thus, for example, in a journal entry dated August 20, 1990 (written at 4:20 in the morning), she lists her current "Writing Projects": ten books, six papers, six additional pieces (short stories, autohistorias, and essays) she had been invited to submit for publication, and five grant proposals.[32] Even during a single night, Anzaldúa typically shifted among several projects. On February 19, 1989, for instance, she wrote in her journal,

> I feel good @ myself today. Last night I did some work; had phone conf. with N[orma] Alarcón for 1–1/2 hrs; worked on *Theories by chicanas* notebook, making holes & putting in articles; then I spent a couple of hours on *Entremuros, Entreguerras, Entremundos*, also punching holes, switching stories from one section to another, consolidating editing suggestions on "The Crossing" and "Sleepwalker." Of course this was time spent away from [completing the] intro to *Haciendo caras*—my rebelling again.[33]

This journal entry captures so much about Anzaldúa's multitasking. In addition to juggling various projects in a single evening, she demonstrates a stubborn resistance to externally imposed deadlines. At a time that she had a specific due date for one project (the introduction to *Making Face, Making Soul/Haciendo Caras*), Anzaldúa worked instead on *other* projects, including some with no deadlines at all. As her reference to this divergence as "rebelling again" indicates, this mobile writing practice, organized by desire rather than deadlines, was typical.[34] Moreover, Anzaldúa consistently underestimated the hours required to complete a piece (especially the time her revisions would take) while overestimating her energy levels. She got lost in the revision process and held open so many projects at once that finishing *anything* to her complete satisfaction was impossible. The final chapter in *Light in the Dark* represents the closest approximation to completion that Anzaldúa achieved, and this achievement was possible only because she took an extra year for her revisions.[35] Is it any wonder, then, that Anzaldúa was so delayed in finishing this book?

In 2001, Anzaldúa recommitted herself to completing her doctoral degree. In the fall of this year, she initiated a writing group, "las comadritas"; reconstituted her doctoral committee; and looked into the UCSC Graduate School's paperwork and other graduation requirements.[36] Although she met regularly with las comadritas, worked diligently on the chapters, and aspired to finish in Winter 2002 or Spring 2003 quarter, she did not meet these deadlines. Nor did she send her dissertation committee any chapters of her project or communicate with them. In spring 2004, Rob Wilson, director of the UCSC Literature Department's graduate program, contacted Anzaldúa and, explaining that the department had a precedent for this procedure, expressed the view that she be awarded the degree for work completed (specifically, for *Borderlands/La Frontera*).[37] After much deliberation and consultation with friends, Anzaldúa declined the offer, both because she felt that it would be unfair to most doctoral students (who must write a traditional dissertation) and because she believed she was within months of completing her book. As she explained in an e-mail to Wilson:

> Though going the non-dissertation route would be easier I think it's unfair to other grad students who have to fulfill all the requirements. I also don't want a "free" ride. But I also feel that the dissertation has to be quality work and I have reservations about pulling it off this quarter. I'll try my best, but my health is shaky (I suffer from diabetes and kidney and other complications) so I can't push myself too hard. I do agree with you that we should work on this while the energy/focus is present.
>
> Contigo, gloria

Anzaldúa passed away in mid-May and was awarded the doctoral degree posthumously.

When Anzaldúa returned to the dissertation/book project in fall 2001, she looked over but did not directly take up her Lloronas book (which at this point was titled *Lloronas—Writing, Reading, Speaking, Dreaming*).[38] Instead, she expanded the focus to encompass ontological investigations while maintaining several previous themes, particularly those related to aesthetics, nepantla, shifting identities, and knowledge transformation as a decolonizing process. The book's table of contents changed multiple times between 2001 and 2004 as Anzaldúa wrote, revised, and rethought her project. In fall 2001, she planned to include three previously published essays (revised to reflect her most recent thinking and the book's themes), several new pieces designed to pull the collection together, and "now let us shift . . . the path of conocimiento . . . inner work, public acts," an extended essay she was writing for our co-edited collection, *this bridge we call home: radical visions for transformation*.[39] By fall 2003, Anzaldúa had come closer to determining the book's table of contents but was still reorganizing the chapters and making other alterations, and by January 2004, she had finalized the table of contents' organization, although she was still considering various chapter and book titles.[40] Chapters 1, 3, 5, and 6 had been previously published in different form. Anzaldúa revised chapters 3 and 5 considerably to align them with her current thinking about Coyolxauhqui and other key themes in this book; she made fewer changes to chapters 1 and 6, which she had drafted entirely in the twenty-first century and (in the case of chapter 6) written with her dissertation/book project in mind.

As mentioned previously, Anzaldúa did not focus exclusively on *Light in the Dark* during the last years of her life. From 2001 to 2004, she worked on other projects, as well, including her foreword to the third edition of *This Bridge Called My Back*; her preface to *this bridge we call home*; another co-edited, multi-genre collection tentatively titled *Bearing Witness, Reading Lives: Imagination, Creativity, and Social Change*; an essay for her friend Liliana Wilson's art exhibition; several short stories; an e-mail interview on indigeneity for *SAILS: American Indian Literatures*; an essay on the "geographies of latinidad identity" (based on a talk she gave in 1999 and promised for a volume on Latinidad); and a testimonio about the terrorist attacks of September 11, 2001.[41] During this time, Anzaldúa's health continued to decline. Torn in so many directions, she missed her self-imposed deadlines for completing *Light in the Dark*.[42] However, at the time of her death in May 2004, Anzaldúa seemed to believe that she would finish the dissertation within the year.

In editing *Light in the Dark* for publication, I assumed that my tasks would focus primarily on proofreading the manuscript and finalizing the bibliographical material, which I knew, from conversations with Anzaldúa, to be in disarray.[43] I worked with the chapter drafts and notes she had saved on her MacBook hard drive, her handwritten revisions on paper copies of these drafts, and her extensive e-mail communication concerning the dissertation. I began with the most recent version(s) of each chapter, as indicated by Anzaldúa's numbering system and the date stamp on each computer file. However, as I delved into her computer files and examined them in dialogue with her writing notes (also located on her computer hard drive), the editorial process became more complex than I had expected, especially concerning chapters 2 and 4. Chapter 2 included several unfinished sections and authorial notes, indicating places where Anzaldúa had planned to expand and revise, and chapter 4 existed in numerous versions, which Anzaldúa was still collating and revising at the time of her death.

I had two editorial goals which shaped my process. First, to adhere to Anzaldúa's intentions as closely as possible—both by following her most recent revisions and by upholding her high aesthetic standards (including her desire to ensure that her book was "quality work").[44] Second, to provide readers with information about the manuscript that would facilitate their analyses, interpretations, and investigations. Because I'd been working on various writing and editing projects with Anzaldúa for more than a decade, I had a solid understanding of her personal aesthetics—the emphasis she placed on *how* a piece sounds and feels.[45] Anzaldúa took exceptional pride in her work, equally valuing form and content; as I explained earlier, she revised each piece numerous times, honing the images to achieve specific cadences and affects. While I did not attempt to replicate Anzaldúa's revision process, I used her standards as I sorted through her chapters and evaluated them for publication. Drawing on my knowledge of Anzaldúa's writing process, I identified the sections in chapters 2 and 4 that would not have met her publication standards but would have been further revised or entirely deleted. Rather than revise or delete this material, I moved it to the endnotes and appendixes because it contains important clues about Anzaldúa's theories (especially the directions she might have pursued had she been given more time) and about the concepts she was drawing from but in the process of rejecting. I have also included discursive endnotes throughout *Light in the Dark* to assist readers interested in tracking the development of Anzaldúa's theories or other aspects of her writing process, including some aspects of the choices she made as she produced this text.

Tracing Coyolxauhqui . . . chapter overviews

One of the most pronounced differences between the twentieth-century and twenty-first-century versions of Anzaldúa's dissertation/book project is the shift from Llorona to Coyolxauhqui. According to Aztec mythic history, when Coyolxauhqui tried to kill her mother, her brother, Huitzilopochtli (Eastern Hummingbird and War God), decapitated her, flinging her head into the sky and throwing her body down the sacred mountain, where it broke into a thousand pieces. Depicted as a "huge round stone" filled with dismembered body parts, Coyolxauhqui serves as Anzaldúa's "light in the dark," representing a complex holism—both the acknowledgment of painful fragmentation and the promise of transformative healing. As she explains in chapter 3: "Coyolxauhqui represents the psychic and creative process of tearing apart and pulling together (deconstructing/constructing). She represents fragmentation, imperfection, incompleteness, and unfulfilled promises as well as integration, completeness, and wholeness" (see figure FM.1).

Drawing from Coyolxauhqui's story, Anzaldúa develops a complex healing process and a theory of writing that she variously named "The Coyolxauhqui imperative," "Coyolxauhqui consciousness," and "Putting Coyolxauhqui together."[46] She offers one of her most extensive discussions of this theoretical framework in chapter 6, where she describes Coyolxauhqui as "both the process of emotional psychical dismemberment, splitting body/mind/spirit/soul, and the creative work of putting all the pieces together in a new form, a partially unconscious work done in the night by the light of the moon, a labor of re-visioning and re-membering." The product of multiple colonizations, Coyolxauhqui also embodies Anzaldúa's desire for epistemological and ontological decolonization.[47] As the following chapter summaries suggest, Coyolxauhqui hovers over *Light in the Dark*. Appearing in every chapter, "Ella es la luna and she lights the darkness."[48]

In a short preface, "Gestures of the Body—Escribiendo para idear," Anzaldúa introduces her book by explaining its multilayered focus and inviting readers to participate in her literary desires. Reflecting on her own experiences and struggles as an author, Anzaldúa calls for a new aesthetics, an entirely embodied artistic practice that synthesizes identity formation with cultural change and movement among multiple realities. As she interweaves theory with practice, Anzaldúa

FM.I | Coyolxauhqui

briefly touches on issues developed in the chapters that follow: She defines writing as "gestures of the body"; offers a preliminary definition of her theory of the "Coyolxauhqui imperative"; provides an overview of her aesthetics; introduces her genre theories of autohistoria and autohistoria-teoría; expands her previous definitions of nepantla to include aesthetic and ontological dimensions; and posits the imagination as an intellectual-spiritual faculty. "Gestures of the Body" sets the tone for the entire book and reveals the driving force behind it: Anzaldúa's aspiration to evoke healing and transformation, her desire to go beyond description and representation by using words, images, and theories that stimulate, create, and in other ways facilitate radical physical-psychic change in herself, her readers, and the various worlds in which we exist and to which we aspire.

First drafted shortly after the September 11, 2001 terrorist attacks on the United States, chapter 1 elaborates on and enacts Anzaldúa's theory of the Coyolxauhqui imperative, illustrating one form the embodied "gestures" she calls for in her preface can take. Encapsulating Anzaldúa's aesthetic journey, "Let us be the healing of the wound: The Coyolxauhqui imperative—La sombra y el sueño" also explores key elements in her onto-epistemology ("desconocimientos," "the path of conocimiento"); her aesthetics ("the Coyolxauhqui imperative"); and her ethics ("spiritual activism"). Interweaving the personal with the collective, Anzaldúa uses these concepts to bridge the historical moment with recurring political-aesthetic issues, such as U.S. colonialism, nationalism, complicity, cultural trauma, racism, sexism, and other forms of systemic oppression. She calls for expanded awareness (conocimiento) and develops an ethics of interconnectivity, which she describes as the act of reaching through the wounds—wounds that can be physical, psychic, cultural, and/or spiritual—to connect with others. In its intentionally non-oppositional approach, the chapter offers a provocative alternative to portions of Borderlands/La Frontera and some of Anzaldúa's other work. While acknowledging her intense anger, Anzaldúa converts it into a sophisticated theory of relational change. Thus, "Let us be the healing of the wound" can be read as Anzaldúa's invitation to move through and beyond trauma and rage, transforming it into social-justice work. Anzaldúa simultaneously illustrates and instructs, offering readers guidelines (a methodology of sorts) for how to enact this difficult transformative work, how to heed the Coyolxauhqui imperative.

Chapter 2, "Flights of the Imagination: Rereading/Rewriting Realities," contains Anzaldúa's most sustained discussion of the imagination as an epistemological-political tool and the most direct statement of her metaphysical framework. Likening the Coyolxauhqui process to "shamanic initiatory dismemberment," Anzaldúa draws on curanderismo, chamanismo/shamanism, transpersonal psychology, anthropology, fiction, and her childhood experiences to develop her theories of art's transformational power and imagination's role in (re) creating reality.[49] I bracket the prefix to underscore Anzaldúa's complex speculations about ontological issues; she posits multiple, interlayered worlds which we discover and co-create, "decolonizing reality." This chapter also provides the ontological foundation for Anzaldúa's innovative theory of spiritual activism, which she further develops in the chapters that follow. As she defines the term, "spiritual activism" is neither a naïve, watered-down version of religion nor some kind of "New Age" fad that facilitates escape from existing conditions. It is in many ways the reverse: For Anzaldúa, spiritual activism is a completely embodied, highly political endeavor. While Anzaldúa did not coin the term "spiritual activism," she introduced the term and the concept into feminist scholarship.[50] As she connects her theory of spiritual activism with her transformational aesthetics, Anzaldúa returns to her earlier definition of writing as "making soul" and expands it, linking it both with mainstream canonical British literature and with Mexican indigenous traditions. Other topics covered are "shamanic imaginings"; "nagualismo" as epistemology and writing practice; her theories of the "nepantla body" and "spiritual mestizaje"; the relationship between writing, reading, and social change; and her personal aspirations as a writer.

Structured around Anzaldúa's visit in 1992 to an exhibition of Mesoamerican culture and art at the Denver Museum of Natural History, chapter 3, "Border Arte: Nepantla, el lugar de la frontera," builds on and expands the previous chapter's discussion of spiritual mestizaje and aesthetics, grounding them in a theory of "border arte"—a disruptive, potentially transformative, decolonizing creative practice, or what Anzaldúa calls "the Coyolxauhqui process." As she retraces her journey through the museum's exhibition, she explores issues of colonialism, neocolonialism, and the subjugated artist's role in the decolonization process. Emphasizing both the personal and collective dimensions of border arte, Anzaldúa connects her aesthetics to the work of other border artists—particularly visual artists such as Santa Barraza, Liliana Wilson, Yolanda M. López, and Marcia Gómez. For Anzaldúa, the term "border artist" goes beyond geographical boundaries to include other types of risk takers: artists who straddle multiple (often oppressive, colonized, neo-colonized) worlds and use their negotiations to decolonize the various spaces in which they exist. Anzaldúa connects her revisionist mythmaking with her epistemology while expanding her previous definitions of the borderlands, mestizaje, and her own mestiza identity. This chapter explores other identity-related issues as well, including questions of authenticity, appropriation, and the commodification of indigenous art; debates between indigenous and Chican@ authors;[51] and the possibilities of developing identities that are simultaneously ethnic-specific and transcultural. "Border Arte" also contains an important discussion of "el cenote," a term Anzaldúa uses to describe the imagination's source of previously untapped, collective knowledge. Anzaldúa concludes the chapter by introducing her innovative theory of "nos/otras"—a theory she takes up in the chapter that follows.

In chapter 4, "Geographies of Selves—Reimagining Identity: Nos/Otras (Us/Other), las Nepantleras, and the New Tribalism," Anzaldúa expands the previous chapter's analysis of border art and artist-activists to explore nationalism, identity formation, "Raza studies," decolonizing education, and conflict resolution—especially as these are enacted by her nepantlera "escritoras, artistas, scholars, [and] activistas." Focusing on "Raza Studies y la raza," she applies the Coyolxauhqui process to individual and collective identity (re)formation and develops her theory of "the new tribalism." Anzaldúa's new tribalism represents an innovative, rhizomatic theory of affinity-based identities and a provocative alternative to both assimilation and separatism.[52] As she explains in an earlier draft of this chapter: "The new tribalism disrupts categorical and ethnocentric forms of nationalism. By problematizing the concepts of who's us and who's other, or what I call nos/otras, the new tribalism seeks to revise the notion of "otherness" and the story of identity. The new tribalism rewrites cultural inscriptions, facilitating our ability to forge alliances with other groups."[53] With her theories of the new tribalism and nos/otras, Anzaldúa develops a careful, sophisticated critique of narrow nationalisms and other conservative versions of collective identity while remaining sympathetic to the identity-related concerns that generate, motivate, and drive nationalist-inflected politics and desires. These theories represent both an expansion of and a return to her earlier theory of El Mundo Zurdo—a theory she further develops in chapter 6.[54] Significantly, Anzaldúa challenges yet does not entirely reject conventional concepts of identity and racialized social categories, thus offering important interventions into postnationalist thought.[55] This chapter also contains extensive discussions of her innovative theories of "nepantleras" and "geographies of selves."[56]

As the title suggests, in chapter 5, "Putting Coyolxauhqui Together: A Creative Process," Anzaldúa presents her most detailed, extensive discussion of the Coyolxauhqui process. The chapter invites readers inside Anzaldúa's mind; as she writes in her dissertation notes, "This chapter is my creation story. It depicts the psychological dimensions of the writing process and the angst of creativity."[57] Here we see another aspect of Anzaldúa's aesthetics: her own writing practice, played out on the page. This chapter demonstrates—in careful detail, giving us intimate glimpses into Anzaldúa's daily life—the deeply embodied, extremely intentional nature of her work. Anzaldúa takes us through her entire creative process, from the original call (in this particular instance, an invitation to contribute to an edited collection), idea generation, and the pre-drafting phase (or what she terms "componiendo y des-componiendo"); through writing blocks and multiple revisions; to (non)completion and submission of the essay.[58] Because writing's embodiment includes a complex emotional dimension, Anzaldúa also discloses the "shadow side of writing": periods of extreme depression, dissatisfaction, and despair, coupled with self-doubt and feelings of complete inadequacy. Shot through the entire writing process, however, is Anzaldúa's deep love of writing. For Anzaldúa, the personal is always also collective, so in typical Anzaldúan fashion, she uses her experiences to further develop her theories of the Coyolxauhqui imperative, nepantla, el cenote, and the imaginal.[59] Particularly important is Anzaldúa's expansion of nepantla to include additional epistemological dimensions; here and elsewhere in *Light in the Dark*, nepantla also functions as form of consciousness, an actant of sorts. As I suggest later, this expansion has the potential to open new directions in Anzaldúan scholarship.

The final chapter, "now let us shift . . . conocimiento . . . inner work, public acts," represents the culmination of Anzaldúa's personal intellectual-ontological-political journey, a powerful example of her theory of autohistoria-teoría and her aesthetics, as well as the "sister" to chapter 5. Anzaldúa wrote the chapter with her dissertation in mind, viewing it as closely related to "Putting Coyolxauhqui Together,"[60] and thus underscoring the intimate interconnections she posits between aesthetics, ontology, and transformation. Anzaldúa builds on her earlier theories of "El Mundo Zurdo" (1970s), "the new mestiza" (1980s), "nepantla" (1990s), and "nepantleras" (2000s), synergistically expanding them into her relational onto-epistemology, or what she names "conocimiento." While a literal translation of the word *conocimiento* from Spanish to English is "knowledge," Anzaldúa redefines the term, incorporating imaginal, spiritual-activist, and ontological dimensions. An intensely personal, fully embodied process that gathers information from context, Anzaldúa's conocimiento is profoundly relational and enables those who enact it to make connections among apparently disparate events, people, experiences, and realities. These connections, in turn, lead to action.[61] Drawing on her own experiences—her episodes of deep depression, her diabetes diagnosis, her declining health, her literary desires, and her engagements with various progressive social movements—Anzaldúa presents a nonlinear healing journey, or what she calls "the seven stages of conocimiento." A series of recursive iterations, Anzaldúa's theory of conocimiento queers conventional ways of knowing and offers readers a holistic, activist-inflected onto-epistemology designed to effect change on multiple interlocking levels. As Anzaldúa writes in her annotations for this chapter, "The aim of the essay is to transform my personal life into a narrative with mythological or archetypal threads, not in the confessional tone of a participant in the drama who is seeking another form of order. And to do it representing myself without victimization or sentimentality."[62]

Following these chapters are six appendixes that I have added to the original manuscript to provide readers with background information on Anzaldúa's writing process and the history of this book. Appendix 1 contains a draft of Anzaldúa's *Lloronas* dissertation proposal, *Lloronas—Women Who Wail: (Self)Representation and the Production of Writing, Knowledge, and Identity*, and the table of contents for a version of her 1990s dissertation/book, *Lloronas—Writing, Reading, Speaking, Dreaming*. While Anzaldúa's 1990s proposal and table of contents exist in numerous drafts, Anzaldúa viewed the material in this appendix as most representative of her earlier project.[63] I include them here to give readers a sense of the similarities and differences between the

Lloronas book and *Light in the Dark*. Appendix 2 consists of several e-mails that Anzaldúa wrote to her writing comadres during the final years of her life, at a time when she was working consistently on *Light in the Dark*. Because these e-mails were composed quickly (as shown by her use of lower-case letters), they offer a less censored, more immediate entry into Anzaldúa's life, illustrating the severity of her health-related struggles and their impact on her writing practice. Appendix 3 contains additional material (unfinished sections and writing notas) related to chapter 2. Appendix 4 is an alternative opening section that Anzaldúa considered using in chapter 4. Appendix 5 offers historical notes on each chapter's development. Appendix 6 consists of the call for papers and personal invitation that influenced the development of chapter 1. The appendixes are followed by a glossary with brief discussions of key Anzaldúan terms and topics developed in *Light in the Dark*. I hope that this material will enable scholars to retrace Anzaldúa's thinking, develop rich analyses and interpretations of Anzaldúa's words, and in other ways build on her work—creating new Anzaldúan theory.

While some chapters were previously published, Anzaldúa updated and revised them in other ways before her death.[64] As her writing notes indicate, she made these revisions with her dissertation/book project in mind. Thus, they offer additional insights into the development of her thinking and open new avenues into her work. And because context matters, when we read these chapters as parts of the larger whole, each chapter functions synergistically, conversing with, influencing, and building on its sister chapters. Even the book's title—with its Coyolxauhqui-inspired focus on rewriting identity, spirituality, and reality—gives us another lens with which to consider the ideas presented throughout the book. In the next section, I highlight several key innovations in *Light in the Dark* and consider their potential implications. Because Anzaldúa's theories take multiple, interconnected forms; occur in a variety of contexts (contexts that often subtly reshape the theories themselves); and invite readers' collaboration, the following is neither comprehensive nor exhaustive. I intentionally focus on those theories that risk being the most marginalized and ignored; I especially highlight Anzaldúa's potential contributions to twenty-first-century philosophical thought because I believe that her outsider status leads many scholars to ignore this dimension of her work.[65]

"Decolonizing reality": Implications for the scholarship

Written during the final decade of her life, *Light in the Dark* represents Anzaldúa's most sustained attempt to develop a transformational ontology, epistemology, and aesthetics. Through intense self-reflection, Anzaldúa creates an autohistoria-teoría articulating her complex theory and practice of the artist-activist's creative process; she enacts what Sarah Ohmer describes as "a decolonizing ritual"[66] that she invites her readers to share and enact for ourselves. As Ohmer, Norma Alarcón, Ernesto Martínez, and several other scholars have observed, Anzaldúa participates in the twentieth-century and twenty-first-century "decolonial turn." In *Borderlands/La Frontera*, for example, her theories of mestiza consciousness, border thinking, and la facultad decolonize western epistemologies by moving partially outside Enlightenment-based frameworks. Anzaldúa does not simply write *about* "suppressed knowledges and marginalized subjectivities";[67] she writes from *within* them, and it's this shift from writing about to writing within that makes her work so innovatively decolonizing.

In *Light in the Dark*, Anzaldúa takes this "decolonial turn" even further and includes a groundbreaking ontological component (my pun is intentional). Through empirical experience, esoteric traditions, and indigenous philosophies, she valorizes realities suppressed, marginalized, or entirely erased by the narrow versions of ontological realism championed by Enlightenment-based thought—versions that most western-trained scholars (even those of us committed to facilitating progressive change) have often internalized and assumed to be true. Anzaldúa does so by writing from—and not just about—these subaltern ontologies.

I emphasize these ontological dimensions because this aspect of Anzaldúa's work has been underappreciated and often ignored. Perhaps this desconocimiento is not surprising, given the limited attention twentieth-century theorists and philosophers have paid to ontological and metaphysical issues.[68] Indeed, as Mikko Tuhkanen suggests, these "fields [have been] largely exiled from contemporary social sciences and the humanities."[69] Until recently, critical literary studies and western philosophy have focused almost entirely on epistemology, normalizing "paradigms through whose lenses Anzaldúa's metaphysical assumptions seem naive, pre-critical, or, simply, incomprehensible"—and therefore have been ignored.[70] However,

Anzaldúa explores metaphysical and ontological issues throughout her work, from "Tihueque" (her earliest publication) to the end of her career, using them to inspire, empower, and inform her radical social-justice vision.[71]

Nowhere are these explorations more evident (and more impossible to avoid) than in *Light in the Dark*. This book represents the culmination of Anzaldúa's lifelong investigations and demonstrates that, for Anzaldúa, epistemology and ontology (knowing and being) are intimately interrelated—two halves of one complex, multidimensional process employed in the service of progressive social change. She posits a spirit-inflected materialist ontology, a twenty-first-century animism of sorts. Anzaldúa offers her most extensive discussion of this fluid ontology in chapter 2, where she asserts:

> Spirit and mind, soul and body, are one, and together they perceive a reality greater than the vision experienced in the ordinary world. I know that the universe is conscious and that spirit and soul communicate by sending subtle signals to those who pay attention to our surroundings, to animals, to natural forces, and to other people. We receive information from ancestors inhabiting other worlds. We assess that information and learn how to trust that knowing.

According to Anzaldúa, the spiritual, material, physical, and psychic are inseparable aspects of a unified, infinitely complex reality. Stories, trees, metaphors, imaginal figures, and even the essays she writes are ontological beings with lives and various types of agency that at least partially exceed or in other ways escape human knowledge and control. Thus in the preface she distinguishes between "talking *with* images/stories and talking *about* them" (her emphasis), positing an epistemological-ontological dialogue between author and text; in chapter 2, she explains that images can "take on body and life"; in chapter 5, she confesses that "things whisper" to her in the night; and in chapter 6, she encounters "ensoulment in trees, in woods, in streams." To borrow from European philosophical discourse, we could say that Anzaldúa is a monist, positing a reality that includes but exceeds us, existing beyond human life and outside our heads; at best, we "catch glimpses of this invisible primary reality" (chapter 2).

Anzaldúa's complex ontology invites us to situate her writings within recent work in continental philosophy and feminist thought, particularly trends in speculative realism, object-oriented ontology, and neo-materialisms.[72] Like speculative realists and object-oriented ontologists, Anzaldúa sidesteps the Kantian injunction to "adopt an agnostic attitude toward the nature of things-in-themselves"[73] and speculates deeply about ontological and metaphysical questions. Throughout *Light in the Dark*, she employs a non-anthropocentric lens and a broad definition of reality in which spirits are as real as dogs, cats, baseball bats, methane gas, doorknobs, bookshelves, and everything else.[74] But unlike object-oriented philosophers, who generally posit an extreme hyper-individualized realism in which all objects (including human beings) are, ultimately, independent and separated ("withdrawn") from all others, Anzaldúa insists on the radical interrelatedness, interdependence, and sacredness of all existence. Like twenty-first-century neo-materialists, who "tak[e] matter seriously," Anzaldúa posits "the ongoing, mutual, co-constitution of mind and matter" and defines nature as "material, discursive, human, more-than-human, corporeal, and technological."[75] However, unlike these theorists, who often sharply distinguish their work from post-structuralism's "linguistic turn" and thus underestimate (or deny) the concrete, material reality of language, Anzaldúa closely associates language with matter. In her ontology, language does not simply refer to or represent reality; nor does it become reality in some ludic post-modernist way. Words, images, and material things are real, embodying different aspects of reality—ranging from the "ordinary reality" of everyday life (in its physical, nonphysical, and semi-physical iterations) to what Anzaldúa describes in chapter 2 as "the hidden spirit worlds."

Language is a critical strand in Anzaldúa's onto-epistemology and aesthetics, a linchpin of sorts. In chapter 5, for example, she refers to "a spiritual being" who "shares with you a language that speaks of what is other; a language shared with the spirits of trees, sea, wind, and birds; a language which you'll spend many of your writing hours trying to translate into words." Here's where Anzaldúa's transformational aesthetics comes in. Because language, the physical world, the imaginal, and nonordinary realities are all intimately interwoven, words and images matter and *are* matter; they can have causal, material(izing) force.[76] The intentional, ritualized performance of specific, carefully selected words has the potential to *shift* reality (and not just our perception *of* reality). Anzaldúan aesthetics enables writers and other artists to enact, materialize, and in other ways concretize transformation. For Anzaldúa, writing is ontological—intimately connected with physical and nonphysical beings, with ordinary and nonordinary realities.

Anzaldúa can make these bold claims because she does not remain entirely within European philosophical traditions. As I noted earlier, she draws from but also moves partially outside them, incorporating indigenous and esoteric traditions.[77] Because the Enlightenment-based reality we have inherited is too restrictive and prevents us from enacting (or even envisioning) the radical social change we need, she decolonizes this dominant ontology, draws from alternative traditions, and develops a more expansive philosophy embracing spirit, indigenous wisdom, alchemy, mythic figures, ancestral guides, and more. Anzaldúa uses shamanism, curanderismo, alchemy, and the indigenous philosophies they reflect to substantiate and illustrate her transformational ontology and aesthetics, including her insistence on language's material(izing) properties.[78] By thus moving partially outside conventional European-based philosophical and scientific traditions, she obtains additional insights that embolden her to enact an ontological decolonization of sorts. Designed to address "the trauma of colonial abuses, trauma which fragments our psyches, pitching us into states of nepantla," Anzaldúa "rewrite[s] reality" in more expansive terms, incorporating Spirit, ancestral guides, indigenous wisdom, imagination, and cultural-mythic figures.[79] She identifies creativity and storytelling with healing and associates both with progressive sociopolitical change on multiple levels. Defining "illness" broadly to include the effects of colonialism, assimilation, racism, sexism, capitalism, environmental degradation, and other destructive practices, epistemologies, and states of being that occur at individual, systemic, and planetary levels, Anzaldúa maintains that artists can assist in the healing process. As she asserts in chapter 1, "My job as an artist is to bear witness to what haunts us, to step back and attempt to see the pattern in these events (personal and societal), and how we can repair el daño (the damage) by using the imagination and its visions. I believe in the transformative power and medicine of art."

Because the term "shamanism" originated in anthropology's interactions with indigenous peoples, some readers might view Anzaldúa's incorporation of shamanic worldviews as an act of appropriation that romanticizes a homogenous indigenous past, downplays the specificity of contemporary indigenous peoples, and oversimplifies (or entirely ignores) questions of land sovereignty.[80] To be sure, in her early work Anzaldúa sometimes relied on stereotyped thinking about indigenous peoples. While it's important to address these oversimplifications, it's also important to locate them chronologically in the trajectory of her career and acknowledge her intellectual development and subsequent attempts to rectify these simplifications by offering a more nuanced response to indigenous appropriation, misrepresentation, and conquest. The Gloria Anzaldúa who wrote *Light in the Dark* and other later texts is not synonymous with the Gloria Anzaldúa who embraced "my people, the Indians" in *Borderlands/La Frontera*; it's inaccurate and misleading to conflate the two.

Moreover, and as *Light in the Dark* demonstrates, Anzaldúa viewed indigenous thought as a foundational, vital source of decolonial wisdom for contemporary and future life on this planet and elsewhere. She believed that indigenous philosophies offer alternatives to Cartesian-based knowledge systems which we ignore at our peril. As she asserts in her writing notes, "We've come to the time of a shift in consciousness when entire civilizations change the way they know about the world. We need a new and better method of thinking about the world. A new mental operation to improve the human condition. We get hints from the alchemic and shamanistic traditions of the past." The Gloria Anzaldúa who wrote *Light in the Dark* was not interested in recovering "authentic" ancient teachings (whether these teachings had their source in alchemy or shamanism) and inserting them into twenty-first-century life. Nor did she identify herself *as* "Native American." Rather, she learned from and built on indigenous insights; she mixed these hints with other teachings, crafting a philosophy designed to address contemporary needs. Let me underscore this point: Anzaldúa does not reclaim an authentic indigenous practice but instead develops a twenty-first-century approach—a decolonizing ontology—that respectfully borrows from indigenous wisdom and many other non-Cartesian teachings. As she states in her interview with Irene Lara, "I'm modernizing Mexican indigenous traditions."[81]

Like language, imagination is a critical strand in Anzaldúa's decolonizing ontological project, facilitating physical-psychic transformation and knowledge production. Anzaldúa investigates imagination's creative power in chapter 2, where she borrows from transpersonal psychology (particularly James Hillman's imaginal work), curanderismo, indigenous and esoteric philosophies, scholarship on shamanism and neo-shamanism, and her own creative process to articulate the imagination's epistemological, ontological, and creative functions, or what Jeffrey J. Kripal might describe as the "materializing capacity of the empowered imagination"—the imagination's ability "to affect biological bodies and the physical environment in extraordinary ways."[82] According to Anzaldúa, the imagination enables us "to change or reinvent reality"; acquire additional information from previously untapped sources (such as el cenote); and move among different dimensions of reality: "Imagination's soul dimension bridges body and nature to spirit and mind, making these connections in the in-between space of nepantla."

A Nahuatl word meaning "in-between space," nepantla is, arguably, the most expansive (and expanding) theory in *Light in the Dark*, appearing more than one hundred times, within and between almost every aspect of Anzaldúa's autohistoria-teoría. Does Anzaldúa lean too heavily on nepantla—making it do too much work, circulating it through too many aspects of her theories? Perhaps. Or, perhaps, nepantla leans too heavily on—and into—Anzaldúa, compelling her to complicate her theories of individual and collective identity formation, alliance-building, the creative process, the imagination's roles in knowledge production, and spiritual activists' work as mediators and agents of change. (After all, Anzaldúa seriously considered titling her book *Enacting Nepantla: Rewriting Identity*.) Nepantla represents both an elaboration of and an expansion beyond Anzaldúa's well-known theories of the Borderlands and the Coatlicue state (introduced in *Borderlands / La Frontera*). Like the former, nepantla indicates liminal space where transformation can occur; and like the latter, nepantla indicates space / times of chaos, anxiety, pain, and loss of control. But with nepantla, Anzaldúa underscores and expands the ontological (spiritual, psychic) dimensions. As she explained in an interview four years after *Borderlands*' publication,

> I find people using metaphors such as "Borderlands" in a more limited sense than I had meant it, so to expand on the psychic and emotional borderlands I'm now using "nepantla." With nepantla the connection to the spirit world is more pronounced as is the connection to the world after death, to psychic spaces. It has a more spiritual, psychic, supernatural, and indigenous resonance.[83]

In *Light in the Dark*, nepantla extends beyond Anzaldúa's previous theorization and exceeds her conscious control, opening additional epistemological, ontological, aesthetic, and ethical possibilities in each chapter. As Anzaldúa acknowledges in her preface, "Nepantla concerns automatically infuse my writing: I don't have to *will* myself to deal with these particular points; these nepantlas inhabit me and inevitably surface in whatever I'm writing."

These "nepantla concerns" do more than "inevitably surface" in Anzaldúa's writing; they provoke Anzaldúa, pushing her in new directions. This agentic quality is what I referred to earlier when I described nepantla as an actant, a strange collaborative endeavor: Nepantla works *with* Anzaldúa as she invents her theories of las nepantleras, nos/otras, new tribalism, geography of selves, spiritual activism, conocimiento, and the Coyolxauhqui imperative. Take, for example, her theory of las "nepantleras"—the word she coined to describe threshold people, those who move within and among multiple worlds and use their movement in the service of transformation.

Nepantleras are born from nepantla. During an Anzaldúan nepantla, individual and collective self-definitions and belief systems are destabilized as we begin questioning our previously accepted worldviews (our epistemologies, ontologies, and/or ethics). As Anzaldúa explains in chapter 1, "In nepantla we undergo the anguish of changing our perspectives and crossing a series of cruz calles, junctures, and thresholds, some leading to a different way of relating to people and surroundings and others to the creation of a new world." This loosening of restrictive worldviews—while extremely painful—can create shifts in consciousness and, thus, opportunities for change; we acquire additional, potentially transformative perspectives, different ways to understand ourselves, our circumstances, and our worlds. It's as if nepantla shoves us partially outside of our previously comfortable frameworks; pushes us into a frictional, contradictory clash of worldviews; challenges us to make some sort of meaning from chaos; and thus forces us to change.

Some people experiencing nepantla choose to become nepantleras. I emphasize this volitional component to avoid romanticizing the concept.[84] It's not easy to be a nepantlera; it's risky, lonely, exhausting work. Never entirely inside, always somewhat outside, every group or belief system, nepantleras do not fully belong to any single location. Yet this willingness to remain with/in the thresholds enables nepantleras to break partially away from the cultural trance and binary thinking that locks us into the status quo. Living within and among multiple worlds, nepantleras use these liminal perspectives (or what Anzaldúa describes in chapter 4 as "perspective[s] from the cracks") to question "consensual reality" (our status quo stories) and develop alternative perspectives—ideas, theories, actions, and beliefs that partially reflect but partially exceed existing worldviews. They invent relational theories and tactics with which they can reconceive and in other ways transform the various worlds in which we exist.[85] Planetary citizens and world travelers, nepantleras embody Anzaldúa's theory of conocimiento; enact her relational ethics; and facilitate the development of new forms of individual and collective identities, alliance making, and coalition building (articulated in her theories of nos / otras and new tribalism).

In the context of Anzaldúan scholarship, nepantla's implications are immense. Whereas scholars generally subordinate nepantla to borders / borderlands and focus more frequently on the latter, if we take *Light in the Dark* seriously, we must expand our focus. In addition to its previous descriptions as a stage in a larger process, a state of consciousness, and a "liberatory space," nepantla takes on additional meanings that complicate—without negating—previous interpretations.[86]

How, for example, might nepantla's onto-epistemological dimensions affect our understanding of Anzaldúa's revolutionary border thinking, as described by Walter Mignolo, José David Saldívar, and others? If, as Saldívar suggests, "Border gnosis or border thinking, for Anzaldúa, is a site of criss-crossed experience, language, and identity," [87] consider the additional crisscrossing that occurs in nepantla's shamanic world traveling.

Relatedly, by shifting her focus from new mestizas to nepantleras, Anzaldúa takes readers beyond debates about new mestizas' ethnic-sexual identities. Indeed, Anzaldúa's "demythologization of race" (which occurs in "the in-between place of nepantla") invites readers to follow her example and go beyond—without erasing or ignoring— the specific identity labels that she previously embraced. Look, for instance, at chapter 4, where she declares that "being Chicana is not enough—nor is being queer, a writer, or any other identity label I choose or others impose on me. Conventional, traditional identity labels are stuck in binaries, trapped in jaulas (cages) that limit the growth of our individual and collective lives." Significantly, Anzaldúa does not reject her identity as woman, lesbian-dyke-patlache, Chicana, or campesina. However, in *Light in the Dark*, these categories become insufficient, and she self-defines "in more global-spiritual terms instead of conventional categories of color, class, career" (chapter 6). How will readers answer Anzaldúa's call for new approaches to identity, "Fresh terms and open-ended tags that portray us in all our complexities and potentialities"? What connections will we make between these identity-related expansions and the ontological decolonization on which they are based?

Light in the Dark / Luz en lo oscuro—Rewriting Identity, Spirituality, Reality invites us to consider these questions and many others. This book broadens Anzaldúan scholarship and shifts conversations in new directions, demonstrating that Anzaldúa is a provocative philosopher of the highest caliber, weaving together mexicana, Chicana, indigenous, feminist, queer, tejana, and esoteric theories and perspectives in ground-breaking ways.

PREFACE

Gestures of the Body—Escribiendo para idear

> There's something epistemological about storytelling. It's the way we know each other, the way we know ourselves. The way we know the world. It's also the way we don't know: the way the world is kept from us, the way we're kept from knowledge about ourselves, the way we're kept from understanding other people.
> ANDREA BARRETT, WRITER'S CHRONICLE, VOL. 32, NO. 3, DECEMBER 1999

When writing at night, I'm aware of la luna, Coyolxauhqui, hovering over my house. I envision her muerta y decapitada (dead and decapitated), una cabeza con los parpados cerrados (eyes closed). But then her eyes open y la miro dar luz a los lugares oscuros, I see her light the dark places. Writing is a process of discovery and perception that produces knowledge and conocimiento (insight). I am often driven by the impulse to write something down, by the desire and urgency to communicate, to make meaning, to make sense of things, to create myself through this knowledge-producing act. I call this impulse the "Coyolxauhqui imperative": a struggle to reconstruct oneself and heal the sustos resulting from woundings, traumas, racism, and other acts of violation que hechan pedazos nuestras almas, split us, scatter our energies, and haunt us. The Coyolxauhqui imperative is the act of calling back those pieces of the self/soul that have been dispersed or lost, the act of mourning the losses that haunt us. The shadow beast and attendant desconocimientos (the ignorance we cultivate to keep ourselves from knowledge so that we can remain unaccountable) have a tenacious hold on us. Dealing with the lack of cohesiveness and stability in life, the increasing tension and conflicts, motivates me to process the struggle. The sheer mental, emotional, and spiritual anguish motivates me to "write out" my/our experiences. More than that, my aspirations toward wholeness maintain my sanity, a matter of life and death. Grappling with (des)conocimientos, with what I don't want to know, opening and shutting my eyes and ears to cultural realities, expanding my awareness and consciousness, or refusing to do so, sometimes results in discovering the positive shadow: hidden aspects of myself and the world. Each irritant is a grain of sand in the oyster of the imagination. Sometimes what accretes around an irritant or wound may produce a pearl of great insight, a theory.

I'm constantly struggling with my own ways of cultural production and the role that I play as an artist. I call the space where I struggle with my creations "nepantla." Nepantla is the place where my cultural and personal codes clash, where I come up against the world's dictates, where these different worlds coalesce in my writing. I am conscious of various nepantlas—linguistic, geographical, gender, sexual, historical, cultural, political, social—when I write. Nepantla is the point of contact y el lugar between worlds—between imagination and physical existence, between ordinary and nonordinary (spirit) realities. Nepantla concerns automatically infuse my writing: I don't have to will myself to deal with these particular points; these nepantlas inhabit me and inevitably surface in whatever I'm writing. Nepantlas are places of constant tension, where the missing or absent pieces can be summoned back, where transformation and healing may be possible, where wholeness is just out of reach but seems attainable.

Escribo para "idear"—the Spanish word meaning "to form or conceive an idea, to develop a theory, to invent and imagine." My work is about questioning, affecting, and changing the paradigms that govern prevailing notions of reality, identity, creativity, activism, spirituality, race, gender, class, and sexuality. To develop an epistemology of the imagination, a psychology of the image, I construct my own symbolic system.[1] While attempting to create new epistemological frameworks,

I'm constantly reflecting on this activity of idear. The desire or need to share the process of "following" images and making "stories" and theories motivates me to write this text.

Direct interpretive engagements between artists and their images have few precedents. There's very little direct, personal artistic research, so I've had to engage with my own experiences and construct my own formulations. Intento dar testimonio de mi propio proceso y conciencia de escritora chicana. Soy la que escribe y se escribe / I am the one who writes and who is being written. Últimamente es el escribir que me escribe / It is the writing that "writes" me. I "read" and "speak" myself into being. Writing is the site where I critique reality, identity, language, and dominant culture's representation and ideological control.

Using a multidisciplinary approach and a "storytelling" format, I theorize my own and others' struggles for representation, identity, self-inscription, and creative expressions. When I "speak" myself in creative and theoretical writings, I constantly shift positions—which means taking into account ideological remolinos (whirlwinds), cultural dissonance, and the convergence of competing worlds. It means dealing with the fact that I, like most people, inhabit different cultures and, when crossing to other mundos, shift into and out of perspectives corresponding to each; it means living in liminal spaces, in nepantlas. By focusing on Chicana/mestiza (mexicana tejana) experience and identity in several axes—writer/artist, intellectual, scholar, teacher, woman, Chicana, feminist, lesbian, working class—I attempt to analyze, describe, and re-create these identity shifts. Speaking from the geographies of many "countries" makes me a privileged speaker. I "speak in tongues"—understand the languages, emotions, thoughts, fantasies of the various sub-personalities inhabiting me and the various grounds they speak from. To do so, I must figure out which person (I, she, you, we, them, they), which tense (present, past, future), which language and register, and which voice or style to speak from. Identity formation (which involves "reading" and "writing" oneself and the world) is an alchemical process that synthesizes the dualities, contradictions, and perspectives from these different selves and worlds.

In these auto-ethnographies I am both observer and participant—I simultaneously look at myself as subject and object. In the blink of an eye, I blur subject/object, class, gender, and other boundaries. My methodological stances emerge in the writing process, as do the theories. I treat all work, including these chapters, like fiction or poetry.

In formulating new ways of knowing, new objects of knowledge, new perspectives, and new orderings of experiences, I grapple, half-unconsciously, with a new methodology—one that I hope does not reinforce prevailing modes. I come to know how to "read" and "write"; I come to knowledge and conocimiento through images and "stories." I use various storytelling formats consistent with the experiences that I reflect on, and I use whatever language and style correspond to the ways I do the work. I believe that meditation on and conscious awareness of the image's significance for me, its maker, and for you, its reader/interpreter/co-creator, furthers (not obstructs) the making of art. I gain frameworks for theorizing everyday experiences by allowing the images to speak to and through me, imagining my ways through the images and following them to their deep cenotes, dialoguing with them, and then translating what I've glimpsed. Sometimes the shadow blocks this process and rules my behavior, making the process painful.

I cannot use the old critical language to describe, address, or contain the new subjectivities. Using primary methods of presentation (auto-historia) rather than secondary methods (interpreting other people's conceptions), I reflect on the psychological/mythological aspects of my own expression. I scrutinize my wounds, touch the scars, map the nature of my conflicts, croon to las musas (the muses) that I coax to inspire me, crawl into the shapes the shadow takes, and try to speak with them.

Methods have underlying assumptions, implying theoretical positions and basic premises. There are two standpoints: perceptual, which has a literal reality; and imaginal, which has a psychic reality. In putting images together into story (the story I tell about the images), I use imagistic thinking, employ an imaginal awareness. I'm guided by the spirit of the image. My naguala (daimon or guiding spirit) is an inner sensibility that directs my life—an image, an action, or an internal experience.[2] My imagination and my naguala are connected—they are aspects of the same process, of creativity. Often my naguala draws to me things that are contrary to my will and purpose (compulsions, addictions, negativities), resulting in an anguished impasse. Overcoming these impasses becomes part of the process. This mode of perception is magical thinking: It reads what happens in the external world in terms of my personal intentions and interests. It uses external events to give meaning to my own mythmaking. Magical thinking is not traditionally valued in academic writing.

My text is about the imagination (the psyche's image-creating faculty, the power to make fiction or stories, inner movies like *Star Trek*'s holodeck), about "active imagining," ensueños (dreaming while awake), and interacting consciously with them. We are connected to el cenote via the individual and collective árbol de la vida, and our images and ensueños emerge from that connection, from the self-in-community (inner, spiritual, nature/animals, racial/ethnic, communities of interest, neighborhood, city, nation, planet, galaxy, and the unknown universes). I use "dreaming" or ensueños (the making of images) to figure out what's wrong; foretell current and future events; and establish hidden, unknown connections between lived experiences and theory. This text is about ordeals that trigger thoughts, reflections, and imaginal musings.[3] It deals indirectly with the symbols that I associate with certain archetypal experiences and processes:

> *Thoughts pass like ripples through her body, causing a muscle to tighten here, loosen there. Everything comes in through skin, eyes, ears. She experiences reality physically. No action exists outside of a physical context. Every action is the result of a decision, internal conflict, struggle, resolution, or stalemate. The body always reflects inner activity.* "Espanto," in Los Ensueños de la Prieta[4]

For me, writing is a gesture of the body, a gesture of creativity, a working from the inside out. My feminism is grounded not on incorporeal abstraction but on corporeal realities. The material body is center, and central. The body is the ground of thought. The body is a text. Writing is not about being in your head; it's about being in your body. The body responds physically, emotionally, and intellectually to external and internal stimuli, and writing records, orders, and theorizes about these responses. For me, writing begins with the impulse to push boundaries, to shape ideas, images, and words that travel through the body and echo in the mind into something that has never existed. The writing process is the same mysterious process that we use to make the world.

There's a difference between talking *with* images/stories and talking *about* them. In this text I attempt to talk *with* images/stories, to engage with creative and spiritual processes and their ritualistic aspects. In enacting the relationship between certain images and concepts and my own experience and psyche, I fuse personal narrative with theoretical discourse, autobiographical vignettes with theoretical prose. I create a hybrid genre, a new discursive mode, which I call "autohistoria" and "autohistoria-teoría." Conectando experiencias personales con realidades sociales results in autohistoria, and theorizing about this activity results in autohistoria-teoría. It's a way of inventing and making knowledge, meaning, and identity through self-inscriptions. By making certain personal experiences the subject of this study, I also blur the private/public borders.

In writing this book, I had to figure out how to imagine/create/discover certain concepts/theories, how to shape each essay's structure and design—in other words, I had to map out each essay's universe, the sweep and body of its terrain. I make these discoveries as I write, and not before. I uncover and release the energy shaping each piece, discover its premise, ideas, counter ideas, controlling ideas, and arch plot. I track what lies beyond the originating idea, trace its turning point, its emotional dynamic, and the linking of its parts. I treat each essay as "story" with antagonism, dialogue, crisis, climax, resolution, and poetics. I consider various aspects of craft: narrative technique, use of language—when Spanish is appropriate, theoretical language pertinent, vernacular language suitable.

I don't write from any single disciplinary position. I write outside official theoretical/philosophical language. Mine is a struggle of recognizing and legitimizing excluded selves, especially of women, people of color, queer, and othered groups. I organize and order these ideas as "stories." I believe that it is through narrative that you come to understand and know your self and make sense of the world. Through narrative you formulate your identities by unconsciously locating yourself in social narratives not of your own making.[5] Your culture gives you your identity story, pero en un buscado rompimiento con la tradición you create an alternative identity story.

This book contains the various kinds of "narratives" that make up my life: feminism, race, ethnicity, queerness, gender, and artistic practice. It deals with the processes that occur in reading, writing, and other creative acts. Shamanic imaginings happen while reading or writing a book. The controlled "flights" that reading and writing send us on are a kind of "ensueños" similar to the dream or fantasy process, resembling the magical flights of the journeying shamans. My image for ensueños is of la Llorona astride a wild horse taking flight. In one of her aspects she is pictured as a woman with a horse's head. I "appropriate" Mexican indigenous cultural figures, such as Coyolxauhqui, symbols, and practices. I use imaginal figures (archetypes) of the inner world. I dwell on the imagination's role in journeying to "nonordinary" realities, on the use of the imaginal in nagualismo and its connection to nature spirituality. This text is about acts of imaginative flight in reality and identity construction and reconstructions.

In rewriting narratives of identity, nationalism, ethnicity, race, class, gender, sexuality, and aesthetics, I attempt to show (and not just tell) how transformation happens. My job is not just to interpret or describe realities but to create them through language and action, symbols and images. My task is to guide readers and give them the space to co-create, often against the grain of culture, family, and ego injunctions, against external and internal censorship, against the dictates of genes. From infancy our cultures induct us into the semitrance state of ordinary consciousness, into being in agreement with the people around us, into believing that this is the way things are. It is extremely difficult to shift out of this trance.

This text questions its own formalizing and ordering attempts, its own strategies, the machinations of thought itself, of theory formulated on an experiential level of discourse. It explores the various structures of experience that organize subjective worlds and illuminates meaning in personal experience and conduct. It enters into the dialogue between the new story and the old and attempts to revise the master story.

I hope to contribute to the debate among activist academics trying to intervene, disrupt, challenge, and transform the existing power structures that limit and constrain women. My chief disciplinary fields are creative writing, feminism, art, literature, epistemology, as well as spiritual, race, border, Raza, and ethnic studies. In questioning systems of knowledge, I attempt to add to or alter their norms and make changes in these fields by presenting new theoretical models. With the new tribalism I challenge the Chicano (and other) nationalist narratives. My dilemma, and that of other Chicana and women-of-color writers, is twofold: how to write (produce) without being inscribed (reproduced) in the dominant white structure and how to write without reinscribing and reproducing what we rebel against. Our task is to write against the edict that women should fear their own darkness, that we not broach it in our writings. Nuestra tarea is to envision Coyolxauhqui, not dead and decapitated, but with eyes wide open. Our task is to light up the darkness.

1 | Let us be the healing of the wound

The Coyolxauhqui imperative—La sombra y el sueño

The day the towers fell, me sentí como Coyolxauhqui, la luna. Algo me agarró y me sacudió, frightening la sombra (soul) out of my body. I fell in pieces into that pitch-black brooding place. Each violent image of the towers collapsing, transmitted live all over the world then repeated a thousand times on TV, sucked the breath out of me, each image etched on my mind's eye. Wounded, I fell into shock, cold and clammy. The moment fragmented me, dissociating me from myself. Arresting every vital organ in me, it would not release me.

Bodies on fire, bodies falling through the sky, bodies pummeled and crushed by stone and steel; los cuerpos trapped and suffocating became our bodies. As we watched we too fell, todos caímos. What occurred on September 11, 2001, to the people in the four hijacked airplanes, the World Trade Center twin towers of New York City, and the Pentagon happened to us, too. I couldn't detach from the victims and survivors and their pain. This wounding opened like a gash and widened until a deep chasm separated me from those around me.

In the weeks following éste tremendo arrebato, susto trussed me in its numbing sheath. Suspended in limbo in that in-between space, nepantla, I wandered through my days on autopilot, feeling disconnected from the events of my life. My house whispered and moaned. Within its walls the wind howled. Like la Llorona lost and alone, I was arrested in susto, helplessness, falling, sinking. Swamped with sadness, I mourned all the dead, counted our losses, reflected on our country's role in this tragedy and how I was personally responsible. It was difficult to acknowledge, much less express, the depth of my feelings—instead me lo tragé.

Now, months later, I'm still trying to move through my depression and into another state of mind. I'm still trying to escape my shadow beasts (desconocimientos): numbness, anger, and disillusionment. Besides dealing with my own personal shadow, I must contend with the collective shadow in the psyches of my culture and nation—we always inherit the past problems of family, community, and nation. I stare up at the moon, Coyolxauhqui, and its light in the darkness. I seek a healing image, one that reconnects me to others. I seek the positive shadow that I've also inherited.

With the imperative to "speak" esta herida abierta (this open wound) before it drowns out all voices, the feelings I'd buried begin unfurling. Vulnerable once more, I'm clawed by the talons of grief. I take my sorrow for a walk along the bay near my home in Santa Cruz. With the surf pounding in my ears and the wind's forlorn howl, it feels like even the sea is grieving. I struggle to talk from the wound's gash, make sense of the deaths and destruction, and pull the pieces of my life back together. I yearn to pass on to the next generation the spiritual activism I've inherited from my cultures. If I object to my government's act of war I cannot remain silent. To do so is to be complicitous. But sadly we are all accomplices.

My job as an artist is to bear witness to what haunts us, to step back and attempt to see the pattern in these events (personal and societal), and how we can repair el daño (the damage) by using the imagination and its visions. I believe in the transformative power and medicine of art. As I see it, this country's real battle is with its shadow—its racism, propensity for violence, rapacity for consuming, neglect of its responsibility to global communities and the environment, and unjust treatment of dissenters and the disenfranchised, especially people of color. As an artist I feel compelled to expose this shadow side that the mainstream media and government denies. To understand our complicity and responsibility we must look at the shadow.

Our government's hasty handling of the 9/11 terrorist attacks profoundly disturbs me. We are a nation in trauma, yes. I know that in sudden shocking, stressful situations, a person's or nation's habitual response (usually a variant of anger, fear, helplessness, and depression) overrides all others. When others wound us, we want to hurt them back. Like the terrorist we hunger for retribution, though for different reasons. In the beginning we're provoked into wanting to strike back with deadly force, but later, reason and compassion usually prevail.

However, reason and compassion did *not* prevail with our president, his right-wing allies in the media, and over half of the nation. In the guise of protecting our shores,[1] Bush sought to shore up his image and our national identity. He didn't seek a deeper understanding of the situation; he didn't seek justice through international law. Instead, he engaged the terrorists in a pissing contest. Hiding behind the rhetoric of "good versus evil," us versus them, he daily doled out a racialized language attributing all good to us and complete evil to the terrorists, thus forging a persuasive reactionary nationalistic argument. If we didn't support the "war" to defend civilization, the war against terrorism, we were siding with the terrorists. This ruse threw dust in our eyes, preventing us from looking too closely at our foreign policies. We turned a blank eye (desconocimiento) to those we killed in other countries and had buried in our basement.[2] I ponder what price this country will pay for the secret narrative of Bush and the other predators in power whose agenda allows them to act against the well-being of people in this nation and other countries and against the health of the planet.[3] *Abre los ojos, North America; open your eyes, look at your shadow, and listen to your soul.*

On October 7, my country beat the drums of war; with military might we fell into barbarism. Championing the show of power and the use of fear and force to control, we became the terrorists. We attacked Afghanistan, a nation that had not attacked us—the nineteen terrorists belong to the transnational Al-Qaeda terrorist network, most from Saudi Arabia. The world's lone superpower swiftly shed civilians' blood, as well as that of the Taliban whose atrocities against women and ethnic minorities had been ignored by the U.S. until 9/11. Despite Afghani women's resistance against the Taliban, we had veiled our eyes to the role we played in their oppression. As Sunera Thobani (a Canadian immigrant who writes about violence against women and criticizes American foreign policy and the war against Afghanistan) put it, "Afghani women became almost the poster child for women's oppression in the Third World," a fact we also ignored.

Except for Congresswoman Barbara Lee (representing Berkeley/Oakland), I have no respect for our government leaders. On September 14, she voted against the bill giving Bush carte blanche to deploy the military against those our government perceived to be responsible for the attacks. Out of a congressional body of 421 members, hers was the only dissenting vote. A real "hero" who throws into light Bush's false bravado, her courage made her a target of hate groups and could have cost her political career. In her address she urged that we step back a moment; think through and understand the implications of our actions; use restraint; and not rush to judgment, counterattack, or open-ended war.[4]

By bombing "the enemy," we sentence to slow death by starvation 7.5 million Afghan refugees (thirty-five times the number that died in Hiroshima and Nagasaki combined) who rely on food and medical aid to survive; relief efforts are blocked by the bombings.[5]

By dismissing them as "collateral damage,"[6] we regard their deaths as less valuable than those who died on 9/11. Our hasty retaliatory war against a small, impoverished nation, whose Taliban regime the U.S. formerly funded, shocked the world's conscience.[7] The U.S. lost the world's sympathy; many now view us not only as imperialist neo-colonizers but also as terrorists.[8] Many look at Bush/the U.S. as a modern Hitler, but the genocidal tally may triple Hitler's. Saying evil was done to us, our government claims the moral high ground and role of victim. But we are now, and have been for decades, the bullies of the planet.

Many accuse the U.S. of using the military to advance economic and political interests around the world and point to a history of colonialism, imperialism, and supporting right-wing dictatorships at the expense of freedom and democracy. The U.S. manipulated the overthrow of independent nations in Latin America, Asia, and Africa to establish puppet dictators, giving them military aid to fund corporate businesses and sweatshops.[9] According to Sunera Thobani, the CIA-backed coup against the elected government of Salvador Allende in Chile resulted in the deaths of more than thirty thousand people. The U.S.-backed regime in El Salvador used death squads to kill seventy-five thousand people. The U.S.-sponsored terrorist contra war in Nicaragua led to the deaths of more than thirty thousand people. As a result of the United Nations–imposed sanctions (enforced by U.S. power), the initial bombings in Iraq in 1990 resulted in two hundred thousand dead. The United Nations Children's Fund (UNICEF) estimates that more than one million Iraqis have died and that five thousand more have died every month in the past ten years. One hundred fifty thousand were killed and fifty thousand disappeared in Guatemala after the CIA-sponsored coup in 1954. More than two million were killed in Vietnam. U.S.-backed authoritarian regimes include Saudi Arabia, Egypt, the apartheid regime in South Africa, Suharto's dictatorship in Indonesia, Marcos in the Philippines, and Israel's various occupations of Palestinian territories.

Osama bin Laden alludes to our support of Israel and our indifference to the plight of the Palestinians as the reason for his terrorist attacks on the United States. Others blame the U.S. for the worldwide abuse of globalization (destruction of traditional ways of living and exploitation of the poor by the wealthy). Whatever the reason, nothing can justify an act of terrorism, whether it's committed by religious fundamentalists or private militia or prettied up as a war of "just" retribution by our government.

"We're the victims here," the war-for-profit mongers proclaimed, pushing a nation-sponsored "war against terrorism" by invoking the names of the dead in New York City. By justifying the war they hope to veil their efforts to reestablish control in the Middle East and exploit its natural gas and oil reserves.[10] They drove us into the "perceived" enemy's trap of exchanging one wound for another, of justifying the killing of women and children.[11] To boost his cowboy self-image, Bush comes riding on his white horse, a gunslinger at high noon, bragging that he'll bring in Osama bin Laden "dead or alive" and save the world for us.

In a 180-degree turn, Bush assumes a feministic guise and intimates that he'll emancipate the Afghan women from their backward, uncivilized Third World culture. Yeah, sure he'll save these women behind veils whom our policies silenced, reduced to meeting in secret to learn and teach, diminished to begging in the streets. With his war toys he'll ejaculate bombs into their bodies, disremembering that the U.S. supported Pakistan's empowerment of the Taliban, which, in turn, silenced and veiled its women. He ignores our own culture's attempt to silence and gag women and men of color. Cable News Network (CNN) and most of the U.S. media disseminate Bush's savior perspective and the government's propaganda, which originates from the boardrooms of Texas oil companies and other corporations that thrive on a war economy, imperialism, and globalization. We remain un- and misinformed about the military's role in enforcing policies benefiting U.S. corporations while costing the lives of millions around the world.

All U.S. media (except for alternative) censors news of the massive opposition to the war in every country, including the United States.[12] Bush and his administration accuse those who protest the war of being unpatriotic, an accusation tantamount to treason. You're siding with the terrorists, they tell us when we demand a peaceful resolution or protest the theft of our human rights in the name of fighting terrorism. No dissent is tolerated, especially if it comes from feminists, progressives, people of color, immigrants, and Arab and Islamic Americans. According to an October 2001 editorial in *Sojourner*, Bush's Justice Department and the new Office of Homeland Security could turn into a witch-hunting squad targeting peace and human rights activists, documented and undocumented immigrants, and those seeking alternatives to Bush's war agenda. His efforts to eliminate civil liberties such as legal and due processes puts many of us in danger of terrorist attacks from our own government. Attacks on activist organizations violate the First Amendment giving us the right to advocate for change and guaranteeing free speech. Illegal search and seizures violate the Fourth Amendment, and being forced to answer the FBI's or INS's questions violates the Fifth Amendment (the right to remain silent). When people are jailed without being charged and are indefinitely detained, the land becomes a police state invasive with security checks and surveillance.

Racialized language leads to racial profiling, which leads to targeting dark-skinned, Middle Eastern–looking, and other people of color earmarked as potential terrorists. So that white Americans can keep their illusions of safety and entitlement unmarred, our government sets up oppressive measures such as racial profiling, which make people of color feel disposable, perpetually unsafe, and torn apart like Coyolxauhqui. Bush's attempts to make the country "safe" from terrorism endanger some of our residents. Under martial law, we would lose most of our rights.[13] In a television appearance, Barbara Bush, bearing limited knowledge of what goes on in this country, exhibited her singular and myopic reality by stating that after 9/11 Americans were no longer safe. She's oblivious to the fact that for women of color, home and homeland have not been safe places—our bodies are constantly targeted, trespassed, and violated. Poor white women and young Black and Latino men have never been safe in this country—a country that internally colonizes people of color, enforces women's domestication through violence, and continues the slow genocide of Native Americans.

By ignoring the ramifications of his headlong actions, Bush and his yes-men dishonored the 2,792 dead and the 300 firefighters and police who died saving lives. They betrayed the people killed in the hijacked jets and the towers; they sold out the children, families, and friends of these victims. They broke faith with the Ground Zero rescue workers who hunt through the burning rubble looking for the remains of the dead. They delivered into the hands of the "assumed" enemy the young men and women in our military who will become casualties of war.[14] They abandoned the 574,000 workers who have lost their jobs since 9/11 when they gave IBM a $1.4 billion tax rebate and large sums to other corporations but refused to give unemployment insurance to those laid off from their jobs.[15] Bamboozled, many Ground Zero rescue workers, as well as the recently unemployed, believe that Bush honors them. Unlike progressives and radicals, these "Bush-rescued" people turn their faces away from our collective shadow and pretend not to see how torn apart this country is internally. But I suspect that the masses have a growing suspicion that Bush is not acting in the best interests of this nation or of the world.

Bush and half of U.S. Americans fell into fear and hate. The instinct toward violence has become so normalized in this country that many succumbed, reacting inhumanely instead of responding compassionately. It's unfortunate that we get our national identity and narrative from this majority who refuse to recognize that conflict is not resolved through war. They refuse el conocimiento (spiritual knowledge) that we're connected by invisible fibers to everyone on the planet and that each person's actions affect the rest of the world. Putting gas in our cars connects us to the Middle East. Take a shower squandering water and someone on the planet goes thirsty; waste food and someone starves to death. Although we make up approximately 4.5 percent of the people on the planet, we consume 82 percent of its resources.[16] And fear, ignorance, greed, overconsumption, and a voracious appetite for power is what this war is about. Our rapacious demands have made plunderers of us all. We allow predators like Bush to take control of our nation and kill off the dream (el sueño) of what our culture could be—a model of democracy. Similarly, western neo-colonialism sucks the resources (life force) from Third World countries.

Casting a long shadow before me, I continue walking along the sea trying to figure out what good, if any, can come from death and destruction. Death and destruction do shock us out of our familiar daily rounds and force us to confront our desconocimientos, our sombras— the unacceptable attributes and unconscious forces that a person must wrestle with to achieve integration. They expose our innermost fears, forcing us to interrogate our souls. As I continue andando (walking), other people's shadows glide over mine, reminding me of our collective shadow beasts. I see Bush and his cohorts not as the cultural heroes they profess to be but as our collective psyche's darkest aspects, the parts of our culture that act without corazón y sin razón (without compassion or intelligence) and do so with impunity. Their unconscionable, destructive aspects represent the predators we must brave and whose fangs we must pull out. We're responsible for the failure of our collective imagination that gave us such poor choices that we were forced to put Bush in office (the legitimacy of Bush's election as president was silenced after 9/11 in the name of patriotism and "standing by" our man). It's up to us to either prune his powers or kick him out of office.

I'm aware that we all harbor a Bush-type raptor within our psyches. I know that Bush and his gang are not totally evil or one-dimensional, though their motives are suspect. I think he acted as though he was showing restraint by waiting for the Taliban to turn bin Laden over to the United States before declaring "war." But here I suspect he was pandering to his ego, acting tough to hide his fear of being weak. Surely he can't be so tapado (mentally clogged) that he can't see beyond black and white into the gray areas and other versions of reality? Right now it's hard for me to be charitable. Our nation is a powerful horse, and he is riding it badly.

A momentous event such as that of 9/11 es un arrebatamiento con la fuerza de una hacha. Carlos Castaneda's Don Juan would call such times the day the world stopped, but the world doesn't so much stop as it cracks. What cracked is our perception of the world, how we relate to it, how we engage with it. Afterward we view reality differently— we see through its rendijas (holes) to the illusion of consensual reality. The world as we know it "ends." We experience a radical shift in perception, otra forma de ver.

Este choque shifts us to nepantla, a psychological, liminal space between the way things had been and an unknown future. Nepantla is the space in-between, the locus and sign of transition. In nepantla we realize that realities clash, authority figures of the various groups demand contradictory commitments, and we and others have failed living up to idealized goals. We're caught in remolinos (vortexes), each with different, often contradictory forms of cognition, perspectives, worldviews, belief systems—all occupying the transitional nepantla space (see figure 1.1).

Torn between ways, we seek to find some sort of harmony amid the remolinos of multiple and conflictive worldviews; we must learn to integrate all these perspectives. Transitions are a form of crisis, an emotionally significant event or a radical change in status. During crisis the existential isolation all people experience is exacerbated. Unruly emotions and conflicts break out. In nepantla we hang out between shifts, trying to make rational sense of this crisis, seeking solace, support, appeasement, or some kind of intimate connection. En este lugar we fall into chaos, fear of the unknown, and are forced to take up the task of self-redefinition. In nepantla we undergo the anguish of changing our perspectives and crossing a series of cruz calles, junctures, and thresholds, some leading to a different way of relating to people and surroundings and others to the creation of a new world. Nepantleras such as artistas/activistas help us mediate these transitions, help us make the crossings, and guide us through the transformation process—a process I call conocimiento.[17]

The ending of one way of being and the beginning of another brings to mind the prophecies of ancient indigenous cultures, which predict that the materialistic present cycle is coming to an end and a more spiritual cycle is commencing. In terms of evolutionary stages, the world is currently between el quinto sol y el sexto. According to Mayan knowledge, the sixth world starts December 2012. It is this nuevo mundo, this new order, we need to create with the choices we make, the acts we perform, and the futures we dream.

Chaotic disruptions, violence, and death catapult us into the Coyolxauhqui state of dissociation and fragmentation that characterizes our times. Our collective shadow—made up of the destructive aspects, psychic wounds, and splits in our own culture—is aroused, and we are forced to confront it. In trying to make sense of what's happening, some of us come into deep awareness (conocimiento) of political and

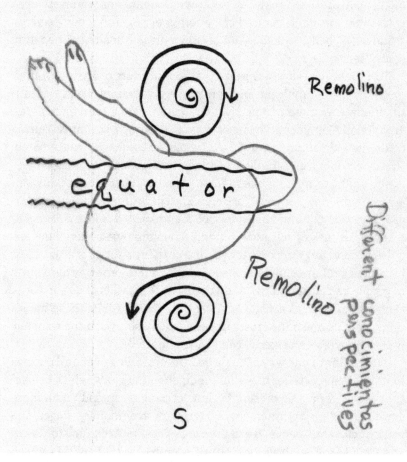

1.1 | Remolinos

spiritual situations and the unconscious mechanisms that abet hate, intolerance, and discord. I name this searching, inquiring, and healing consciousness "conocimiento."[18]

Conocimiento urges us to respond not just with the traditional practice of spirituality (contemplation, meditation, and private rituals) or with the technologies of political activism (protests, demonstrations, and speakouts), but with the amalgam of the two: spiritual activism, which we've also inherited along with la sombra. Conocimiento pushes us into engaging the spirit in confronting our social sickness with new tools and practices whose goal is to effect a shift. *Spirit-in-the-world* becomes conscious, and *we* become conscious of spirit in the world. The healing of our wounds results in transformation, and transformation results in the healing of our wounds.

In the days after September 11, many of us heard a different kind of call to action, a psycho-spiritual/political call. Americans in great numbers gathered in public spaces to pray. We set up peace organizations, vigils, marches, and interfaith prayer meetings. We gave speeches, donated blood, frequented Middle Eastern restaurants, sent e-mail, signed petitions, connected to activist organizations through the Internet, and made art. For me, this call to respond is symbolized by la Llorona, whose cry initiates my will.

As we thrash about in our inner and external struggling grounds trying to get our bearings, we totter between two paths: The path of desconocimiento leads human consciousness into ignorance, fear, and hatred. It succumbs to righteous judgment and withdraws into separation and domination, pushing most of us into retaliatory acts of further rampage, which beget more violence. This easier path uses force and violence to socially construct our nation. Conocimiento, the more difficult path, leads to awakening, insights, understandings, realizations, courage, and the motivation to engage in concrete ways with the potential to bring us into compassionate interactions. Self-righteousness creates the abyss; conocimiento builds bridges across it. En estos tiempos de la Llorona we must use creativity to jolt us into awareness of our spiritual/political problems and other major global tragedies so that we can repair el daño. The Coyolxauhqui imperative is to heal and achieve integration. When fragmentations occur, you fall apart and feel as though you've been expelled from paradise. Coyolxauhqui is my symbol for the necessary process of dismemberment and fragmentation, of seeing that self or the situations you're embroiled in differently. Coyolxauhqui is also my symbol for reconstruction and reframing, one that allows for putting the pieces together in a new way. The Coyolxauhqui imperative is an ongoing process of making and unmaking. There is never any resolution, just the process of healing.

I think of the humbleness, compassion, and generosity that the people of our nation are capable of, donating millions of dollars to the victims' families, driving across the country to assist at Ground Zero. Devastating events can help us overcome our desconocimientos, which dehumanize other people and deny their suffering, prompting us to realize our common humanity. As we see beyond what divides us to what connects us, we're compelled to reach out beyond our walls of distrust, extend our hands to others, and share information and resources. The human species' survival depends on each one of us connecting to our vecinos (neighbors), whether they live across the street, across national borders, or across oceans. A calamity of the magnitude of 9/11 can compel us to think not in terms of "my" country or "your" nation but "our" planet.

What we do now counts even more than the frightening event, close call, shock, violation, or loss that made cracks in our worlds. En estos tiempos of loss, fear, and confusion the human race must delve into its cenotes (wells) of collective wisdom, both ancient and modern. Though only a small percentage of the world's six billion people have achieved a high level of awareness, this collective consciousness has the power to counterbalance the negativity of the rest of humanity.[19] Ultimately, each of us has the potential to change the sentience of the world.

In addition to community building, we can transform our world by imagining it differently, dreaming it passionately via all our senses, and willing it into creation. As we think inspiring, positive, life-generating thoughts and embody these thoughts in every act we perform, we can gradually change the mood of our days, the habits of years, and the beliefs of a lifetime. Changing the thoughts and ideas (the "stories") we live by and their limiting beliefs (including the national narrative of supreme entitlement) will enable us to extend our hand to others con el corazón con razón en la mano. Individually and collectively we can begin to share strategies on peaceful coexistence y desparamar (spread) conocimientos. Each of us can make a difference. By bringing psychological understanding and using spiritual approaches in political activism we can stop the destruction of our moral, compassionate humanity.[20] Empowered, we'll be motivated to organize, achieve justice, and begin to heal the world.

As I walk along the ocean seeking a medicine, watching the waves rise and fall, my mind opens to the horizon's crimson line between water and sky. I seek a way to bring all my feelings and thoughts together to create un testimonio that's harmonious, cohesive, and healing. Only by speaking of these events and by creating do I become visible to myself and come to terms with what happens. Though it is hard to think and act positively en estos tiempos de Coyolxauhqui, it is exactly these times of dislocation/separation that hold the promise of wholeness. We must bear witness to what our bodies remember, what el corazón con razón experiences, and share these with others though we be branded unpatriotic and un-American. These healing narratives serve not just as self-nurturing "therapy," but actually change reality. We revise reality by altering our consensual agreements about what is real, what is just and fair. We can trans-shape reality by changing our perspectives and perceptions. By choosing a different future, we bring it into being.

I listen to waves impact the shore, waves originating from beyond the far edge of the sea, perhaps caused by a storm in a distant corner of the earth or the ice melting in the Arctic. Our actions have ripple effects on all people and the planet's environment. We are accountable for all the wars, all human disasters—none of us are blameless. We ourselves have brought this great turmoil upon ourselves. We are all wounded, but we can connect through the wound that's alienated us from others. When the wound forms a cicatrix, the scar can become a bridge linking people split apart. What happened may not have been in our individual control, but how we react to it and what we do about it is. Let's use art and imagination to discover how we feel and think and to help us respond to the world. It is in nepantla that we write and make art, bearing witness to the attempt to achieve resolution and balance where there may be none in real life. In nepantla we try to gain a foothold on los remolinos and quagmires, we try to put a psycho-spiritual/political frame on our lives' journeys.

Levántate, rise up in testimony. Let's begin by admitting that as a nation we're killing the dream of this country (a true democracy) by making war and depriving many of life and basic human rights. Let's acknowledge the harm we've done, the need to be accountable. Let's stop giving energy to only one side of our instinctual nature, to negative consciousness. When we own our shadow, we allow the breath of healing to enter our lives. Let's look at these events as catalysts that allow us to reframe global disasters, prompt us into remapping our priorities—figuring out exactly what we believe in, what our lives mean, and what our purpose is as individuals, as a nation, and as world citizens. Let's call on our inner resources to help us in times of rising and falling, peace and war, compassion and violence. Let's have compassion for all those who suffer from violence. Let's use internal and external conflicts and wounds to enter the soul.

Like the moon rising over the scintillating blue waters, let's be resilient, let's persevere and prevail with grace. Like Coyolxauhqui, let's put our dismembered psyches and patrias (homelands) together in new constructions. It is precisely during these in-between times that we must create the dream (el sueño) of the sixth world. May we allow the interweaving of all the minds and hearts and life forces to create the collective dream of the world and teach us how to live out ese sueño. May we allow spirit to sustain and guide us from the path of dissolution. May we do work that matters. Vale la pena, it's worth the pain.

Down on the beach, drummers serenade Yemayá, ocean mother. I'd like to think they're beating the drums of peace, calling our souls back into our bodies. We are the song that sings us. It begins with "Let us fight no more but heal the wounds of nations. Let us be the healing of the wound." I watch the gray pelicans rise up, up. As day swallows itself la luna rises, rises, guiding me home—she is my third eye. Her light is my medicine.

Contigo en la lucha,
Gloria E. Anzaldúa
February 2002

2 | Flights of the Imagination

Rereading/Rewriting Realities

I pick the ground from which to speak
a reality into existence.
I have chosen to struggle against unnatural boundaries.

El árbol de la vida/the tree of life

I sit on the knuckled roots of la Virgen's tree and talk to it when I'm feeling jubilant or when painful memories take over and the whispering waves can't soothe the pangs. A severe winter storm broke off a section of this Monterrey cypress one February several years ago, and the park arborist sawed off the hewn branch and the trunk's damaged flank. That day, spirits flagging, I walked toward the cypress on West Cliff along the sea. In the mist and the fog and the stinging wind, I suddenly saw her coming out of the hollowed trunk: It was la Virgen de Guadalupe, head tilted, arms extended, halo spread all around. From a distance, the bright live tans and browns of the raw newly cut wood and dangling trunk fibers looked like the folds of her robe. Since then they've leached into a weathered gray like the sun-bleached houses of Mexicans in South Texas. But once I saw la Virgen emerging from the tree, my imagination picks her out every time I walk toward her, no matter how age, storm, or sea alters the cypress's trunk.

When I go for walks with my friends, they don't see la Virgen until I call their attention to her. Later, they always see and point her out to their friends. It's sort of like hunting for hidden animals in children's coloring books; it requires a slight shift in perspective to bring them up from the foliage. It feels like the tree is teaching me how to perceive not only with the physical eyes but also with the whole body, and especially to *see* with the eyes of my other body. The Guadalupe tree reminds me of something I'd forgotten—that my body has always sensed trees' special relationship to humans, that we have a body awareness of trees and they of us. Awareness is not just in the mind, but also includes body knowledge. This awareness awakens some deep hidden memory or lost knowledge of times past, reminding me that I'm doing something I didn't know I knew. It reminds me that I've been developing an ongoing relationship with the spirit of trees and nature sites since I was a child and that I can alter consciousness in order to communicate with them.[1] To chamanas, consciousness refers to that part of our being called "spirit"; trees, rocks, rivers, and animals have consciousness.[2] I came to the conocimiento that this personal, private, spiritual practice of healing focuses on our daily lives—the work, people, places, emotions, and personal experiences that make up our existence.[3] This story of la Virgen's tree is a healing vision; stories ("teachings") are also healers.

Spirit and mind, soul and body, are one, and together they perceive a reality greater than the vision experienced in the ordinary world. I know that the universe is conscious and that spirit and soul communicate by sending subtle signals to those who pay attention to our surroundings, to animals, to natural forces, and to other people. We receive information from ancestors inhabiting other worlds. We assess that information and learn how to trust that knowing. The mind does not make things up; it just imagines what exists and tells the soul to remember. The soul forgets and must be reminded again and again by signals from nature whose spirits exist in fields, forests, rivers, and other places, and from arrebatamientos (traumatic events). "The imagination conversely illumines us, speaks with us, sings with us," writes Joy Harjo.[4]

Today with the sea's scent rising up and the cypress's fragrance wafting down, I ask the tree for an inspiration. I ask it to help me imagine and open to el cenote, that underground well of memories and shamanic images, and find a frame for this essay. Instantly an image comes to me: Es el árbol de la vida, el árbol de Tamanzuchan, an image I've written about many times. The tree is a link between worlds. Just as the cosmic tree connects under, middle, and upper world, I'll connect this essay's sections: from the roots to the ground and up its trunk to the branches and on to the sky, a journey from the depths of the underworld that ascends to the concrete physical world, and then to the upper realities of spirit, in a constant descend/ascend movement. But the problem with this up/down, linear description is that these three worlds aren't separate. Interconnected and overlapping, they occupy the same place.

Now I have a paradigm, a framework or scheme for understanding and explaining certain aspects of reality, and I'll organize my images, ideas, and knowledge via this mind map. Next I must think in images, hunt for symbols, and engage in conceptual interpretations of those images—that is, I must translate images as symbols for concepts and ideas. I must do it not by controlling the images as my conscious mind wants but by surrendering to them and letting them guide me.

The world tree

The world tree, axis mundi, is tripartite. The underworld exists below the Earth's surface and is represented by the roots; it is the realm of Earth energies, animal spirits, and the dead who have not moved on to the next level of existence. In this realm, soul is knowledge of seasons, weather, animal and plant life, and the dead, as well as healing techniques for illness and disease. The post-Jungian imaginal/archetypal psychologist James Hillman defines the underworld as "the mythological style of describing a psychological cosmos."[5] What is the nature of the underworld itself? According to Hillman, the underworld refers to the psychic perspective, the soul's attitude: "We are not presenting images of the underworld. . . . No, the underworld is a perspective within the image by means of which our consciousness enters or is initiated into the underworld viewpoint."[6] The middle world, the physical plane where we live our ordinary lives, is symbolized by the trunk; it is the realms of the planet and the outer reaches of the universe. Journeying to the middle world can show la chamana ordinary reality's actual conditions and their spiritual aspects; she can discover the location of something, influence weather, view people and events at a distance, journey to meet spirits of place, and perform rituals to honor or propitiate nature spirits. Represented by the branches, the upper world above the sky is the world of noncorporeal energies, spirits who are gods and goddesses, spirits of the dead who have progressed beyond the land of the dead. I'm not sure whether Tlatlayan—the hereafter, the other world—is represented by the upper- or the underworld.[7]

These three interconnected, overlapping worlds are the same place. Shamans journey into these worlds of the cosmos to gain knowledge of the universe beyond Earth, explore parallel universes, and receive divine inspiration. Knowledge and help from the upper world instruct us in our roles as spiritual beings who participate in a larger, more cosmic existence. These three worlds' geographies, types of spirits, and spiritual experiences differ culturally.

Pregnant with story

I was the girl whose imagination swallowed the house, lagoon, corrals, and woods. My imagination made me pregnant with story. I literally ate my grandmothers' and mother's stories. "Don't go in the water," my mother would say. "A snake will crawl into your vagina and make you pregnant."[8] Hers was a cautionary tale so that I wouldn't bare my body like the gringa girls. "Don't go out late at night; a snake will enter your vagina." But my mother was really saying, "Don't go out late at night; a man will rape you." This association between rape and a snake or lizard entering through the vagina and incubating in the uterus has its origin in a story recorded in the sixteenth century by Bernardino de Sahagún. As Rosan A. Jordan explains, women were warned: Don't bathe in lakes and rivers (that is, don't expose your womanly charms to the eyes of others); the axolotl (the larval stage of the salamander) will get inside you, make you pregnant with little animals.[9] Some thought that sperm lived in rivers and lakes. But the snake of my imagination is female: Serpent Woman, another name for la Llorona whose ghostly body carries el nagual (a human who shape-shifts into an animal or one's guardian spirit) possessing la facultad, the capacity for shape-changing form and identity. Since childhood I've been fascinated by wereanimals (and I'm not referring to werewolves here).[10] I view Serpent Woman/la Llorona as a coiled snake with the head of a woman and as a woman's body with the head of a horse.[11]

El nagual in my house

As I walk into my living room, a shadowy figure undulates across my carpet. My heart leaps. Es una víbora, a familiar thing, and my heart settles when I recognize it. I've encountered "real" snakes countless times in my life, but this snake has entered my house—for the second time in ten years. This snake lives under my house; it came into my living room, up through a hole in the square of uncovered ground in the entryway where a large plant grows. On this night sueño con la víbora; an imaginal snake (a psychic inner figure), appears in one of my dreams, and two days later, as I'm walking across Lighthouse Field Park, another "real" snake crosses my path.[12] Whether material or imaginal, este animal symbolically represents transformation for me: encounters where nature—a bird, a tree, the wind—catches my attention and awakens me to another reality, a healing spirituality that calls for soul recovery.[13] I hear the snake warn me, "You're leaking energy, and parts of your spirit have gone missing. Get back the missing pieces of your soul." En estos encuentros I feel that I've "met" my guardian animal, my daimon, known as "el nagual" in Toltec spiritual traditions.[14]

When I encounter la víbora, my guardian spirit, a deep stillness comes over me. I'm aware of my breath and my heartbeat, but nothing else. Time collapses. My body shifts gears. Mi cuerpo becomes part of, merges with, "disappears" into my surroundings. I feel my body's intense focus on and awareness of the snake—I'm seeing it, and it's seeing me. My body sends tendrils of awareness from my solar plexus to the snake's body, and my consciousness flows out along these threads and into la víbora. My tongue becomes her tongue, testing and tasting the air. When my consciousness flows into an animal, it becomes my vehicle to see, feel, touch, hear, taste, and smell in the underworld or otherworld. Psychoanalysis calls these realms the "unconscious," an abstract concept, the unknown lands. This real/imaginal animal initiates me into these worlds via its perspective and "language."

All my life I've encountered serpents—rattlesnakes slithering under the porch, egg-sucking black king snakes in the chicken coop, bullwhips streaking across the arid land, garden snakes sleeping en el jardín. Though snakes de carne y hueso, they activate imaginal, symbolic images in my mind. This confluence of physical and imaginal snakes becomes indistinguishable one from the other. According to Hillman, animal images do not represent instincts; nor do they stand for our bestiality. They are not our images; they are not images *of* animals but images *as* animals. They show us that images are daimonic forces, equivalent to "spirits."[15] Images are animals, helping beings who assist us on our underworld journey each night. All inner images, says Hillman, are "power animals," and the power is imagination.[16] Animal images in dreams are "carriers of soul . . . there to help us see in the dark."[17] Power animals and spirit teachers may be aspects of their "higher selves," or Jungian archetypes. A lower-world journey may be viewed as contacting the personal or collective unconscious or as an excursion into a parallel universe. Snakes may symbolize the life of the unconscious.[18]

SOUL WORK, IMAGE WORK

Nepantla: Bridge between worlds

Perceiving something from two different angles creates a split in awareness that can lead to the ability to control perception, to balance contemporary society's worldview with the nonordinary worldview, and to move between them to a space that simultaneously exists and does not exist. I call entering this realm "nepantla"—the Nahuatl word for an in-between space, el lugar entre medio. Nepantla, palabra indígena: un concepto que se refiere a un lugar no-lugar. In the murals of Teotihuacan, nepantla represented the afterlife. My concept of nepantla is similar to Victor Turner's theory of liminal space. Turner modified Arnold van Gennep's concept of liminality to describe a zone of impetuous transition, the point of contact between the worlds of nature and spirit, between humans and the numinous (divine). This liminal space facilitates the bridging and joining of these worlds through ritual transformation.

Tuning in to the "other" mind or "other" self, the creative unconscious taps into el cenote, an inner, underground river of information. By attending to the stream of mental experience, one becomes aware of the connective tissue, nepantla, the bridge between the compartments or, to use Santa Teresa of Ávila's phrase, between the "mansions" of the self. Nepantla is the bridge between the material and the immaterial; the point of contact y el lugar between ordinary and spirit realities; the midground in the vertical continuum of spirit/soul that places spirituality at the top end (heaven) and soul at the opposite end (underworld). According to Mexican indigenous spirituality, el alma es una entidad que puede desprenderse del cuerpo. Soul is interiority of both the human personality and the external world, the anima mundi. Imagination's soul dimension bridges body and nature to spirit and mind, making these connections in the in-between space of nepantla. Nepantla is also where spiritual transformation or rebirth occurs during visionary states of consciousness.[19]

Soul loss and susto

The process of falling apart (the Coyolxauhqui process), of being wounded, is a sort of shamanic initiatory dismemberment that gives suffering a spiritual and soulful value. The shaman's initiatory ordeal includes some type of death or dismemberment during the ecstatic trance journey. Torn apart into basic elements and then reconstructed, the shaman acquires the power of healing and returns to help the community. To be healed we must be dismembered, pulled apart. The healing occurs in disintegration, in the demotion of the ego as the self's only authority.[20] By connecting with our wounding, the imaginal journey makes it worthwhile. Healing images bring back the pieces, heal las rajaduras. As Hillman notes, healing is a deep change of attitude that involves an adjustment and abandonment of "ego-heroics." It requires that we shift our perspective.

La curandera, the folk healer

If the world is a construct and meaning is rendered by the mind and does not inhere in objects, it would follow that what one knows and experiences is a projection. So what is real? "Do you think spirits are real?" a friend asked me.[21] I've been asked this question many times, and each time the question takes me back to my childhood, when I learned, witnessing las curanderas de mi mamagrande, that the physical world is not the only reality.

My grandmother Ramoncita believed that an older woman had bewitched her son, my uncle Rafa, into falling in love with her. Esa mujer que había embrujado a mi tío tenía papeles, pero the town's people always called her a mojada. Rafa was obsessed with her. He couldn't eat, he couldn't sleep, and he'd walk around como un becerro perdido. El resto de la familia attributed his condition to los nervios, not bewitchment. Rafa went to doctors in Edinburgh, McAllen, and Reynosa, but they couldn't find a thing wrong with him. Finally, as a last resort, Mamagrande Ramona hired a curandera from Las Flores, a town across the border, para que viniera a curar mi tío de su enfermedad.

The next day I saw the curandera arrive in an old, beat-up Chevy. She was a small woman with prominent Indian features. La curandera claimed to be one of Don Pedrito Jaramillo's apprentices. My grandmother had had much respect for the curer and holy man Don Pedro, who had lived in Olmos, a settlement near the town of Falfurias in South Texas. Mi abuela me platicaba que gente from all over the Southwest and places as far as New York would go to him to be healed. As many as five hundred people would camp at Los Olmos Creek and wait for him to heal with a blend of shamanism, herbs, and invocations to Catholic saints. He died when my grandmother was a young girl, but he had trained others to carry on his work. People still travel long distances to place wreaths and letters on his grave, to meditate and pray. If you walk into a botánica anywhere in the Southwest or northern Mexico, you will find candles with his picture and a prayer. He has become a folk hero, one whom the Catholic Church has not canonized.

The curandera began by taking some small branches tied together with herbs and sweeping them over my tío's body. Con té hecho de hierbas y hojas de eucalipto, frotó su cuerpo. This was a limpieza, she said. Then she took un huevo fresco, a fresh egg, and rubbed it over his body. El huevo, she claimed, would absorb the disease caused by the bad spirit invading him. She cracked open the egg into a bowl and examined it for spots or marks. The spots and condition of the egg, she said, helped her divine the cause and origin of the sickness. Después enterró el huevo en la tierra. She buried the egg in the backyard.

Next she stood in the middle of the dining room with her eyes half-closed, rocking back and forth for about ten minutes, not saying a word. Just as I thought she was going to fall, she came out of her trance and walked out of the house through the back door. We trailed after her. She squatted at the edge of the kitchen and stared into the crawl space. Then she reached her thin brown arm up to the floor's foundation and pulled out a round ball that seemed to be covered with wet fur. She reached up two more times. The three balls were identical.

They looked like curled up dead rats. Con mis dos ojos los ví. I had watched her closely since she arrived—she hadn't had time to plant those balls under the house.

That night Rafa slept well, and the next morning he ate a huge breakfast of huevos rancheros with beans and six tortillas. He was back to his own spritely self y yo empezé a tenerles fé a las curanderas and the reality of spirits. People said she had "el don," the gift for healing, along with special sight, or "vista," enabling her to know the causes and cures of illnesses.

During my childhood, curanderismo and hechicerismo were an accepted yet disdained part of the Chicano community. Most Mexican Americans, having swallowed the whites' contempt for indigenous medicine, did not believe that curanderas could restore the soul and heal the body. They thought all curanderas and curanderos were charlatans, out to hoodwink dollars from the gullible. But many others continued practicing curanderismo, along with western traditional medicine. Those of us who believe in curanderismo know that all illnesses have psychological causes; in order to cure, the whole person must be treated. We also know that there are certain Anglo diseases that only western medicine can cure. It wasn't until some years ago that academic researchers and their documentary films gave curanderos a new respectability, conferring cultural legitimacy on traditional medicine.

Chamanas, curanderas, artistas, and spiritual activists, like nepantleras, are liminal people, at the thresholds of form, forever betwixt and between.[22] They move among different realities and psychic states, journeying beyond the natural order or status quo and into other worlds. Often curanderas express an oppositional worldview. For them, life is a struggle between forces of good and evil, and their lives and therapeutic philosophies have an adversarial quality. They mediate between life-giving and life-taking forces, bring the opposites together in some meaningful fashion. They seem to perform a balancing act by standing above the contest and mastering both sides. Curanderos' cultural ideology represents an adaptation to—not an adoption of—the Christian ethos. The shamanic balance is not achieved by synthesis; it is not a static condition acquired by resolving opposition, a tension that exists when two forces encounter each other headlong and are not reconciled but teeter on the edge of chaos. This balance is not that of the highest good as the golden mean. One pole cannot exist without its opposite, as westerners would like to think, seeking good without evil, pleasure without pain, god without the devil, love without hate. But la chamana stands at the juncture of opposing forces and moves between them.

Shamanic journeying

A type of Mesoamerican magic supernaturalism, nagualismo is an alternative epistemology, a folk theory of knowledge conditioned by a long-standing ideology and belief system. Nagualismo's basic assumptions (worldview) are shapeshifting (the ability to become an animal or thing) and traveling to other realities. These journeys require a different kind of "seeing": the ability to perceive the world in a different way, the perceptual experience of what Carlos Castaneda calls "nonordinary" reality.[23] To "see," one must "stop the world" (accomplished by interrupting the flow of thoughts and interpretations of the everyday world). To "see," says Don Juan, one has to sneak between the worlds of ordinary reality and the world of the sorcerers.[24] This way of "reading" reality is central to chamanería.

El chamanismo es una alianza entre los humanos y "los dioses"—La chamana explica, alivia, y previene las desgracias. A system of healing based on spiritual practices, chamanería has survived for more than forty thousand years. It is the oldest known religious practice, one in which the shaman or nagual undertakes a "journey" (or trance journey) to the underworld, upper world, or other worlds, moving from one zone to another to encounter "spirits" from whom she or he obtains healing insights and brings them back to help their community. Chamanería is an animistic system; a "nature religion"; a system of healing; and a personal, private, spiritual practice that focuses on our daily lives—the work, people, places, emotions, and individual experiences that compose our existence. Chamanería awakens some deep, hidden memory or lost knowledge of times past. The shaman acquires this knowledge and power from the helping spirits she encounters on journeys to other realities. She uses specific techniques for altering consciousness so that she can access spiritual realities unseen by those whose awareness focuses entirely on the ordinary reality of daily life. She is a "walker between the worlds," intentionally entering realms that others encounter only in dreams and myth and bringing back information (treasure for healing others, the community, the Earth).

It is not the service or specific activities the shaman renders to others that make her a shaman but the method of deriving knowledge and power to perform these activities. She consults with her spirit advisers before prescribing an herb, or she may even journey into the spirit realms and consult directly with the spirits of the plants before prescribing them. When interpreting dreams, she might ask spirit teachers about the meaning or she may journey back into the dream to question the figures who appeared there. Her knowledge and power come from the spirits. These spirits who advise and empower may be animal spirits; the spirits of place; the elemental spirits of air, water, fire, and earth; or ancestral spirits of the dead.

When chamanas go on an inner journey, they break through this plane of reality and find their allies within the unconscious realm; they have encounters with ancestors or mythical archetypes, wrestle with the demonic forces of the subconscious and the negative characteristics of the psyche. The shaman is torn to pieces by these figures and reassembled (an ego death and spiritual rebirth sequence). The journey is a sort of dying. She has integrated her knowledge of the separate reality into her normal faculties of perception, incorporating a wider vision.

Healing involves the restoration of power, life force, or soul. First, the shaman determines whether a "foreign" spirit or form of energy has entered through a "hole" or "gap" in the person's energy and then extracts or removes this harmful energy or spirit in ritual context—pulling it out by hand or sucking it out of the body into her own mouth and then spitting it into water or blowing it into a fetish that is then buried, burned, or in some other way destroyed. Second, she journeys into the spirit world to bring back some object that contains life force and either blows its essence into the patient or presents it to the patient in some symbolic form, such as a spirit helper, telling the patient to honor the spirit and use it for protection. Or she may journey into the spirit world to hunt for the lost soul or soul part, bring it back, and blow it into the patient.

Carlos Castaneda (and Arnold Mindell after him) use the term "dreaming body" to describe a sense of self untied to space, time, or society. This imaging body—or what I call the "nepantla body"—can be sensed during shamanistic states or whenever you shift attention from the everyday to some feeling, fantasy, or fiction. Everyday reality "disappears" or is momentarily suspended. Why shift to this dreaming body? Western psychology would explain that the purpose is to work out a problem; you'll continually run into certain problems or issues, and repeat certain behaviors, until eventually you confront them and work them out. But according to an ancient indigenous concept, when you fall into a problem, a spirit has entered you and is influencing your mind. If you apply this concept to modern-day problems, you could say that compulsions, obsessions, and negative reenactments are forms of "spirits" that provoke us to leave everyday reality. Unusual events upset your notion of who you are. Listening to the environment (like Castaneda's Don Juan) and taking unusual events (illness, near-death, near-insanity periods, dreams of wise spirit figures, meetings with ghosts, sudden healings, spiritual awakenings, and other paranormal events) seriously brings you closer to your personal myths (according to Mindell[25]). Paying deep attention to irrational events, messages from the environment, dreams, fantasies, and other imagining processes are attempts to understand, to reach awareness.

We are able to "see" when we shift our stance from the perceptual to the imaginal, from what Castaneda calls the first attention (the world of ordinary everyday reality) to the second attention (the other reality). When we shift our attention, we enact "dreaming," . . . "seeing" from the other side, seeing the ego as other and seeing familiar elements from that other alien perspective. Dreaming is the nagual's journey.

Ensueños: Willed interactions with imaginal realities

Each day curled up in my bed before sleeping or after waking, I spend time in particular imaginal places. "Stories" unravel in these inner worlds—some I consciously construct or will into being; others emerge out of images that don't originate with me and whose stories I "watch" as I would a movie someone else has made. I call these "fantasies" "ensueños." In these imaginings I process feelings, traumas, negativities resulting from gender, racial, or other oppressions, and I mourn my losses. These stories—both those I create and those created for me by something outside of myself (soul, spirit, the universe's consciousness)—nourish me, heal me in ways I don't completely understand. Estos ensueños serve a healing function.

I use the word "ensueño" in several guises: as illusion and fantasy; as un sueño que se hace realidad, a dream that becomes a reality; as a way to bridge the reality of the dream with the reality of the non-dream; and as a type of lucid dreaming where one is in full awareness (or perhaps even control) of the dreaming process. In the vernacular, it's a compliment to say, "Eres un ensueño, that is, una persona mágica." "Es un ensueño" may be also said of viajes or lugares maraviosos. A type of creative fantasy, ensueños are simply another reality. The reasoning mind's reality is not higher than the imagination's. I am interested in the place/space (nepantla) where realities interact and imaginative shifts happen. Some images stimulate changes; certain images change the images that live within a person's psyche, altering the stories that live within rather than trying to "fix" the person that "houses" these images.

The creative process is an agency of transformation. Using the creative process to heal or restructure the images/stories that shape a person's consciousness is a more effective way of healing. When you allow the images to speak to you through the first person rather than restricting these images to the third person (things of which you speak), a dialogue—rather than a monologue—occurs. Dreams, too, are a form of experience, a dimension in which life and mind seem to be embedded. Dream reality is a parallel continuum. While the shaman accesses this continuum with hallucinogens and other techniques, the rest of us access it through dreams.

Literal encounters, traumatic happenings—arrebatamientos such as illness, loss, depression, dislocations, accidents, and the like—can function as initiatory ordeals; they trigger imaginal musings of the sort put forth by post-Jungian archetypal or "imaginal psychology," in which the imagination (the psyche's image-creating faculty, the power to make fictions or stories) and "active imagining" (an interactive dialogue with imaginal realities) are central when we consciously interact with them.[26] Jung suggests the following process: Start with any image, contemplate it, carefully observe how the picture begins to unfold. Don't force it; just observe, and sooner or later the picture will change through a spontaneous association that causes a slight alteration. Note all these changes. Step into the picture yourself. If it's a speaking figure, talk to it and listen to what he or she has to say.[27] You alter your state of awareness into what Robert Bosnak calls an image consciousness.[28]

This intentional interaction is similar to fiction writing's willed, active fantasy; without any partial control on the dreamer/writer's part, the artist's conscious and unconscious personality unite to create the art produced. The writer records the conversation between these inner images and her ego. You could say that the writer, through her interactive participation, merges herself in the conscious/unconscious processes and gains possession of her characters by allowing them to possess her. Imagination is an active, purposeful creativity.

Imaginal identities and imagination

The "I" is only one of the many members, imaginal figures, that compose a psyche. Other imaginal figures wander in and out within and without a person, all with lives of their own. "I" am not in charge of "my" images. Images have lives of their own and walk around as they choose, not as "I" choose. Nor do "I" create these images; they emerge from my personal psyche. All images have body and exist in three-dimensional space. Although contemporary theories of identity leave out our innermost spiritual core identity, I'm interested in the connective membrane between the interiority and the exteriority of subjectivity.

The ability to spontaneously generate images in the mind is what is meant by the imagination. Imagination is the realm of soul, and the psyche's language is metaphorical. The imaginal's figures and landscapes are experienced as alive and independent of the dreamer. They speak with their own voices; move about at will. They possess an intelligence and an inner knowing. As a child I depended on this "imaginal intelligence" for guidance, companionship, and comfort. My imagination allows me to use my intuition, to figure things out in images. Imagination is my musa bruja. The images are a gateway to el cenote, the place where they take on body and life. It feels as though I'm looking through a veil at a world previously unseen but suddenly populated with significance. The images become my intimates. Sometimes their visitations are sudden and startling. I remember the coiled serpent as big as my bedroom. These figures "see" me; I'm not the only one "seeing" them. Sueños y ensueños se pueden definer como encuentros con un "doble," the dreaming self.

Inner figures in the psyche versus the reality of spirits

Is the idea of chamanería real, or is it a work of imagination and therefore of fantasy, not reality? When a chamana "journeys," does she move outward in her body around the Earth, or does she move inward into an altered state of consciousness where she experiences realities outside normal perception? Such questions keep cropping up, but their framework is too narrow. To explore them, we must redefine the imagination not as a marginal nonreality nor as an altered state but, rather, as another type of reality.

Judging stories of nonliteral realities, such as chamanas' flights to other worlds, as "made up," our western society invalidates the meanings and healing they offer. Are dreams real? Do they represent a separate reality? Do we make dreams, or does something outside us originate and orchestrate them? Is imagination's nonordinary reality real? Does it matter whether the journey comes from a waking dream, the unconscious in symbolic representation, or a nonordinary parallel world? Who cares, as long as the information (whether metaphorical or literal) gained from a shamanic journey makes positive changes in a person's life. We must avoid the snares of literalism. Are spirits literally present or are they imaginally present? They are both. Fantasy is not just a way to cope with, correct, or supplement reality. A dream/fantasy frees you from the confines of daily time and space, from your habitual identity. Science denies reality to fantasy because scientific belief sees only the literal as real. But according to Jung, neither the conscious world's literal reality nor the unconscious world's nonliteral reality is absolutely real.[29]

Since we live in a modern western setting, spiritual needs and belief in spirits are roughly equated with psychological needs, a blending of chamanerías and psychotherapy.[30] The notion that the gods are forces and potencies within the human mind and that humans have, at the deepest levels of the mind, personifications of the great archetypal experiences is the current theory—more "rational" than the belief that spirits are real. Though imaginal spirits are just as "real" (in a different sense) as "real" spirits, these spirits and the indigenous experience of spirits are denied their reality. For psychologists, the split-off parts are lost in an undifferentiated region called the unconscious, while for shamans the soul parts live a parallel existence in nonordinary worlds.

Some anthropologists define spirits as metaphor and symbol, thinking they are only mental images. But as the anthropologist Edith Turner notes, this view is "intellectual imperialism." According to Turner, spirits are "manifestations [that] constitute the deliberate visitation of discernable forms that have the conscious intent to communicate, to claim importance in our lives."[31] Mary Watkins (a Jungian developmental psychologist) sees her "imaginals" as conscious beings with self-determination, with autonomy.[32] She asserts that something Other is in us: "There is another force influencing our thoughts, emotions, movements, and actions. One can no longer say it is a god or a spirit and yet one has those ancient feelings of possession and movement by a force that does not answer to logic or common space and time."[33]

Spirituality: The connection between different forms of consciousness & realities

Spirituality is an ontological belief in the existence of things outside the body (exosomatic), as opposed to the belief that material reality is a projection of mentally created images. The answer to the question, "If a tree falls in the forest, does it make a sound if no one is there to hear it?" is yes. Spirituality is a symbology system, a philosophy, a worldview, a perspective, and a perception. Spirituality is a different kind and way of knowing. It aims to expand perception; to become conscious, even in sleep; to become aware of the interconnections between all things by attaining a grand perspective. A source reality exists, and both physical and nonphysical worlds emanate from it, forming a secondary reality. When you catch glimpses of this invisible primary reality and realize you're connected to it, feelings of alienation and hopelessness disappear. Coming to terms with spirit means bringing yourself into harmony with the world within and around you. One finds one's way to spirit through woundings, through nature, through reading, through actions, through discovering new approaches to problems.

Through spirituality we seek balance and harmony with our environment. According to indigenous belief, we are embedded in nature and exist in reciprocity with it. We are bonded to this planet in ways we don't even imagine. We are in partnership with the Earth, but the partnership must go both ways; we must demonstrate trust, love, respect, and reciprocity to make this bond work. A human yearning and an essential human need to witness the flow of life and the patterns (including individual patterns) manifested in life, the spiritual is a deep sense of belonging and participation in life. Spirit represents the zest for living—the energizing power for life. It is the inner voice, the electrical charge, that says, "I'm going to do it. I *will* do it."

But made to feel embarrassed for using a spiritual vocabulary, we bear the negative connotations it carries. Academics disqualify spirituality except as anthropological studies done by outsiders, and spirituality is a turn-off for those exposed to so-called New Agers' use of flaky language and Pollyanna-like sentiments disconnected from the grounded realities of people's lives and struggles. And no wonder. Most contemporary spiritual practitioners in this country ignore the political implications and do not concern themselves with our biggest problem and challenge: racism and other racial abuses. They're not concerned with violence against children and women, with poverty and the attacks against nature. I describe the activist stance that explores spirituality's social implications as "spiritual activism"—an activism that is engaged by a diverse group of people with different spiritual practices, or spiritual mestizaje.[34]

The artist as chamana

The artist uses the imagination to impose order on chaos; she gives psychic confession form and direction, provides language to distressed and confused people—a language that expresses previously inexpressible psychic states and enables the reader to undergo in an ordered and intelligible form real experiences that would otherwise be chaotic and inexpressible.[35] For both la chamana and the artist, this inner journey is one of turmoil and distress. By recounting intense psychic details through transpersonal language, the psyche organizes itself and gives significance and direction to human suffering. Through creative expression, the human experience is mythologized and collectively understood.

The mind's unconscious workings play a huge part in both reading and creating a work of art. After receiving/dreaming the initial inspiration (which exists as an inner vision), the work demands to come into being during periods of incubation. A heightened consciousness or awareness that I call "conocimiento" and some call "love" (which may be the same thing) stirs the artist to take action, propels her toward the act of making. This conocimiento initiates the relationship between self-knowledge and creative work. Because the artist must keep watch on her inner responses, she becomes more aware, more alive, and thus she "makes" the story of herself as she makes her art. This self-creation persists through a series of traumatic dislocations and is recorded by words and images—that is, by language. Through her métier, her art, she both remembers her personal history and "forgets" herself and her world. A good fiction or other creation takes her out of herself, allowing her to "forget" herself. The paradox in reading, making art, and making self is that the artist must simultaneously remember and forget self and world. The stories she believes shape her perceptions of reality. She lives her life according to these stories, and according to these stories she shapes the world. Creation is really a rereading and rewriting of reality—a rearrangement or reordering of preexisting elements.

This creation process takes various forms. In the western Promethean story, the artist acts independently and often against god the creator. She steals the power of creativity from god and creates out of her own ego or her own limitations. In other stories, the artist surrenders to the creative process, the creative urge—in other words, to god—and allows the story/artwork to be channeled through her. An alert and active receptivity, an openness to the moment when she has exhausted everything, all ideas and emotions—she surrenders. It is then that something new may emerge and she just follows instead of controlling it.

Creativity is a liberation impulse, an activity that transforms materials and energy. It stems from the impulse to use the capacities of your mind, body, soul, and other inner resources collaboratively, to create. The creative process demands the reconciliation of conflicting impulses and ideas; it calls forth conocimiento, a higher awareness and consciousness that brings you into deeper connection with yourself and your materials. When art functions as a spiritual discipline, the work of mind and body come together in acts of imagination. In wanting fullness of expression artists seek inner wholeness.[36]

In creating artistic works the artist's creative process brings the imagination's unconscious process to the page/canvas. Books and other art forms initiate us into the imagination and often into shamanic states of consciousness. Shamanic imaginings occur while writing or reading; these controlled "flights" send us on a kind of "dreaming" similar to the dream or the fantasy process, similar to the journeying chamanas' magical flights. The artist awakens and activates the imagining process in readers or viewers, thus empowering them.

You make soul when you make art, a concept from the romantic poet John Keats, who coined the word "soul-making," and also from the Mexican indigenous spiritual tradition of making face, making soul.[37] My naguala/daimon is my relationship with my own active, creative power (see figure 2.1).

The aim of good writing is to decrease the distance between reader, writer, and text without "disappearing" any of these players. It's to involve the reader in the work as completely as possible without letting the reader forget that it's a work of art even as s/he interacts with it as if it were reality. In creating an identification or sympathy between reader and character and presenting an immediacy in the fiction's scenes and events, the writer allows the reader to create temporary unities and imagine/project possible wholes out of the given fragments. Both reading and writing are ensueños, willed interactions. Perhaps, as the poet Stanley Plumly suggests, the imagination is the real reality, the ultimate arbiter.[38]

REVISING NOTIONS OF REALITY

How real is reality?

Versions of un/reality: Does perception determine experience, or does experience determine perception? What comes first: the experience or the ideology framed by language? Does experience/life create reality, or does language/ideology interpret experience and therefore create reality? The world is already constructed (by the consensus of human beings) when you come into it. You can reconstruct the world

Aaah
Naguala

..reader

..inner
dweller

..imaging bo-
dy
..watcher

2.1 | Naguala, Inner Dweller

and your life, consciously or unconsciously, con conocimiento o con desconocimiento, but you must always mediate and negotiate your position between and among your cultures. Your reconstructions may be wholly within the bounds and dictates of your culture and cultures; or one culture may contradict another culture's givens; or your reconstruction may be partially outside society's bounds. Because your reconstructions are always in progress, the world, society, and culture are always in compositional/decompositional states.

The dominant western worldview holds that an "objective" external reality exists independently of the knower, a reality that science can accurately describe. Though it recognizes individual fallibilities, it contends that these can be overcome collectively through careful application of the scientific method and that the picture of reality thus obtained will more closely approximate what is actually "out there."[39]

For followers of Tao, all realities are our minds' projections, and we are always creating stimulating dramas. I buy the second statement, but not the first. The outside world does exist beyond our small individual and collective minds, and we as physical flesh-and-blood entities must participate fully with that world. There may be a universal consciousness that encompasses the consciousness of all life forms, including ecosystems, planets and galaxies, bacteria, and all matter. The writer struggles to capture an elusive life from the imagination, but reality is too big for any ideological system to contain, and literary realism is too small to contain it. To explore experience in an indeterminate world such as the one we inhabit, one in which anything that can be imagined can happen, I need a different mode of telling stories, one that can simultaneously hold the different models of what I think reality is. I need a different way of organizing reality.[40]

Decolonizing reality

Knowledge is relative, and reality is a composition. You reconstruct yourself and, to a lesser extent, your culture, society, and world by the decisions you make. Your decisions may be conscious but probably are most often at least partially unconscious, depending on which part or parts of your personality makes them. It basically comes down to awareness when you make your choices—awareness of yourself, of your acts, of the acts of others, and of the world. Formal education enhances some aspects of awareness and gives access to certain kinds of knowledges.

Decolonizing reality consists of unlearning consensual "reality," of seeing through reality's roles and descriptions by what Don Juan calls acts of not-doing.[41]

To change or reinvent reality, you engage the facultad of your imagination. You must interrupt or suspend the conscious "I" that reminds you of your history and your beliefs because these reminders tie you to certain notions of reality and behavior. You then insert the idea, with accompanying images of the new reality. To invent this new reality, you cultivate a pretend reality and act as though you're already in that pretend reality. Eventually that reality becomes the real one, at least until you change it again.

Imagination opens the road to both personal and societal change—transformation of self, consciousness, community, culture, society. We have different kinds of imaginings, each with similar yet different processes: a political process of imagining, a spiritual process of imagining, and an aesthetic process of imagining. Without imagination, transformation would not be possible. Without creativity, "other" epistemologies—those of the body, dreams, intuitions, and senses other than the five physical senses—would not reach consciousness.[42]

Proposal for a new perspective

I propose a new perspective on imagining and a new relationship to the imagination, to healing, and to shamanic spirituality. Art, reading, and writing are image-making practices that shape and transform what we are able to imagine and perceive. In honoring the creative process, the acts of writing and reading, and border arte, I use cultural figures to intervene in, make change, and thus heal colonialism's wounds. I delve into my own mythical heritage and spiritual traditions, such as curanderismo and Toltec nagualism, and link them to spirituality, spiritual activism, mestiza consciousness, and the role of nepantla and nepantleras. I enact spiritual mestizaje—an awareness that we are all on a spiritual path and share a desire that society undergo metamorphosis and evolution, that our relationships and creative projects undergo transformations.

This book explores the quest for greater consciousness and other dimensions of reality by challenging the basic premises on which our concepts are built. It discusses how we might overcome the limits of perception, extend perception beyond bodily confines, transform our consciousness and our perception from ordinary reality to a spiritual/magical/other reality, and enter states of nonordinary reality. By transferring our consciousness, we can move from one world/dimension to another. If reality is only a description of a particular world, when a shift of awareness happens we must create a new description of what's perceived—in other words, create a new reality. When we have access to this type of expanded perceptive universe, our viewpoint, identity, and character change, and we can no longer view the world as a constant.

We are all on a path of empowerment. We must empower the imagination to blur and transcend customary frameworks and conceptual categories reinforced by language and consensual reality. To explore the "cracks between the worlds" (rendijas, rents in the world), we must see through the holes in reality ("seeing" is another type of perception). According to Caroline Myss, we fear becoming empowered because every time we take on a challenge and become empowered, our whole life will change; the setting (and, I would add, the people) that have disempowered us have to disintegrate because we don't need them anymore.[43] Our interpretation of what's happening (our reality) is different from our society's, parents', or lovers' descriptions; their versions of reality disempower us. But creating our new self, new life, new project will cost us. This cost is the emotional pain of cutting off the old self, the old lover, the old job.

Each reality is only a description, a system of perception and language. When you learn to access other "realities," you undo one description or plane/level of reality and reconstruct another or others. You learn a new language and a new way of viewing the world, and you bring this "magical" knowledge and apply it to the everyday world. According to Don Juan, you must "stop the world" before you can apprehend this separate reality. You learn that the world's former description and framework were inadequate; henceforth, you see the world with two sets of eyes, with dual vision. Your personality undergoes transformation in the quest to make yourself whole (or, to use Jung's term, to attain individuation); you gain rapport with what was formerly your unconscious mind and eventually achieve a total integration and harmonize the subconscious's conflicting energies. An integration of polarities, a union of opposites, and mastery over duality is the ultimate goal.

This book is a celebration of a story—our story—of the thresholds between the worlds. By enacting the seven rites of passage of the path of conocimiento, we mark the beginning, transitions, and ending of our journey to return "home."

3 | Border Arte

Nepantla, el lugar de la frontera

Border artists inhabit the transitional space of nepantla. The border is the locus of resistance, of rupture, and of putting together the fragments. By disrupting the neat separations between cultures, Chicana artists create a new culture mix, una mestizada.

I stand in front of the Denver Museum of Natural History watching a Native woman bless the four directions: the Black, Red, Yellow, and White. Accompanied by drumming, I listen to Niba and her son (Lakota) chant/pray in a native tongue I don't recognize. As she speaks of "all my relations," I'm aware of the mix of people participating in this opening ceremony. Around me are the museum director, the state governor, the Black mayor of Denver, a representative of the Mexican president, the consulates-general from Mexico, and the former "Hispanic" mayor of Denver. Being among so many different kinds of people I feel that I'm standing on a borderlands.

The museum gatekeeper takes each person's ticket. We enter the simulation of the Aztec capital city, Tenochtitlan, as it was thought to exist before the European colonizers destroyed it. It's September 26, 1992, opening day of the *Aztec: The World of Moctezuma* exhibition. Presented here is el legado indígena, the culture de unos de nuestros antepasados indígenas. Sus símbolos y metáforas todavía viven en la gente chicana/mexicana. Viewing the figures, I am again struck by how strongly Chicana/o artists feel the impact of ancient Mexican art forms, foods, and customs. We consistently reflect back these images in revitalized and modernized versions in theater, film, performance, painting, dance, sculpture, literature, and other arts. Floricanto (flower and song), reenacted by literary and performance artists on college campuses and at community festivals, is one example among many that incorporates these ancient forms in modern ways.[1]

La negación sistemática de la cultura mexicana-chicana en los Estados Unidos impede su desarrollo, haciéndolo este un acto de colonización. As a people who have been stripped of our history, language, identity, and pride, we attempt again and again to find what we have lost by digging into our cultural roots imaginatively and making art from our findings. I ask myself, "What does it mean for me—esta jotita, this queer Chicana, this mexicatejana—to enter a museum and look at indigenous objects that were once used by my ancestors? Will I find my historical Indian identity here at this museum among the ancient artifacts and their mestizaje?"

As I pull out a pad to take notes on the clay, stone, jade, bone, feather, straw, and cloth artifacts, I am disconcerted with the knowledge that I, too, am passively consuming and appropriating an indigenous culture. I walked in with a group of Chicano kids from Servicio Chicano Center, and now we are being taught secondhand our cultural roots twice removed by whites. The essence of colonization: rip off a culture, then regurgitate its white version to the "natives."

I am jostled amid a white middle-class crowd. I look at videos, listen to slide presentations, and hear museum staff explain portions of the exhibit. It angers me that these people talk as though the Aztecs and their culture have been dead for hundreds of years when in fact there are still ten thousand Aztec survivors living in Mexico. The museum itself is a colonized structure; it enacts a psychosis of sorts, implying that all Aztecs are dead and only inhabit prehistory. It induces a double being-ness in me: feeling my Mexican indigenous aspects represented while at the same time feeling these parts of myself "disappeared." It reminds me of the Native Americans' bones shown in the Museum of Natural History in New York City alongside prehistoric artifacts.[2] What does it mean that this exhibit takes place in Denver? It means that the border itself moves, is mobile.[3]

The museum, if it is daring and takes risk, can be a kind of "border-lands" where cultures coexist in the same site. This exhibition bills itself as an act of goodwill between the United States and Mexico, a sort of bridge across the border. The Mexico-U.S. border is a site where many different cultures "touch" each other, and the permeable, flexible, ambiguous shifting grounds lend themselves to hybrid images. Border artistas cambian el punto de referencia. By disrupting the neat separations between cultures, they create a culture mix, una mestizada in their artworks. Each artist locates her/himself in this border *lugar*, tearing apart and then rebuilding the *place* itself. The border is the locus of resistance, of rupture, of implosion and explosion, and of putting together the fragments and creating a new assemblage. For me, this process is represented by Coatlicue's daughter, Coyolxauhqui, la diosa de la luna.[4]

I stop before Coyolxauhqui's dismembered body. The warrior goddess's eyes are closed; she has bells on her cheeks, and her head is in the form of a snail design. Decapitated by her brother, Huitzilopochtli (Eastern Hummingbird and War God), Coyolxauhqui exemplifies women as conquered bodies. Her bones jutting from sockets call to mind the dominant culture's repeated attempts to tear U.S. Mexican culture apart and scatter the fragments to the winds. First it took our land (our actual bodies), then our cultures through commercialization, and then our tongues, though not the underground tongue of our psyche's images (images precede language). Today the U.S. "commemorates" our culture in Quincentennial, cinco de mayo, and other "Spanish" holidays, but these celebrations Anglicize and rip off our culture. This slick, prepackaged exhibition costing $3.5 million exemplifies that dismemberment. I stare at the huge round stone of la diosa. She seems to be pushing at the restraining orb of the moon. Though I sense a latent whirlwind of energy, I also sense a timeless stillness—patiently waiting to explode into activity. To me Coyolxauhqui also embodies Chicana/mexicana writers' resistance and vitality. I see resemblances between the moon goddess's vigorous and warlike energy and Yolanda López's *Portrait of the Artist as the Virgin of Guadalupe* (1978), which depicts a Chicana/mexicana woman emerging and running from an oval halo of rays that look like thorns, with the traditional virgen's mantle in one hand and a serpent in the other. She wears running shoes, has short hair and powerful bare legs—a very dykey-looking woman. *Portrait* represents the cultural rebirth of the Chicana struggling to free herself from oppressive gender roles. The struggle and pain of this rebirth is also represented eloquently by the female figures emerging from the earthworks and stoneware sculptures by Marsha Gómez, such as *This Mother Ain't for Sale*.

Coyolxauhqui also represents the "me" tossed into the void by traumatic events (an experience of the unconscious). I disintegrate into hundreds of pieces, hundreds of separate awarenesses. A plurality of souls splits my awareness so that I see things from a hundred different viewpoints, each with its own intelligence that can "do" a hundred different things (think, feel, sense, observe) in a continuously changing consciousness moment to moment. Yet while experiencing the many, I cohere as the one reconstituted and restructured by my own unconscious urge toward wholeness. Coyolxauhqui represents the psychic and creative process of tearing apart and pulling together (deconstructing/constructing). She represents fragmentation, imperfection, incompleteness, and unfulfilled promises, as well as integration, completeness, and wholeness. The light of the full moon encourages crossing over and entering the other world, what Don Juan calls the left side of awareness and what I call El Mundo Zurdo.

As part of the tour, I don headphones and clip on a Walkman. The sibilant whispery voice of the Chicano actor Edward James Olmos interrupts my thoughts and snaps me from my "dreaming" back to the "real" world. Olmos guides me to the serpentine base of a reconstructed sixteen-foot temple where the human sacrifices were flung down, leaving bloodied steps. Around me I hear the censorious, culturally ignorant words of Anglos, who focus on bloodthirsty images and voraciously consume the more sensational and exoticized ones. Though I, too, am a gaping consumer, I feel that these artworks are part of my legacy; my appropriation differs from the misappropriation by "outsiders."

I remember visiting the Chicana tejana artist Santa Barraza at her Austin studio in the mid-1970s and advocating the merger and appropriation of cultural symbols and techniques by artists in search of their spiritual and cultural roots. As I walked around her studio, I was amazed at the vivid Virgen de Guadalupe iconography on her walls and drawings strewn on tables and shelves. The three "madres"— Guadalupe, la Malinche, y la Llorona—are cultural figures that Chicana writers and artists "reread" in our works.

And now, years later, Barraza expands her focus, interpreting pre-Columbian codices as a reclamation of cultural and historical mestiza/o identity. Her "codices" are edged with milagros and ex-votos.[5] Using the folk art format, Barraza paints tin testimonials known as retablos: traditional popular miracle paintings on metal, a medium introduced to Colonial Mexico by the Spaniards. One of her devotional retablos is of la Malinche with maguey (the maguey cactus is Barraza's symbol of rebirth; see figure 3.1). Like that of many Chicana artists, her work explores indigenous Mexican "symbols and myths in a historical and contemporary context as a mechanism of resistance to oppression and assimilation."[6]

Painted on small tin sheets, on copper, or on cloth, retablos depict the divine intervention inspired by beliefs in the reality of the supernatural. These paintings include a narrative feature: the retelling of the witnessed events of a profoundly religious experience. Inscribed at the painting's lower edge (drawn or painted with a brush, sometimes written in pencil or engraved with an etching tool that exposes the metal background) is the donor's description of his or her experience (an ex-voto); these inscriptions end with: "dedico este retablo a. . . ." The space above the text shows scenes portraying the event, and to one side often appears a kneeling figure of the donor giving thanks for the miracle or the favor granted. Votive paintings are intended as offerings of thanksgiving to holy personages, saints, or, most often la Virgen for their intervention in the life of the donor, usually by saving her or him from some misfortune. The donors of votive paintings also cross the threshold between the real world and the celestial miracle through their offerings.

Once again, my eyes return to Coyolxauhqui. Nope, she's not "for sale," despite las vendidas, the sellouts, who may be tempted to sell out indigenous images for money. Nor are the original la Lupe, la Llorona, and la Chingada or their current artistic renditions "for sale," though they have arrived at market. Often when the mainstream culture "uses" them (as in the Milk industry's "Got Milk" commercial featuring la Llorona), it's for commercial purposes.

These cultural figures inform and inspire Chicana/Latina artists who "use" them to further inform and inspire others.[7] Appropriating these figures is part of the cultural "recovery" and "recuperation" work Chicana artists and writers have been doing for the past couple

3.1 | *La Malinche*. Oil paint on metal, 8" × 9", 1991. Used by permission.

of decades, finally acknowledging and accepting our native origins (which we denied fifteen years ago). Only now, we've gone to the other extreme, "becoming," claiming, and acting as though we're more indigenous than Native Americans themselves—something that Native Americans rightfully resent and thus the source of recent Chicana/ Native conflict. Being assimilated into white culture, being part indigenous, being artists yet having to survive in the "real" world puts us in a precarious position, with our feet in different worlds. Though Chicanas are aware that we aren't "Indian" and don't live in a Native American culture, and though our roots are indigenous, we often do misappropriate and collude with the Anglos' forms of misappropriation.

I wonder about the genesis of el arte de la frontera. Border art remembers its roots—sacred and folk art are often still one and the same. I recall the nichos (niches or recessed areas) and retablos that I had recently seen in several galleries and museums, like the Denver Metropolitan State University Art Museum. The altar pieces are placed inside open boxes made of wood, tin, or cardboard. Las cajitas contain three-dimensional figures such as la Virgen, photos of ancestors, candles, and sprigs of herbs tied together. They are actually tiny installations. I make mine out of cigar boxes or vegetable crates that I find discarded on streets before garbage pickups. Los retablos range from the strictly traditional to the modern, more abstract forms. A secret feeling for the sacred and intuition inspire the artists of retablos. These artists are intermediaries between the miraculous events and their representations.

Santa Barraza, Yolanda M. López, Marcia Gómez, and other Chicana artists connect their art to everyday life with political, sacred, and aesthetic values. Haciendo tortillas becomes a sacred ritual in literary, visual, and performance arts, as in Carmen Lomas Garza's paintings or the depiction in Jose Montolla's *Tortilla Art* series of tortillas in animals' shapes.[8] Tortillando (making tortillas) also connotes the slap tickle of the lesbian sex act.

Olmos's occasional musical recitations in Nahuatl further remind me that the Aztecs, their language and indigenous cultures, are still very much alive. Although I wonder if Olmos and we Chicana/o writers and artists also are misappropriating Nahuatl language and images, hearing the words and seeing the images boosts my spirits. I feel that I am part of something profound outside my personal self. This sense of connection and community compels Chicana/o writers/artists to delve into, sift through, and rework Native imagery.

I walk from the glass-caged exhibits of the sacred world to the Tlatelolco (Tla-te-LOL-ko), the open mercado. The people's market is strewn with baskets overflowing with chiles, avocados, corn, and beans. Nopalitos lie on petates, and ducks hang in wooden cages. Life-size statues of people in arrested activity look on. I think of how border art, in critiquing old, traditional, and erroneous representations of the Mexico-U.S. border, attempts to represent the "real world" de la gente going about their daily lives. But it renders that world and its people in more than mere surface slices of life. If one looks beyond the tangible, one sees a connection to the spirit world, to the underworld, and to other realities. In the "old world," art was/is functional and sacred, as well as aesthetic.

When folk and fine art separated, the metate (a flat porous volcanic stone with rolling pin used to make corn tortillas) and the huipil (blouse) were put in museums by the western curators of art.[9] Many of these officiators believe that only art objects from dead cultures should end up in museums. According to a friend who recently returned from Central America, a museum in Guatemala City solely houses indigenous clothing as though the items were garments of the past.[10] There was little mention of the women she saw still weaving the same kind of clothing and using the same methods as their ancestors—despite the marks of colonization. For instance, indigenous peoples were forced to wear clothing of a certain color so that their patrones could distinguish "their" peons from those of other bosses. Thus, the men in Todos Santos, a Guatemalan community, wear red pants, while men from another area wear another color. These red pants reflect a colonization of their culture. Colonization influences the lives and objects of the colonized and, as a result, alters artistic heritage.

I come to a glass case where the skeleton of a jaguar with a stone in its open mouth nestles on cloth. The stone represents the heart. My thoughts trace the jaguar's spiritual and religious symbolism from its Olmec origins to present-day jaguar masks worn by people who no longer know that the jaguar was connected to rain, who no longer remember that Tlaloc, jaguar, serpent, and rain are tightly intertwined.[11] The jaguar symbolizes the shaman's journey to the underworld. According to Carlos Castaneda's Don Juan, hunting/stalking is a symbolic description of the psychological attitude needed for obtaining information from the nagual (unconscious).[12] By focusing energy, assuming an attitude of receptivity, and observing the unconscious's movements, we can look for meaning in its appearance. In archetypal psychological terms, you could say that the jaguar symbolizes the consciousness that stalks in the darkness of the underworld, searching for knowledge and seeking to fulfill one's personal myth. According to Burr Cartwright Brundage, the same Mayan word, *balam*, is used for jaguar and sorcerer.[13]

Throughout the centuries, one culture touches and influences another, passing on its metaphors and its gods before it dies. Metaphors *are* gods. According to archetypal psychology, we have internalized the old deities, animals, and forces of nature that our ancestors considered gods. We could say that metaphors are allies, spirits (transformative aspects of the unconscious seeking to enter consciousness). (In my case, snake is one of my allies or guardian animals.) The new culture adopts, modifies, and enriches these images, and it, in turn, passes them on changed. In the case of Native American spiritual practices such as the vision quest, the practices, rituals, and ceremonies have been disrespectfully appropriated and misappropriated by whites, Chicanos, and Latinos. Some Native Americans call these thieves "white shamans" or "plastic medicine men."[14] Vine Deloria Jr., a Lakota writer, accuses non-natives of pirating misunderstood pieces of indigenous shamanism to feed the white man's fantasies, forcing the Indians "to deal with American fantasies about the Indians of white imagination rather than the reality of the present."[15] Castaneda's Don Juan novels initiated the new shamanism spiritual movement. In workshops such as those conducted by Michael Harner, Joan Halifax, and other "white" shamanic practitioners, trance journeys are "sold" to participants.[16] Don Miguel Ruiz, a Mexican nagual, has "passed on" Toltec shamanism to a large number of U.S. shaman aspirants.[17]

The process of "borrowing" is repeated until the images' original meanings are pushed into the unconscious, and images more significant to the prevailing culture and era surface. However, the artist on some level still connects to that unconscious reservoir of meaning, connects to that nepantla state of transition between time periods, connects to the border between cultures. Chicana/o artists currently are engaged in "reading" that nepantla, that border, and that cenote—from which direction and renewal spring forth. Imagination, the mundis imaginalis—the source of creativity, dreams, fantasies, intuitions, and symbolic events—resides in el cenote. For those of us who are receptive, el cenote offers the unconscious's resources for self-knowledge and transformation. Nepantla is the threshold of transformation. Art and la frontera intersect in a liminal space where border people, especially artists, live in a state of nepantla. The Nahuatl word for an in-between state, nepantla is that uncertain terrain one crosses when moving from one place to another; when changing from one class, race, or sexual position to another; when traveling from the present identity into a new identity. The Mexican immigrant at the moment of crossing the barbed-wired fence into a hostile "paradise" of El Norte (the U.S.) is caught in a state of nepantla. Liliana Wilson, a Chilean artist, captures nepantla's characteristic tension in her painting *El color de la esperanza* (1987), which depicts a modern-day girl sleeping and dreaming on the U.S. side of the border fence. Images of a giant ancient sun (Tonatiuh) and la Virgen de Guadalupe (images grounded in ancient indigenous Mexican spiritual history and thus holding mythic power) observe and guard her from the "other" side of the border.

En este lugar entre medio, nepantla, two or more forces clash and are held teetering on the verge of chaos, a state of entreguerras. These tensions between extremes create cracks or tears in the membrane surrounding, protecting, and containing the different cultures and their perspectives. Nepantla is the place where at once we are detached (separated) and attached (connected) to each of our several cultures. Here the watcher on the bridge (nepantla) can "see through" the larger symbolic process that's trying to become conscious through a particular life situation or event. Nepantla is the midway point between the conscious and the unconscious, the place where transformations are enacted. Nepantla is a place where we can accept contradiction and paradox.

Others who find themselves in this bewildering transitional space may be people caught in the midst of denying their projected/assumed heterosexual identity and coming out, presenting and voicing their queer, lesbian, gay, bi, or transgendered selves. Crossing class lines, especially from working class to middle class-ness and privilege, can be just as bewildering. The marginalized starving Chicana/o artist who suddenly finds her or his work exhibited in mainstream museums, or sold for thousands of dollars in prestigious galleries, as well as the once neglected writer whose work is in every professor's syllabus for a time, inhabits nepantla.

I think of the borderlands as Jorge Luis Borges's Aleph,[18] the one spot on earth containing all other places within it. It's like el árbol de la vida which crosses all dimensions—the sky, spiritual space, the earth, and the underworld. It's also like el cenote, the Mayan well—un ombligo (an umbilical cord) connecting us to the earth and to concrete reality. All people in nepantla—Natives, immigrants, colored, white, queers, heterosexuals, from this side of the border, del otro lado—are personas del lugar, local people, and relate to the border and to the nepantla states in different ways.

I continue meandering from room to room, noticing how different parts of Aztec culture are partitioned off from others and how some are placed together in one room and a few feet apart but still seem to be in neat little categories that leave no space. That bothers me. Abruptly, I meet myself in the center of the room with the sacrificial knives. I stand rooted there for a long time, thinking about spaces and borders and moving in them and through them. According to Edward Hall, early in life we become oriented to space in a way that is tied to survival and sanity. When we become disoriented from this sense of space we risk becoming psychotic.[19] I question this view; to be disoriented in space is the "normal" way of being for us mestizas living in the borderlands. It's the sane way of coping with the accelerated pace of this complex, interdependent, and multicultural planet. To be disoriented in space is to be en nepantla. To be disoriented in space is to experience bouts of disassociation of identity, identity breakdowns and buildups. The border, in a constant nepantla state, is an analog of the planet. This is why the borderline is a persistent metaphor in el arte de la frontera, an art that explores such themes as identity, border crossings, and hybrid imagery. *Imágenes de la Frontera* was the title of the Centro Cultural Tijuana's exhibition in June 1992.[20] Malaquís Montoya's *Frontera Series* and Irene Pérez's *Dos Mundos* monoprint are examples of the multi-subjectivity, split-subjectivity, and refusal to be split themes of the border artist creating a counter-art.[21]

The nepantla state is artists' natural habitat—most specifically, for mestizo border artists who partake of the traditions of two or more worlds and who may be binational. They thus create a new artistic space, a border mestizo culture. "Beware of el romance del mestizaje," I hear myself saying silently. Puede ser una ficción. Don't romanticize mestizaje—it is just another fiction, a way of ordering, understanding, or interpreting reality, something made up, like "culture" or the events in a person's life. But I and other writer/artists of la frontera have invested ourselves in it. Mestizaje, not chicanismo, is the reality of our lives.[22] Mestizaje is the heart of our art. We bleed in mestizaje, we eat and sweat and cry in mestizaje. The Chicana/o is inside the greater mestiza/o umbrella.

There are many obstacles and dangers in crossing into nepantla. Popular culture and the dominant art institutions threaten border artists from the outside with appropriation. "Outsiders" jump on the border artists' bandwagon and work their territory, as when Anglos and other people of color "adopt" el día de los muertos celebrations. The present unparalleled economic depression in the arts gutted by government funding cutbacks threatens los artistas de la frontera. Sponsoring corporations that judge projects by "family values" criteria force multicultural artists to hang tough and brave out financial and professional instability. I walk into the Aztec Museum gift shop where we are "sold" and see feathers, paper flowers, and ceramic statues of fertility goddesses priced at ten times what they sell for in Mexico. Border art is becoming trendy in these neo-colonial times of art tourism and pop culture rip-offs. Of course, colonizing, commercializing, and consuming the art of ethnic people (and of queer writers and artists) is nothing new; however, our art is now being misappropriated by pop culture. Diversity is sold on TV, on billboards, in fashion lines, in department store windows, and, yes, in airport corridors and "regional" stores where you can take home the Navajo artist R. C. Gorman's *Saguaro* or Robert Arnold's *Chili Dog* and a jar of Tex-Mex picante sauce and drink a margarita at Rosie's Cantina.

I touch the armadillo pendant hanging from my neck and think: frontera artists have to grow protective shells. We enter the silence, go inward, attend to feelings and to that inner cenote—the site of imagination, the creative reservoir where earth, female, and water energies merge. We surrender to the rhythm and the grace of our artworks. Through our artworks we cross the border into other subjective levels of awareness, shift into different and new terrains of mestizaje. Some of us have a highly developed facultad and may intuit what lies ahead. Yet the political climate does not allow us to withdraw completely. In fact, border artists are engaged artists. Most of us are politically active in our communities, making community-based art. If disconnected from la gente, border artistas/activistas would wither in isolation. The community feeds our spirits, and the responses of our "readers" inspire us to continue struggling with our art and making aesthetic interventions that subvert cultural genocide.

A year ago I was thumbing through the catalogue CARA, *Chicano Art: Resistance and Affirmation.* My eyes snagged on some lines by Judy Baca, a Chicana muralist: "Chicano art comes from the creation of community. . . . Chicano art represents a particular stance which always engages with the issues of its time." Chicana/o art is a form of border art, an art shared with our Mexican counterparts from across the border, with Native Americans, and with other groups of color and non-color folks living in the vicinity of the Mexico-U.S. border or near other cultural borders elsewhere in the United States, Mexico, and Canada.[23] Both Chicana/o and border art challenge and subvert U.S. imperialism and combat assimilation by either the U.S. or Mexico, yet they acknowledge its affinities to both.[24]

"Chicana" artist, "border" artist: These adjectives label identities. Labeling affects expectations. A white poet doesn't write "white" in front of his name, nor is s/he referred to as "white" by others. A doctor is presumed to be white and male unless labeled otherwise. Is "border" artist just another label that strips legitimacy from the artist, signaling that s/he is inferior to the adjective-less artist? Is "border" a label designating that s/he is capable only of handling ethnic, folk, and regional subjects and art forms? Yet the dominant culture consumes, swallows whole, the ethnic artist, sucks out her/his vitality, and then spits out the hollow husk along with its labels, such as "Hispanic" and, more recently, "Latino" (as I discuss in the next chapter). Though "Latino" preceded "Hispanic," Latinos didn't become such a huge buying power until recently. The dominant culture shapes the ethnic artist's identity if s/he does not scream loud enough and fight long enough to name her/himself. Until we live in a society where all people are equal and no labels are necessary, we need them to resist the pressure to assimilate.

I cross the room. Codices hang on the walls. I stare at the hieroglyphics. The ways of a people, their history and culture put on paper beaten from maguey leaves. Faint traces of red, blue, and black ink left by their artists, writers, and scholars. The past is hanging behind glass. We, the viewers in the present, walk around and around the glass-boxed past. I wonder who I used to be (the chicanita del rancho totally immersed in mexicano culture), I wonder who I am now (living in a California beach town known as paradise). My identity keeps constantly shifting—being Chicana or queer or writer is not enough. I'm more mestiza than any particular identity. The border artist constantly reinvents her/himself. Through art, s/he is able to reread, reinterpret, re-envision, and reconstruct her/his culture's present, as well as its past. More than twelve years ago, I switched from using flow charts during my speaking engagements to using what I call pictograms or rough glifos (pictograms or hieroglyphs), which I sketch on transparencies. The images I place on overhead projectors "contain" or "illustrate" my ideas and theories (see figure 3.2). Recently I learned that the ancient teachers and wise people used the images they painted on accordion-unfolding codices to teach.

The capacity to construct meaning and culture privileges the artist. As a cultural icon for her/his ethnic community, s/he is highly visible. But this artistic and cultural power has its drawbacks: the relentless pressure to produce, being put in the position of representing an entire pueblo and carrying all the ethnic culture's baggage on her/his espalda while trying to survive in a gringo world. Power and the seeking of greater power may create a self-centered ego or a fake public image, one the artist thinks will make her/him acceptable to an audience. It may encourage self-serving hustling; while all artists have to sell themselves to get grants, get published, secure exhibition spaces and good reviews, for some the hustling outdoes the art making, and we concentrate more on the career than on the writing or art making. Some of us are invested in our "image" or our personality, doing ego-driven work. But for most, our art is our mission, a lifetime task of teaching tolerance and respect for the Earth and the people of the Earth, of making bridges. Our work is spiritual, and we try to make sure that what we put out in the world is true to our deepest convictions.

The Chicana/o border writer/artist has finally come to market. The problem now is how to resist corporate culture while asking for and securing its patronage and dollars without resorting to "mainstreaming" the work. Is the border artist complicit in the appropriation of her or his art by the dominant dealers of art? And if so, does this complicity constitute a self-imposed imperialism? The artist, in making plata from the sale of their sculpture, "makes it." Having money means having power. The access to privilege that comes with the

↳ ID Crisis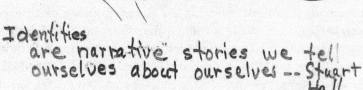

of individual
of community
of ethnic group
of the nation

Identities
are narrative stories we tell
ourselves about ourselves -- Stuart
Hall

Id labels are roles we take on tempor

defense mechanism comes on when
some aspect of your identity
is criticized/attacked/threatened
+ when a value/belief assoc.
w/ that identity is challenged

Identity is performance
an act of projection
an artifice
a fabrication
a fiction

3.2 | Identity Crisis

bucks and the recognition can turn artists on their ears in a nepantla spin. ¿Adónde nos vamos de aquí?

Artistic ideas that have been incubating and developing at their own speed have come into their season—now is the time of border art. Border arte is an art that supersedes the pictorial. It depicts both the soul del artista y el alma del pueblo. It deals with who tells the stories and what stories and histories are told. I call this form of visual narrative "autohistorias." This form goes beyond the traditional self-portrait or autobiography; in telling the writer/artist's personal story, it also includes the artist's cultural history—indeed, it's a kind of making history, of inventing our history from our experience and perspective through our art rather than accepting our history by the dominant culture. The altars I make are not just representations of myself; they are representations of Chicana culture. El arte de la frontera is community—and academically—based. Many Chicana/o artists have master's degrees and doctorates and hold precarious teaching positions on the fringes of universities. They are overworked, overlooked, passed over for tenure, and denied the support they deserve. To make, exhibit, and sell their artwork, and to survive, los artistas have had to band together collectively.

Finally, I find myself before the reconstructed statue of the newly unearthed dios murciélago, the bat god with his big ears, fangs, and protruding tongue representing the vampire bat associated with night, blood sacrifice, and death.[25] I make an instantaneous association of the bat man with border artists' nepantla stage—the dark cave of creativity where they hang upside down, turning the self upside down to see from another point of view, one that brings a new state of understanding. Or it may mean transposing the former self into a new one—the death of the old self and the old ways, breaking down former notions of who you are. Though the bat god does not cause or represent susto, it does lend itself to night fear and other kinds of susto when every button is pushed.[26]

The border person constantly moves through that birth canal, that nepantla. If you stay too long in nepantla, you are in danger of being blocked, resulting in a breech birth or being stillborn. What meaning will this bat figure have for other Chicanas/os? What artistic symbol they will make of it? What political struggle will it represent? Perhaps like the home/public altars, which expose both the United States' and Mexico's national identity, the murciélago god questions the viewer's unconscious collective and personal identity and its ties to her/his ancestors, los muertos. The specter of death always haunts the backgrounds in border art. Often las calaveras (skeletons and skulls) take a prominent position—and not just of el día de los muertos (November 2). De la tierra nacemos, from earth we are born; a la tierra regresaremos, to earth we shall return; a dar lo que ella nos dió, to give back to her what she has given. "Yes," I say to myself, "the earth eats the dead, la tierra se come los muertos."

I walk out of the Aztec exhibition hall and turn in the Walkman with the Olmos tape. It is September 26, mi cumpleaños. I seek out the table with the computer, key in my birthdate, and there on the screen is my Aztec birth year and ritual day name: 8 Rabbit, 12 Skull. In that culture I would have been named Matlactli Omome Mizuitzli. I stick my chart under the rotating rubber stamps, press down, pull it out, and stare at the imprint of the rabbit (symbol of fear and of running scared in western culture) pictograph and then of the skull (night, blood sacrifice, and death). Very appropriate symbols in my life, I mutter. It's so raza. ¿y qué?[27]

At the end of my five-hour "tour," I walk out of the museum to the parking lot with aching feet and questions buzzing around my head. As I wait for my taxi, I ask myself, What direction will el arte fronterizo take in the future? The multi-subjectivity and split-subjectivity of border artists creating various counter-arts will continue, but with a parallel movement in which a polarized us/them, insiders/outsiders culture clash is not the main struggle, and a refusal to be split will be the norm. We are both nos (us) and otras (others)—nos/otras. Art makes a wider community, one that transcends the artist's culture and lifetime.

The border is a historical and metaphorical site, un sitio ocupado, an occupied borderland where single artists and collaborating groups transform space, and the two home territories, Mexico and the United States, become one. The museum, like the borderlands, is occupied space. Border arte in a sense tries to decolonize that space. It deals with shifting identities, border crossings, and hybridism—all strategies for decolonization.

There are other borders besides the actual Mexico-U.S. frontera and other border artists occupying other nepantlas. Wuthering Heights (1990), an oil painting by Juan Davila (a Chilean artist who has lived in Australia since 1974), depicts Juanito Leguna, a half-caste, mixed-breed transvestite. Juanito's body is a simulacrum parading as the phallic mother with hairy chest and hanging tits.[28] Another Latino artist, Rafael Barajas (who signs his work "El Fisgón"), has a mixed-media piece titled *Pero eso si . . . soy muy macho* (1989). It shows a Mexican man wearing the proverbial sombrero taking a siesta against the traditional cactus, tequila bottle on the ground, gun belt hanging from una penca de nopal. But the leg sticking out from beneath the sarape-like mantle is wearing a garter belt, panty hose, and high-heeled shoe. It suggests another kind of border crossing—gender bending.[29]

As the taxi whizzes me back to my hotel, my mind reviews image after image. Something about who and what I am and the two hundred "artifacts" I have just seen does not feel right. I pull out my "birth chart." Yes, cultural roots are important, *but I was not born at Tenochtitlan in the ancient past nor in an Aztec village in modern times.* I was born and live in that in-between space, nepantla, the borderlands. Hay muchas razas running in my veins, mescladas dentro de mi, otras culturas that my body lives in and out of. Mi cuerpo vive dentro y fuera de otras culturas, *and a white man* who constantly whispers, "Assimilate, you're not good enough," and measures me according to white standards. *For me, being Chicana or any other single identity marker is not enough—is not my total self.* It is only one of my multiple identities. Along with other border gente, it is at this site and time, en este tiempo y lugar where and when, *I help co-create my identity* con mi arte. Neither art nor a person's identity is an entirely willed activity. Other forces influence, impact, and construct our desires—including the unconscious and collective unconscious forces and residues of those that came before us, our ancient ancestors.

4 | Geographies of Selves—Reimagining Identity

Nos/Otras (Us/Other), las Nepantleras, and the New Tribalism

Amor es . . . amar la plenitude del árbol. . . .
en el ansia de la semilla ciega
que perdió el rumbo de la luz,
Aprisionada por su tierra,
vencida por su misma tierra.
DULCE MARIA LOYNAZ, "AMOR ES"

Reimagining identities

My body is sexed; I can't avoid that reality, although I could change it through transgendering or transsexing.[1] My body is raced; I can't escape that reality, can't control how other people perceive me, can't de-race, e-race my body, or the reality of its raced-ness. U.S. society is gendered and racialized; it expects certain behavior from women, certain bearings from men, certain comportment from queer mujeres, certain demeanor from queer hombres, certain conduct from disabled, and so on. If you're a person of color, those expectations take on more pronounced nuances due to the traumas of racism and colonization. Though there are aspects of gender, sexual, and racial identity that no single person can change, together we can alter cultural beliefs, behaviors, attitudes about their meanings. These identity categories—categories based primarily on history, biology, nationality—are important aspects of personal and collective identity; however, they don't contain our entirety, and we can't base our whole identidad on them. It's not "race,"[2] gender, class, or any single attribute but the interaction of all of these aspects (as well as others) that creates identity.

For me, being Chicana is not enough—nor is being queer, a writer, or any other identity label I choose or others impose on me. Conventional, traditional identity labels are stuck in binaries, trapped in jaulas (cages) that limit the growth of our individual and collective lives. We need fresh terms and open-ended tags that portray us in all our complexities and potentialities. When I think of "moving" from a sexed, racialized body to a more expansive identity interconnected with its surroundings, I see in my mind's eye trees with interconnected roots (subterranean webs). When I was a child I felt a kinship to a large mesquite.

> El mesquite and its gnarled limbs reign over the portal, the house, and the yard. Its fifty- or sixty-feet-deep roots tap the same underground water source as the windmill. When she [Prieta] stays still long enough her feet worm themselves like roots into the moist core, forming an umbilicus that connects her to el cenote, la noria interior, and to the earth and all its creatures.—"El Paisano Is a Bird of Good Omen"

El árbol de la vida—la Virgen de Guadalupe's tree

Struggling with a "story" (a concept or theory), embracing personal and social identity, is a bodily activity. The narrative works itself through my physical, emotional, and spiritual bodies, which emerge out of and are filtered through the natural, spiritual worlds around me. Tengo una ancia como la de "la semilla ciega / que perdió el rumbo de la luz." Nature is my solace; it allows my imagination to stir. Sea, wind, trees evoke images, feelings, thoughts that I acknowledge as sacred. If I'm receptive, a new conocimiento/insight will flash up through the cracks of the unconscious, what I call el cenote, la noria interior, a subterranean reservoir of personal and collective knowledge. Its surge provokes a new clarity inspiring me to formulate ideas that may transform my daily existence.

Today I walk to the ocean, to my favorite tree, what I call la Virgen's tree.[3] Most days, I put my arms around the tree and we have una "platica" (talk), but today I straddle and stretch out on la Virgen's gnarly protruding roots, thick as a horse's back, absorbing the tree's energy, in kinship with it. Al espíritu del árbol I pray for strength, energy, and clarity to fuel este trabajo artistico. In return le hago una promesa: to offer it un milagrito.[4] With my back against its trunk, I meditate, allowing it to absorb my body into its being; my arms become its branches, my hair its leaves, its sap the blood that flows in my veins. I look at the broken and battered raíces dangling down the edge of the cliff, then stare up at the trunk. I listen to the sea breathing us in and out with its wet sucking sounds, feel the insects burrow into our skin, observe the birds hopping from rama to rama, sense people taking shade under our arms.

El árbol de la vida (the tree of life[5]) symbolizes my "story" of the new tribalism.[6] Roots represent ancestral/racial origins and biological attributes; branches and leaves represent the characteristics, communities, and cultures that surround us, that we've adopted, and that we're in intimate conversation with. Onto the trunk de mi árbol de la vida I graft a new tribalism. This new tribalism, like other new Chicano/Latino narratives, recognizes that we are responsible participants in the ecosystems (complete set of interrelationships between a network of living organisms and their physical habitats) in whose web we're individual strands.[7]

I must forsake "home" (comfort zones, both personal and cultural) every day of my life to keep burgeoning into the tree of myself. Luckily, the roots of my tree are deep enough in la cultura mexicana and strong enough to support a widespread branch system.[8] Las raíces that sustain and nourish me are implanted in the landscape of my youth, my grandmother's stories of la Llorona, my father's quiet strength, the persevering energy de la gente who work in the fields. I lived the first seven years of my life in a house with dirt floors. Los ranchos de mi tierra (Jesús María y Los Verjeles) cradled me and gave me strong Mexican indigenous roots embedded in preconquest tierra. For some, home-ethnic roots may not be as clear-cut as those connected to the land, nor as portable and potable as the diasporic roots clinging to immigrants' feet and carried from one community, culture, or country to another. Some immigrants are cut off from ethnic cultures. Como cabezas decapitadas, they search for the "home" where all the pieces of the fragmented body cohere and integrate like Coyolxauhqui.[9] Many urban, multiethnic people, as well as others adopted out of their racial group, have mixed or tangled, distant or mangled roots. Others, like Richard Rodriguez (known for his anti-bilingualism stance), have in some respect severed their raíces. Many try to recuperate their roots by becoming the most ardent Chicanas or Salvadoreñas, etc., turning into border patrols bearing rigid nationalistic tendencies.

Regardless, cada uno somos una semillita del árbol de la Raza. Roots are embedded not only in the soil but also in inner city asphalt and in the spirit, psyche, incorporeal ground of being. We're not just the individual or material árbol de la vida that is our life; we are also las cosas y gente que pasan a nuestros alrededores, whether these be concrete metropolis or green environments. To partake of the new tribalism, you don't have to be connected to your home-ethnicity; other root systems will suffice. The "root" you connect to becomes your spiritual ground of being, your connection to your inner self, which is your greatest strength. Gilles Deleuze and Félix Guattari use a similar structural model, the rhizome, for the self. They define it as "an underground stem composed of segments that . . . connect freely and unrestrictedly with one another. . . . Unlike a plant with a single tap root, rhizomes spread in all directions, creating a . . . network in which every point can be connected to every other point."[10]

Geographies of Selves

> She feels the world gradually slip inside her, first the streets, then the skyscrapers. As though from a distance she, herself, closes in on her body and slips inside herself. Her body glows, thickens, expands. But no, her body is the same. It is she who extends in all directions, who is both inside and outside her body. She feels present, feels visible in the world. She's in the gestures of the body, in its movements. Her heart palpitations soothe her. She thinks of it as her guardian animal beating its wings inside her chest, soothing away the pain. She, the watcher, watches the inner dweller, and watches itself watching the others. She is full of people. Ella es gente, y no una sola persona. Why hadn't she realized this before?
> "SUSTO," IN LOS ENSUENSU DE LA PRIETA

The places where I've lived have had an impact on my psyche, left a mark on every cell in my body. As a queer Chicana living in New York City in a Puerto Rican neighborhood, surrounded by Russians, Jews, and other "racially" different peoples, I bore my "differentness" and negotiated my identity. Like others, I've had to pick and choose among competing definitions and categorizations of otherness. Along with the roar of the N train rushing from Brooklyn to Manhattan and the reek of urine in the subways, I carried the processes and experiences negotiated by my urban self when I moved on.

After speaking at a conference in Houston, I flew south to the Rio Grande Valley. (Yes, on a "real" plane, not an astral flight.) Through the Plexiglas I peer down at the long arc of the Gulf of Mexico shoreline made jagged by estuaries and deltas of rivers that deposit sands washed down from higher inland grounds. These sands become mud and eventually form barrier islands along the entire coast. Over my left shoulders I can see the long thin body of Padre Island. The plane banks to the right. The citrus, corn, and vegetable fields stretch in long lines, swell into squares and rectangles framed by palm trees. The plane descends into Harlingen. As soon as my feet touch the ground, I know I am on Chicanoland. As I walk on the bedrock of this timeless land of bronzed faces, a tribal sense of belonging, of continuity surges up.—"Interviewing Remedios," in Los ensueños de la Prieta

Strands/Webs of identity

Our bodies are geographies of selves made up of diverse, bordering, and overlapping "countries."[11] We're each composed of information, billions of bits of cultural knowledge superimposing many different categories of experience. Like a map with colored web lines of rivers, highways, lakes, towns, and other landscape features en donde pasan y cruzan las cosas, we are "marked" (see figure 4.1).[12] Life's whip makes welts and thin silver scars on our backs; our genetic code digs creases and tracks on our flesh. As our bodies interact with internal and external, real and virtual, past and present environments, people, and objects around us, we weave (tejemos), and are woven into, our identities. Identity, as consciously and unconsciously created, is always in process—self interacting with different communities and worlds.

Identity is relational. Who and what we are depends on those surrounding us, a mix of our interactions with our alrededores/environments, with new and old narratives. Identity is multilayered, stretching in all directions, from past to present, vertically and horizontally, chronologically and spatially. People's mass movements

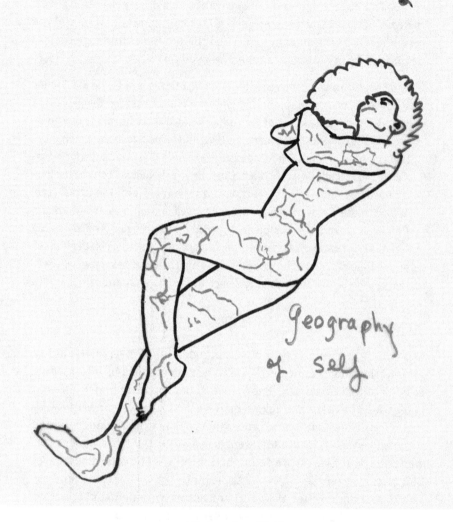

4.1 | Geography of Self

across neighborhoods, states, countries, and continents, as well as the instant connection via satellites, Internet, and cell phones, make us more aware of and linked to each other. Soon our consciousness will reach other planets, solar systems, galaxies. Pictured like a diagrammatic model, the universe is a web—tightly woven connections of all living things past, present, and future, containing both positive and negative forces.

I see Raza as a set of attitudes, expectations with no geographical limits. The terrain, the planes (and plains) of identity alter when a person moves (immigrates) into another community or social position. One ends up living in a different physical and symbolic environment while retaining the former "home" culture and position. After leaving the home culture's familiar cocoon, you occupy other ideological spaces, begin seeing reality in new ways, questioning both the native culture's and the new culture's descriptions of reality. The new culture, like the old one, inculcates you with its values and worldviews. Like immigrants, those in the academy find themselves constantly trafficking in different and often contradictory class and cultural locations; they find themselves in the cracks between the world (see figure 4.2).

In the cracks between the worlds; dwelling in liminalities

Negotiating with borders results in mestizaje, the new hybrid, the new mestiza, a new category of identity.[13] Mestizas live in between different worlds, in nepantla. We are forced (or choose) to live in categories that defy binaries of gender, race, class, and sexuality. Living in intersections, in cusps, we must constantly operate in a negotiation mode.

Mestizas don't fit with the norm. Depending on the degree of cultural hybridization, we are caught between cultures and can simultaneously be insiders, outsiders, and other-siders. You may think, "I'm the only one who's different. I'm the only one who lives between the cracks." You may be a blond, light-skinned Latina; a red-haired Jew; a blue-eyed Asian; a gringa who grew up in Mexico and speaks perfect Spanish; a Chicana dyke who's lost her tongue and ethnicity but doesn't feel she belongs in the white lesbian community. Some may be vulnerable to social inequities, while others can "pass" as members of Euro-American cultures. Possessing more than one heritage, people

Mestisaje

mixed heritage, many cultures

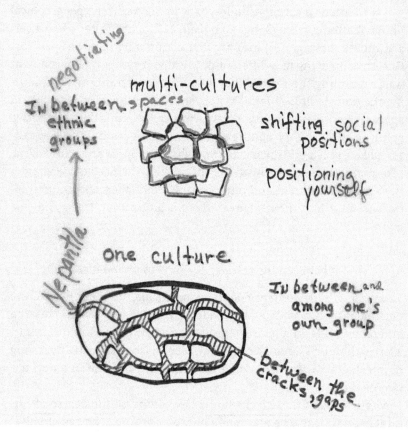

negotiating

In between spaces

In between ethnic groups

multi-cultures

shifting social positions

positioning yourself

Nepantla

one culture

In between and among one's own group

between the cracks, gaps

4.2 | Between the Cracks

of mixed races are often pressured to choose one tribe over another or to adhere to standards of ethnicity that are often contradictory, such as being too Mexican or not Mexican enough. People who refuse to pick sides and identify exclusively with one group trouble the majority, disturbing the dominant discourse of race, just as bisexuals trouble that of sexuality, transpeople confound that of gender. Cracks in the discourses are like tender shoots of grass, plants pushing against the fixed cement of disciplines and cultural beliefs, eventually overturning the cement slabs.

Constant trafficking, negotiating, and dialoguing across borders results in a profound new mestizaje, one that transgresses the biological and encompasses cultural mixtures. This new mestizaje eschews the racial hierarchies inherent in older mestizaje. We do not allow ourselves to shelter in simplistic colonialist notions of racial difference, exclusionary boundaries, and binaries (such as other-insider). We must unchain identity from meanings that can no longer contain it; we must move beyond externalized forms of social identity and location such as family, race, gender, sexuality, class, religion, nationality.

War of identities (and cultural meanings)—when our tribes are legion

Composed of numerous Latino groups en conocimiento y desconocimiento (knowledge and ignorance) of each other's histories, cultures, and experiences, and with vast differences among us, we live entremedios in a tense balance with each other and with other groups.[14] Immersed entreguerras—in collisions and conflicts with those bearing different views—we perpetuate mental and emotional violence against each other. Somos semilla ciegas que han perdido el rumbo de la luz. Disquieted by fears that some "other" will take whatever small or great privileges we have garnered, those of us in academia compete furiously, often turning our backs on our own gente and "biting at our shadows" (to borrow Wendy Rose's words from "For My People"). Yet because we're forced to deal with interracial conflicts and negotiate our numerous and varied social positions in the cracks between realities/mundos, we may access experiences and abilities that can catapult us into creating innovative, inclusive identities. This could be our moment in history, when we clarify collective and personal vision and purpose, transcending the "us" versus "them" dichotomy inscribed by society or psychology. Our steps have carried us to the brink of a great cultural understanding and awakening, of giving ourselves over to, de entregarnos a, las nuevas concepciones acerca de identidad.

To re-image identity in new ways requires that we change the focus of the lens trained on our faces and shift our perceptions. It requires letting go of the old identifications and behaviors. The who-we-are is currently undergoing disintegration and reconstruction, pulled apart, dismembered, then reconstructed—a process I envision symbolized by Coyolxauhqui. It may be necessary to adopt some type of pan-ethnic term other than "Latino" (given to us by mainstream media) or "Chicano/Latino" (cumbersome at best). To derive an appropriate pan-ethnic term we need to identify our common conditions and our different circumstances while honoring our diversity. We must explore the ramifications of what we're becoming and confront the shadow beasts that color the realities of our times before being totally subsumed under any broad social category or totally homogenized by the dominant culture. To continue la herencia que la huelga estudiantil de 1968 in the U.S. and Mexico nos dejó tenemos que re-pensar (we need to rethink) nuestra identidad racial y escribir new identity narratives.

Our various histories of mestizaje, and the contradictions inherent in the term and its mixtures, give us the ability and flexibility—the tools necessary—to realize great changes in personal and collective identity. Like corn, a primary staple of Mexicans and indígenas, mestizos have been, and continue to be, subject to genetic mixtures and extensive hybridity.[15] But we find our sense of self threatened by our shadow aspects and by the very liminal spaces (las nepantlas) we inhabit, aspects and spaces with the potential to push us into new avenues of growth. Like other new Raza narratives, mine are replete with contradictions, riddled with cracks. Though these holes allow light/insights to enter, they also cast shadows. Acknowledging and exploring estas sombras is more difficult when I myself have created them, and I risk reducing the complexities of race and culture. I'm always, already, a traitor por escribir y por mi lengua, and rewriting cultural narratives makes me even more of a malinchista.

Rewriting identity

To protect ourselves from oppressors, we idealize and hesitate to criticize Raza. We exclude from the vast geographies, from the round disk of wholeness, the concerns of the smaller groups and the issues of women. The inner, personal, and intrapersonal conflicts and misperceptions among women and men, queer and straight, are basically struggles of identity. It's not race, gender, class, sexuality, or any single aspect of the self that determines identity but the interaction of all these aspects plus as yet unnamed features. We discover, uncover, create our identities as we interrelate with others and our alrededores/surroundings. Identity grows out of our interactions, and we strategically reinvent ourselves to accommodate our exchanges. Identity is an ongoing story, one that changes with each telling, one we revise at each way station, each stop, in our viaje de la vida (life's journey).[16] Though the words for identity components used by each generation, each Latino group, each individual may be the same, the definitions may be slightly different. Concepts such as self, culture, race, hybridity, mestizaje, and spirituality have become more nuanced. We must challenge the present concepts, creating frameworks that span the fissures among us and link us in a series of interconnected webs (telarañas).

We must push against any boundaries that have outlived their usefulness. Rigid borders hinder communication and prevent us from extending *beyond* ourselves. While pondering both the necessity and the futility of fences, I paced up and down my side yard looking at my tall new redwood fence. I missed seeing into my neighbor's yard. Though the barrier insures my privacy and lessens noise and intrusion, it limits my visual space.

It's vital that we maintain our heritages' useful, nurturing aspects but release the unproductive and harmful components. When an individual realizes that she doesn't fit into a particular collective-conditioned identity and when the tribe cannot contain all that she is, she must jettison the restrictive cultural components and forge new identities. The point may not be to move beyond a nationalistic search for indigenous roots but rather to undertake transformative work that processes and facilitates evolving as a social group, becoming an extended tribe, and developing a new tribalism. What's important is negotiating alliances among the conflicted forces within the self, between men and women, among the group's different factions, and among the various groups in this country and the rest of the world. The story of mestizaje must also include other planetary groups. It must cultivate major transformations in spiritual and soul identities.

NOS/OTRAS: BRIDGING SPLITS, LEAPING ACROSS ABYSSES

Estamos peliados

While speaking at various universities, I've witnessed gente in professional disciplines a grito herido (with loud cries) badmouth each other. Palabras picantes like jabañer nasal spray sting the air and, like the slash of whips, scar the skin. Jíjole. For people of color and other outsiders, the academy is a wounding field. Our cuerpos are riddled with emotional scars. Heridas fragment and disrupt the self, disturb who and what we are.

The dialogue between the old male vanguard and Chicanas/Latinas feministas who challenge it has become polarized on many campuses. Hombres y mujeres fear the other for similar reasons: being thought less of, ignored, disliked, displaced, not allowed space. Las feministas chingonas in frustration betray their feminisms; liberated men snarl like machos perrones. Los malentendidos llenos de enemistad fall out, become enemies. De mala gana (with reluctance), we work with each other. Las mujeres somos abusadas por boconas y atrevidas. Women (and cultural others) are still the old standby receptors for projections, still demonized as malinches.

Chicanas silence indigenous women, and indigenous women lambast Chicanas for appropriating Indian identity. We hurt an "other" for their identity, race, gender, sexual preference. Wounded, we let our anger stomp on others as if they're ants. We compete for control. Ignoring the fact that colleagues and academic departments are part of a living ecology (like ants living in the same hill), we often overlook how our words and work affect our colleagues, how they deny our interdependence with the world around us. We disregard the fact that we live in intricate relationship with others, that our very existence depends on our intimate interactions with all life forms. Our shadow aspects reveal themselves in caustic and cutting ways, exposing unfulfilled wishes and repressed feelings. Despite living in close proximity to each other at home, school, and work, despite living in overlapping worlds, unconscious forces and unspoken desires divide us. How can we turn this energy exchange from aggression into something else?

Shadow aspects emerge in conflict

Entreguerras (civil wars) arise out of the human effort to define ourselves and our territories when we're up against others who are also determining themselves and their territories but with different and/ or opposing ideas, who try to spin and suck us into the remolinos of their ideologies. We may feel threatened by those who possess a different viewpoint or different kinds of knowledge/conocimiento. Fear and ignorance (desconocimientos) of the other—those who come from a different race or class; have a different skin color or gender; dress, speak, or are "abled" differently—may be the source of our problems. Fear and ignorance produce conflict. When things go wrong, you experience discord in your relationship to environment, nature, time, space, and other objects. Exchanges with self, others, and world arouse antagonism when others don't react as you expected. Inner conflict arises from clashing ideas and emotions in your body, mind, soul, and spirit; personal conflicts arise from antagonism with family, friends, and colleagues; extra-personal conflicts occur when you clash against social institutions such as government, church, school, and business. Like a stone thrown in water, conflict ripples outward from inner to personal to extra-personal to environmental to cosmic. Internal wars between parts of the self escalate into wars with others, then into intertribal strife, and into national and international armed conflicts. Stopping the world's violence begins with las entreguerras at home.

To bridge the fissures among us, to connect with each other, to move beyond us/them binaries (men and women, queer and straight, able and disabled), we must dismantle the identity markers that promote divisions. In our conflicts, we must sometimes put certain aspects of our identities backstage; otherwise we'll be so busy asserting and protecting those identities that we'll miss what's really going on, miss the opportunity to become or gain allies. Our defense mechanisms white out the others' voices. When dealing with other women of color, we must rein in our nationalistic tendencies. We try to contemplate others' sufferings from "safe" places without engaging them with deep feeling. However, to really listen, we must put our corazones y razones

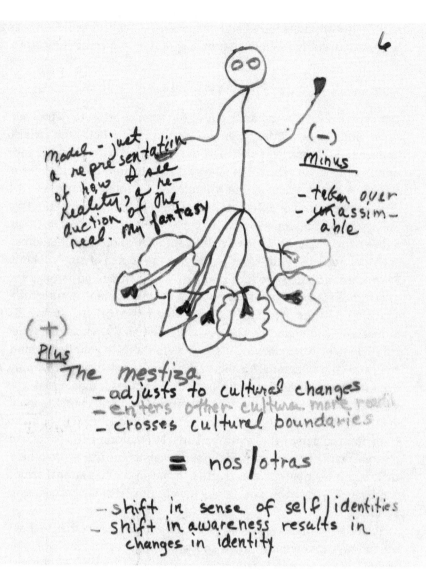

model - just a representation of how I see reality? a reduction of the real. my fantasy

(−)
minus

- taken over
- unassim-
  able

(+)
Plus
The mestiza
  - adjusts to cultural changes
  - enters other culture more readily
  - crosses cultural boundaries

= nos/otras

- shift in sense of self/identities
- shift in awareness results in changes in identity

4.3 | Nos/Otras

(feeling and intellect) in our manos and extend them to others in empathetic efforts to understand. Intimate listening is more productive than detached self-interest, winning arguments, or sticking to pet theories.

Self/other: The slash in nos/otras

Living in a multicultural society, we cross into each other's worlds all the time. We live in each other's pockets, occupy each other's territories, live in close proximity and intimacy with each other at home, school, and work. We are mutually complicitous—us and them, nosotras y los otros, white and colored, straight and queer, Christian and Jew, self and Other, oppressor and oppressed. We all of us find ourselves in the position of being simultaneously both insider and outsider. The Spanish word "nosotras" means "us." I see this word with a slash (rajadura) between "nos" (us) and "otros" (others), and use it to theorize my identity narrative of "nos/otras" (see figure 4.3).

La rajadura gives us a third point of view, a perspective from the cracks and a way to reconfigure ourselves as subjects outside binary oppositions, outside existing dominant relations. By disrupting binary oppositions that reinforce relations of subordination and dominance, nos/otras suggests a position of being simultaneously insider/outsider, internal/external exile (see figure 4.4). The clash of cultures is enacted within our psyches, resulting in an uncertain position. An identity born of negotiating the cracks between worlds, nos/otras accommodates contradictory identities and social positions, creating a hybrid consciousness that transcends the us versus them mentality of irreconcilable positions, blurring the boundary between us and others. We are both subject and object, self and other, haves and have-nots, conqueror and conquered, oppressor and oppressed. Proximity and intimacy can close the gap between us and them.

Navigating the cracks between worlds is difficult and painful, like reconstructing a new life, a new identity. Forced to negotiate the cracks between realities, we learn to navigate the switchback roads between assimilation/acquiescence to the dominant culture and isolation/preservation of our ethnic cultural integrity. But both are necessary for survival and growth. When we adapt to cambio (change), we develop a new set of terms to identify with, new definitions of our academic disciplines, and la facultad (the ability) to accommodate

nos/otras

Disrupts

___ Euroamerican feminist *discoure*
___ dominant racial
___ Western concepts of:

RACE
IDENTITY
REALITY
KNOWLEDGE

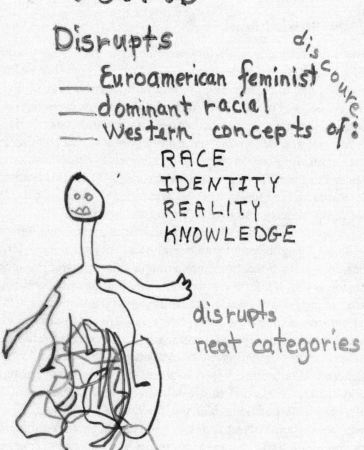

disrupts
neat categories

4.4 | Nos/Otras Disrupts

mutually exclusive, discontinuous, and inconsistent worlds. As world citizens we learn to move at ease among cultures, countries, and customs. The future belongs to those who cultivate cultural sensitivities to differences and who use these abilities to forge a hybrid consciousness that transcends the "us" versus "them" mentality and will carry us into a nos/otras position bridging the extremes of our cultural realities, a subjectivity that doesn't polarize potential allies.

Today, the division between the majority of "us" and "them" is still intact. We are nos/otras. This country does not want to acknowledge its walls—its limits, the places some people are stopped or stop themselves, the lines they're not allowed to cross. Hopefully, sometime in the future we may become nosotras without the slash. Perhaps geography will no longer separate us. We are becoming a geography of hybrid selves of different cities or countries who stand at the threshold of numerous mundos.

As an identity narrative, nos/otras has the potential to overturn definitions of otherness. When we examine the us/them binary deeply, we find that otra-ness may be deceptive, merely a cage we assign to others. According to Buddhism, the primal distinction between self and other is illusory because the existence of self is, itself, an illusion. This distinction is responsible for all evil and sorrow. There is no wrong, no vice, no evil in this world, except what flows from the assertion of entirely independent selfhood. There are no "otras"—we all emerge from humanity's basic shared, communal ground, an emotional-spiritual ground of being. Nos/otras (as the slash becomes increasingly permeable) puede ser el nuevo nombre de seres que escapan de jaulas.[17] The task of remaking our selves and our cultures is in our own hands; the task of las nepantleras is to point the way.

LAS NEPANTLERAS: ALTERNATIVE SENSE OF SELVES

Lugares nepantleras—perspectives from the cracks

While juggling several cultures or forces that clash, nepantleras live in tense balances entremedios, teetering on edges in states of entreguerras. We're not quite at home here but also not quite at home over there. Like queer and bisexual people who must live in both straight and gay worlds, or like rural people living in cities—stuck between the cracks of home and other cultures—we experience dislocation, disorientation.

We are forced (or we choose) to live in spaces/categories that defy gender, race, class, sexual, geographic, and spiritual locations.

Our uncertain positions as mestizas compel us to negotiate the cracks between worlds, to accommodate contradictory identity positions and mutually exclusive, inconsistent worlds. Las rajaduras give us a nepantla perspective, a view from the cracks, rather than from any single culture or ideology. This perspective from the cracks enables us to reconfigure ourselves as subjects outside the us/them binary. Dwelling in liminalities, in-between states or nepantlas, las nepantleras cannot be forced to stay in one place, locked into one perspective or perception of things or one picture of reality. Las nepantleras refuse to turn right onto the dominant culture's assimilation/acquiescence highway. They refuse to turn left onto the nationalistic-isolationism path demanding that we preserve our ethnic cultural integrity. Instead, las nepantleras construct alternative roads, creating new topographies and geographies of hybrid selves who transcend binaries and de-polarize potential allies. Nepantleras are not constrained by one culture or world but experience multiple realities.

Our perspective's stability relies on liminality and fluidity. Rejecting identification with a single position, we shift from one position to another, listening to all sides. We're no longer locked in the outsider/other/victim place so prevalent in the 1970s and '80s. The nepantla mind-set eliminates polarity thinking where there's no in between, only "either/or"; it reinstates "and." Because our perceptions and thinking contain subtle and hidden biases, we need a nepantla brain to prompt the questioning of our usual assumptions and beliefs.[18] Such a brain would facilitate our ability to look at the world with new eyes. Navigating the cracks is the process of reconstructing life anew, of fashioning new identities. Nepantleras use competing systems of knowledge and rewrite their identities.

La nepantlera, artista-activista, with consencia de mestiza offers an alternative self. As intermediaries between various mundos, las nepantleras "speak in tongues"—grasp the thoughts, emotions, languages, and perspectives associated with varying individual and cultural positions. By living on the slash between "us" and "others," las nepantleras cut through isolated selfhood's barbed-wire fence. They trouble the nos/otras division, questioning the subject's privilege, confronting our own personal desconocimientos, and challenging the other's marginal status. Las nepantleras recognize that we're all com-

plicit in the existing power structures, that we must deal with conflictive as well as connectionist relations within and among various
groups. Ensuring that our acts not mirror or replicate the oppression
and dominant power structures we seek to dismantle, las nepantleras
upset our cultures' foundations and disturb the concepts structuring
their realities. Las nepantleras nurture psychological, social, and spiritual metamorphosis.

The web of connection

We are all strands of energy connected to each other in the web of existence. Our thoughts, feelings, experiences affect others via this energy web. Our pervasive, excessive sense of woundedness compels us
to erect barriers that create knots on the web and block communication. When conflict (like a rock thrown into the web) disrupts a sense
of connectedness, las nepantleras call on the "connectionist" or web-
making faculty, one of less structured thoughts, less rigid categorizations, and thinner boundaries that allows us to picture—via dreaming
and artistic creativity—similarities instead of divisions. Las nepantleras develop esta facultad, a realm of consciousness reached only
from an "attached" mode (rather than a distant, separate, unattached,
mode), enabling us to weave a kinship entre todas las gentes y cosas.
It removes hidden agendas driven by fear or ambition, is not invested
in outcomes, and does not favor one view over another. Las nepantleras guard against reproducing exclusions based on racial and class
identity. They see in surface phenomena the meaning of deeper realities, "see through" our own cultural conditioning and dysfunctional
values. As agents of awakening (conocimiento), las nepantleras reveal
how our cultures see reality and the world. They model the transitions our cultures will go through, carry visions for our cultures, pre-
paring them for solutions to conflicts and the healing of wounds. Las
nepantleras know that each of us is linked with everyone and everything
in the universe and fight actively in both the material world and the
spiritual realm. Las nepantleras are spiritual activists engaged in
the struggle for social, economic, and political justice, while working
on spiritual transformations of selfhoods.

Living in nepantla states enables us to create alternative forms of
selfhood. Shifting our perception and acquiring a different self, or
moving the center of the self slightly, allows us to imagine a different

identity. The imagination's power to shift (what I call la naguala) enables la nepantlera to flow from one identity or theoretical position to another.[19] When we shift geographical or social positions, another identity may spring into being. Roots grow and ground us in a particular moment or reality if we're available to the emotional currents among those present. In a particular situation you become a person with particular identifiable features; in another situation, you metamorphose into another type with other distinguishing characteristics. Like train way stations, our "self" stops for a few minutes or a few years on el viaje de la vida; each way station expands the self or creates another self.[20] Nepantleras constantly articulate and redefine identity positions to include what has previously been excluded or has not been part of consensual reality. (Identities such as those of neo-Nazis and other hate groups with unethical behavior are not included.)

Green shoots cracking rock

Nepantleras function disruptively. Like tender green shoots growing out of the cracks, they eventually overturn foundations, making conventional definitions of otherness hard to sustain. Their activism, cultural production—indeed, their very lives—challenge traditional identity politics. Dismantling identity entails unlearning stereotypical labels and questioning consensual reality. It means seeing through identity roles and descriptions of reality. Those of us who live skirting otros mundos, other groups, in this in-between state I call nepantla have a unique perspective. Unlike previous generations of Raza, our academic knowledge and language give us both the vocabulary to look at our own cultures and dominant cultures in new ways and the tools to interrogate them. We notice the breaches in feminism, the rifts in Raza studies, the breaks in our disciplines, the splits in this country. These cracks show the flaws in our cultures, the faults in our pictures of reality. This perspective from the cracks gives us different ways of defining the self, of defining group identity—as in the lines of a Leonard Cohen song, "There is a crack, a crack in everything / That's how the light gets in."[21] The light spilling through these cracks shows the flaws in our cultures, the faults in our pictures of reality. Like green saplings, new viewpoints push up through the cracks and later grow into trees with roots, dislodging foundations of previous beliefs. Perspectives from cracks offer us different ways of defining the self, of deciding group identity. Nepantleras both affirm ethnic/national identities and align with wider social movements. Because Raza is realizing more profound mestizajes and wider diasporic changes, our narratives are beginning to construct identities from multiple cracks between worlds. Like older notions of mestizaje, the new versions cast new shadows.

Bridging the extremes of cultural realities, las nepantleras stand at the thresholds of numerous mundos. As world citizens, las nepantleras learn to move at ease among cultures, countries, and customs. The future belongs to those who cultivate cultural sensitivities to others. Recognizing and engaging in the nos/otras imperative (of removing the slash) will take effort by members of all communities cooperating with others. The new tribalism is about being part of but never subsumed by a group, never losing individuality to the group nor losing the group to the individual. The new tribalism is about working together to create new "stories" of identity and culture, to envision diverse futures. It's about rethinking our narratives of history, ancestry, and even of reality itself.

CHANGING "STORIES" HEALING WOUNDS: THE COYOLXAUHQUI IMPERATIVE

Everyone has a song.
God gave us each a song.
That's how we know who we are.
ROBBIE ROBERTSON, "MAKING A NOISE," CLASSIC MASTERS, CD

Being "worked" through by remolinos (whirlwinds) de cambio

"Cultura" is the fabric of life that the scissors of previous generations cut, trimmed, embroidered, embellished, and attached to new quilt pieces, but it is a cloth that the wash of time discolors, blends the dyes, and applies new tints. If cultura is the story of group identity (what it means to be Chicano, etc.) and its ideas about what is real, then with alterations in story come nips, tucks, and new wrinkles in both self- and cultural identity. Since cultura is rooted in patterns of the past, its design, trimming, blueprint, and so on laid out and co-created by previous generations, it is a social system that is difficult and slow to change. Cultural ideas (such as what's honorable or cowardly, manly or womanly) and their taken-for-granted truisms are imbibed at a young age and become life's givens, a familiarity that makes us feel secure. It can be hard to adopt new ideas and new ways of seeing, especially if these new perspectives seem threatening and make us doubt or distrust our core sense of self. Change generally produces tension because it has no sense of closure, completion, or boundaries. We don't want to risk lo desconocido (the unknown). We want to remain in our cages of custom and habitual thought patterns and behaviors. We resist, dig in our heels when confronted by fast-paced change.

Because we operate in forward mode, we're forced to absorb in ten years or less changes that usually take more than two generations to assimilate. We each have five to one hundred times the amount of sheer human experience of our ancestors just one hundred years ago.[22] We live in the constant suck of remolinos—vortexes composed of new ideas, technological shifts, cyber-age information, new class systems, new communities—demanding our attention. Estos remolinos sweep us up and land us in different places, forcing us to shift our values, beliefs, perceptions, and myths. The bits and pieces swirled up and sucked in the cultural vortex create extreme hybridization. We have to process cambio/change more quickly, and our children will have to process even faster. Right now, the who-we-are is undergoing the Coyolxauhqui process of disintegration and reconstruction. Our trabajo is to figure out how an individual maintains her cultural identity in this blurring of borders.

Our habitual perspective changes when something jars us loose, when something traumatic or joyful (like a cambio in jobs or love partners) shocks us out of our habitual state. When we experience bodily and boundary violations, border shifts, and identity confusions, a flash of understanding may sear us, shocking us into a new way of reading the world. Ideological filters fall away; we realize that the walls are porous and we can "see" through our belief system's fictions and fissures. These fissures disrupt the neat categories of race, gender, class, and sexuality.[23] Without the blindfolds, we begin refiguring our identity and life purpose. This change triggers an identity crisis, cracking us open to other ways of identification. Although painful, this shift or shock is the first step in entering the territory of conocimientos/knowledge, insights the prevailing maintainers of the culture's laws would keep from you. Once recognized, these understandings render identity malleable, allowing greater freedom in constructing identity. Because change often happens in nepantla, we must learn to swim in this liminal space.

Healing sustos and breaches in reality

Breathing the acrid stench of burning rubber, she passes the carcass of a stripped car and the kids playing soccer in a vacant lot carpeted with broken glass. The fetid odor of death wafts from rubble piled high in a bombed-out cavity, brick walls are charred black from fire. She hears a woman's cry coming from the end of the empty alley—la Llorona wailing in the Lower East Side. She stumbles on a piece of cement jutting out of the split sidewalk. Under her feet a crunch, she looks down to shards of broken glass reflecting multiple images of herself like the faces/phases of the moon. Looking up, she sees the full moon, Coyolxauhqui, descending on her, bringing the promise of wholeness.

"SUSTO," IN LOS ENSUEÑOS DE LA PRIETA

For racialized people, managing losses, the trauma of racism, and other colonial abuses affect our self-conceptions, our very identity, fragmenting our psyches and pitching us into states of nepantla. During or after any trauma (including individual and group racist acts), you lose parts of your soul as an immediate strategy to minimize the pain and to cope—hecho pedazos, you go into a state of susto.[24] After a racial or gender wounding, something breaks down; you fall to pieces (you're dismembered). You can't swallow your anger and grief. You struggle to redeem yourself, but you can never live up to the white dominant ideal you've been forced to internalize. Caught in the sticky morass of chaos, unresolved discordance prevents you from pulling yourself together.

When what you expect to happen doesn't happen (getting tenure, curing an illness, and so on), you experience a lack in your life, a loss of control. This breach in reality upsets your sense of equilibrium. A gap (nepantla) or abyss opens up between your desires and what occurred. This disorientation compels you to rethink the situation and the people involved. If you're receptive, you may get an insight that prompts you to revise your sense of things, your vision of reality. With the revised version come new expectations of yourself, others, and the world. When these expectations aren't fulfilled and you can't put your life back on an even keel, can't fill the lack, another breach in reality occurs. Again, you revise the situation and your expectations. The situation becomes even more tangled when beneath the surface of what you want (or what you think you want), you have unconscious contradictory desires (you want tenure, a better job, yet you dread the responsibilities that the rise in status will demand of you). Personal desires may be entangled with racial or gender conditioning. Conflict arises again. Again you make adjustments. Mourning your wounds and losses is part of processing changes.

Grieving losses

Betrayed for generations, traumatized by racial denigration and exclusion, we are almost buried by grief's heavy pall.[25] We never forget our wounds. La Llorona, our dark mother with her perpetual mournful song, has haunted us for five hundred years—our symbol of unresolved grief, an ever present specter in the psyches of Chicanos and mexicanos. For cultural changes to occur, members of that culture must move through stages similar to those in the grieving process: denial, perceiving the damage, anger, blaming others, bargaining, acceptance, and, finally, establishing a new direction. If you name, acknowledge, mourn, and grieve your losses and violations instead of trying to retain what you've lost through a nostalgic attempt at preservation, you learn not just to survive but to imbue that survival with new meaning. Through activist and creative work you help heal yourself and others.

But often grief is so overwhelming that you can't move on with your life. At those times it's hard to accept loss, hard to recognize that loss is a condition of life. Knowing that permanent stability is impossible, that protective walls and other defenses cannot halt life's flux, is small comfort. Even the fact that all people share life's flux does not allay or offer solace. At such times, you must dig deep into yourself. What nourished you in times of chaos and strife may now save your sanity by connecting you to cultural archetypes, the life force or spirit. I picture these sources, like archetypal cultural figures, welling up from el cenote, el fuente fecundo or pool in the personal and cultural unconscious formed by the waters of many rivers: the spiritual and the mundane, indigenous Mexican, Chicano, Basque, Spanish, Latino Euro-American, and cultures of color. As the streams flow upward, they co-mingle to create meaning, customs, and practices that spread to and are "borrowed" from and by other cultures through diffusion.

Travel and the flow of information and communication facilitate cultural change and assist in birthing new cultures. As change works itself through your physical body, it also works itself through your culture. You "work" the culture through yourself and you are "worked" through the culture—both personal and cultural identity change accordingly. Together, you write the new cultural story.

After much struggle and in moments of insight/conocimiento, your life and its scattered parts get reconstituted on a different plane: You gain another identity through change and loss. The process of making yourself whole requires all your parts—you can't define yourself by any single genetic or cultural slice. If one aspect is denied or rejected, if you leave some aspect out of the amalgam, la masa, you will not achieve lasting integration (though integration lasts only until something new jars you off kilter). Remember that while Coyolxauhqui in her dismembered state (depicted as a disk with topsy-turvy body parts) embodies fragmentation, she also symbolizes reconstruction in a new order. Her round disk (circle) represents the self's striving for wholeness and cohesiveness. The Coyolxauhqui process is currently working on each person and her or his culture as both attempt to become more inclusive, more whole. The moon is the Zen emblem of enlightenment.

Con las manos en la masa: Spiritual activism

Our task has always been to heal the personal and group heridas of body, mind, spirit. We must repair the damage/daño that we have perpetuated on members of our own group, that men have rendered to women and women to men, that adults have done to children, that all groups have done to other groups. I define healing as taking back the scattered energy and soul loss wrought by woundings. Healing means using the life force and strength that comes with el ánimo to act positively on one's own and on others' behalf. Often a wound provokes an urgent yearning for wholeness and provides the ground to achieve it. In shadow work, the problem is part of the cure—you don't heal the wound; the wound heals you. First you must recognize and acknowledge la herida. Second, you must "intend" to heal. Then you must fall headlong into that wounding—attend to what the body is feeling, be its dismemberment and disintegration. Rupture and psychic fragmentation lead to dialogue with the wound. This dialogue, in turn, opens imaginings, and images awaken an awareness of something greater than our individual wounds, enabling us to imagine ways of going through nepantla's disorientations to achieve wholeness and interconnect to others on the planet. And finally, you have to plunge your hands into the mess, plunge your hands en la masa, into embodied practical material spiritual political acts. This politics of embodied spiritualities (that I term "conocimiento") es nuestro legado.[26] We struggle to decolonize and valorize our worldviews, views that the dominant cultures imagine as other, as based on ignorance. We struggle to cultivate nuestras facultades that rely on inner knowledges.

> Back in South Texas, soy la rancherita once more. Though she's been dead for over twenty-five years, I "see" mamagrande Ramona, wounded healer, picking orange leaves, making me un té for my menstrual cramps. Today my sister and I pick cactus, cook los nopalitos—a folk medicine for the diabetes we both struggle with. Across the border, I walk along Avenida Juarez in Nuevo Progresso, Tamaulipas, buying diabetes medications—they're much cheaper in Mexico.—Journal entry[27]

Congruent with the previous steps, each of us, alone and as a group, goes about doing the inner/outer work of healing, removing and rewriting negative inscriptions. Activism is engaging in healing work. It means putting our hands in the dough and not merely thinking or talking about making tortillas. It means creating spaces and times for healing to happen, espacios y tiempos to nourish the soul. Meditative prayer, a work of the imagination and a powerful generative and transformative force, often accompanies each stage of this healing process. It's frustrating when healing doesn't happen immediately. Some of us choose to slow down the healing work or choose not to heal because we've become familiar and comfortable with our wounds. We may be afraid that our entire life will change if we heal. And it will. Fear holds us back. We fear that the empowerment we may attain if we take on the challenge and succeed will force us to let go of our surroundings, intimates, and situations that disempower us because we don't need them anymore.[28]

We attempt to heal cultural "sustos" resulting from the trauma of colonial abuses fragmenting our psyches. Pitched into states of nepantla, we step through the gates of change. Fragments and contradictions are stirred en la olla and cooked to a new soup. During this process, the ego/I's will is ousted as the self's sole authority. In the cauldron the culture unseats its gatekeepers, resolves its fragments and contradictions, and recasts its entire heritage. En la olla the culture reorganizes itself, creating order out of chaos.

Conversaciones to sustain us: Deshaciendo el daño through collective knowledge

We're on a path of recuperation on many fronts, a healing of our humanhood, our selves, our very bodies, and our intellectual lives. Engaged en una busqueda intelectual, we're combating the concepts, ideas, and ideologies that control us. We're revising and claiming them. This quest has led us to self-development programs, Alcoholics Anonymous meetings, self-help books, tapes, therapists, and learning institutions, where we're developing mental/spiritual/emotional healing skills. For the most part, we have been alone, isolated in our journeys. But now we're sharing the stress and the skills by connecting with different people through healing therapies and activism. We must foster mentorship programs. We must facilitate funding for the more experienced organizations to do cross-training, giving technical assistance to less experienced organizations in process-oriented, participatory, and collaborative relationships.

To be in conocimiento with another person or group is to share knowledge, pool resources, meet each other, compare liberation struggles and social movements' histories, share how we confront institutional power, and process and heal wounds. In conocimiento, we seek input from communities so as not to fall into elite collective, isolated cells that widen the chasm between campus politics and grassroots activism. Let's not wait for "Hispanic Week" or "Lesbian and Gay Awareness Week" to try to understand each other's cultures. Solidarity work demands a global, all-embracing vision. Let nosotras (without the slash) be el nuevo nombre de mujeres que escapan de jaulas, who struggle with and for differences, who carry differences without succumbing to binaries. How do we survive these wounds and struggles? The path of knowledge requires that we apply what we learn to all our daily activities, to our relationships with ourselves, with others, with the environment, with nature. Escritoras, artistas, scholars, activistas transmit knowledge to help others cope. Through knowledge we liberate ourselves; through knowledge we question the limitations of a single culture/nationalistic identity. Walking el camino de conocimiento by the light of one's knowledge enables us to close the gaps, bridge the abysses.

Many activists think that spiritual work is not a form of activism but a cop-out; however, this view is too limited and ignores the greater picture. How do those of us laboring in the complex environments of an academy indifferent and even hostile to spirit make our professional work into a form of spiritual practice? By joining intellectual work with spiritual work into a spiritual activism. We must build a practice of contemplation into the daily routines of academic and professional life. Contemplation allows us to process and sort out anger and frustration; it gives us time for the self, time to allow compassion to surface. La compasión es una conversación sostenida. In short, we need a spiritual orientation to life. According to Aung San Suu Kyi, "The quintessential revolution is that of the spirit. . . . It is not enough merely to call for freedom, democracy, and human rights. Without a revolution of the spirit, the forces which produced the iniquities of the old order would continue to be operative, posing a constant threat to the process of reform and regeneration."[29]

By cultivating awareness, we minimize wounding; by maintaining compassion and empathy for those of different genders, races, classes, regions, generations, and physical and mental capacities, we link to them. To maintain our connections, we must cultivate liberating insights/conocimientos and radical realizations that burst through the cracks of our unconscious and flow up from our cenotes. We need artistic expressions and efforts that heal and inspire, that generate enough energy to make a difference in our lives and in those of others. We must create new art forms that support transformation.

Revivan tallo, rama, raíz/revive flower, stem, branch, root

The Coyolxauhqui imperative urges, "Revivan tallo, rama, y raíz." It tells us that chaos and disintegration will lead to a reorganization, to a new order and a new kind of being in the world. Raza groups are not yet a "we." We are multiple nos/otras. Integrating the fragmented, dislocated pieces/souls of our separate, divided selves must come before integrating all our ethnicities into cohesive geographies of selves.

Maybe what we call ourselves is not ultimately so important. Maybe the dialogue itself is most significant. Until we respect and care for each other, "nosotras" will mean nothing and socially transforming our selves will fail. To coexist with the other necessitates that we rethink the dichotomy between "us" and "them," that we redefine "enemy" and "ally." Isn't an ally that which empowers you? Isn't an enemy not another person but the ignorance, fear, hate (los desconocimientos) that diminish us? When our "enemies" become conscious of their desconocimientos and act on that awareness, they may become our "allies."

We need nepantleras whose strength lies in our ability to mediate and move between identities and positions. Necesitamos nepantleras to inspire us to cross over racial and other borders. To become nepantleras, we must *choose* to occupy intermediary spaces between worlds, *choose* to move between worlds like the ancient chamanas who *choose* to build bridges between worlds, *choose* to speak from the cracks between the worlds, from las rendijas (rents). We must *choose* to see through the holes in reality, *choose* to perceive something from multiple angles. The act of seeing the holes in our cultural conditioning can help us to separate out from overidentifying with personal and cultural identities transmitted by both our own groups and the dominant culture, to shed their toxic values and ways of life. It takes energy and courage, to name our selves and grow beyond cultural and self-imposed boundaries. As agents of awakening, nepantleras remind us of each other's search for wholeness. Large geographic distances no longer separate us. Because of increasing self-knowledge and interdependence through communication, collaboration, and greater access to information, we're increasingly becoming a part of the greater whole, but also more individualistic.

> The N train crawls through its underground holes, winding in and out of its warrens. On the other side of the glass, the words "7th Ave." flicker faster and faster, like frames in a movie. La Prieta sways to the subway train's jarring yet fluid motion. Her hand, along with seven other hands, grips the pole . . . . The pole is a tree of life, a new ridge pole, the cosmic tree, not of family but of strangers, and their bodies its branches.
>
> When she is spewed out at the other end an hour later, she feels the City pulsating like a live animal. The buildings are watchful trees rooted deep in the bowels of the Earth. Where before she felt drained and exhausted by the energy of thousands of packed people, where before she tired herself out trying to protect herself from the intensity, anger, frustration, and madness

of a million busy souls sardined in the trains, buses, streets, now she rides
on that energy.—"Susto," *in* Los ensueños de la Prieta

Today we (all people, not just Raza) are poised on the brink of a great flowering of our árbol de la vida de "amar la plenitude del árbol," a geography of a new tribalism not foreclosed by traditional categories. For this, our moment in history, we need to spread our branches and increase our capacity for awareness, vision, presence, and compassion. In Gandhi's words, "You have to be the change you want to see in this world." In seeking the truths of our lives, let's not draw back from what frightens us. Let's look toward our nepantleras (poetas, artistas, queer, youth, and differently abled) who have a tolerance for ambiguity and difference, la facultad to maintain numerous conflicting positions and affinity with those unlike themselves. Let's call on las ánimas de nuestros abuelas y abuelos y pedir a diosita que nos de rumbo y destino para seguir el camino de conocimiento.

I take my daily "pilgrimage" to the Guadalupe tree, make la promesa (vow) to write well. When the tree's spirit answers my prayer, I offer it un milagrito, a tiny pluma (pen), gently placed in its hollowed trunk. I look up through the branches and see the moon. El árbol de nuestras vidas has weathered a lot of storms—some branches torn off, trunk gashed, roots severed. Yet still its lifeblood rises, still it faces the storms of life with grace. Ahora sí chispas, quémenos / Now is the time. Echéle ganas Raza, agarremos ánimo—sí se puede.

5 | Putting Coyolxauhqui Together

A Creative Process

Pacing your breathing to the foghorn's doleful sounds, you walk along
the coast of Monterey Bay toward the lighthouse and its beckoning
light. Across the bay to the east, the yolk of the sun, swollen and lop-
sided, is slowly squeezed up by the mountain. Fog creeps up and
swallows the gold. From the precipice you stare down at the waves
crashing against the rocks, incessantly and furiously. In the middle of
the rip, all tides converge and churn a white chaos. Bobbing out at sea
is a small blue boat cradling its lone occupant.

De la orilla del mar you mull over el cuento de tu proceso: a meta-
story tracking the phases of your creative process and touching on your
writing habits, rituals, and emotional upheavals, your beliefs about
writing, your relationship to it, and the support you get from your writing comadres, the "godmothers" who read and encourage the work. To
tell how you write is enormously appealing—like most members of
the tribe of writing, you love talking about it.[1]

Your goal is to cultivate an acute awareness of processes at work in
your own psyche and to create symbols and patterns of its opera-
tions. The problem is that a process is arrested when you stop to
watch it. Another problem is that not only do you want to make the
fleeting process known, but you also want to create a virtual reality of
the experience so the reader goes through it, as well. And you have

only words to do it with. Ultimately, with this story, as with all creative work, you, like all artists, want to alter, however slightly, the way you look at the world. You want to change the reader's sense of what the world is like. You want to make a difference, if only for one other person. A tall order. As you walk back home, hueles la tempestad en el aire.

As you go about your day, the potential story calls to you. At first la llamada is just an intangible longing, a vague yearning for form. Soon it becomes a beat pulsing subliminally. It won't take no for an answer. Symbolically, the call's source is the dark mother, la Llorona, the ghost woman wailing for the loss of her children whom she murdered in crazed anger against a lover's betrayal. Aztecs know her as Cihuacoatl, or Serpent Woman. La Llorona is your musa bruja, la naguala that incites you to write. In her horse aspect, la Llorona will carry you from beginning of story to finish line.

As always when you first take on a call, something in you is ebullient and expands, eager to be filled. You believe you can do anything if you leave no stone unturned. Blessed and cursed by la llamada, you both anticipate the pleasure of using your skills and talent and quail at the toll it will take. Structuring experiences and emotions through language makes life tolerable, meaningful; it allows you to escape your condition through fantasy, only to find yourself confronting the condition you're trying to escape. Mapping the different terra incognitae with their shadowy indwellers enables you to evolve and grow, but only after putting you through a crucible. Creating theories of nearly unconscious processes va ser un jale bruto.

Having taken up the reins of esta historia, the next day as you walk along West Cliff in the early morning hours a tenuous tension begins to stretch in your body. In saying "yes" to the call, you're taking on more than just this essay. You've been mulling over the creative process for years and know that one day a book will emerge. Te espanta el trabajo. You arrive at your arboreal amada, the giant gnarled cypress you're in love with. You sit between its thick exposed roots and let them cradle you. Through the embrace of its branches you see a bit of sky looking like a blue flower. Below, waves break against the jawbones of the bluff, the water cutting itself on its canine teeth. Incessant, enduring.

You assess your situation, plan your strategy. From your pack you pull out your workbook and jot down your thoughts: how you're going to carve out the time and muster the energy to take on this trabajo; what the project means in the scheme of your life. Be realistic, you caution yourself. If you find the task too complex to finish by the deadline, you'll carry the burden of failure, the guilt for a missed opportunity. Remember the demons who always try blocking you before the finish. But even more, remember that a writer must write; remember your readers awaiting new work.

To bring into being something that does not yet exist in the world, a sacrifice will be required. Sacrifice means "making holy." What will you give up in making holy the process of writing? You make a commitment, un compromiso, to create meaning. A commitment to add to the field of literature and not just duplicate what's already there. A commitment to explore untrodden caminos—which means turning over all rocks, even those with worms underneath them. You suspect that your shadow self and its darkness has more to do with creativity than your surface self.

Be realistic about your health—it's precarious, especially your eyes. Fluctuations of blood flow cause the arteries to break and bleed. Besides struggling with diabetes and its complications, you have cross-country travel and speaking engagements from which you make your living, the mentoring of writing interns, and being a resource. Writing is the normal condition of your life—not something you do on the side when you have time. Writing is a given. All else yields before it, except your health, and there will probably be times when you'll sacrifice even that. You'll juggle this work with your novel-in-stories and put other writing projects on hold. And if the winter storms keep lashing the coast and the water keeps rising, you'll have to keep El Niño from swamping your house.

Some things will go wrong—así es la vida. You'll need a contingency plan to deal with the cycles of stress, turmoil, depression that you create for yourself and for the obstacles that are part of your process. When you slam into a block or get bitten by a writing virus, remember to let it work itself through your body like water through a blowhole. You'll have to release stress by taking time out and giving yourself treats—permission to laze, your favorite comidas, escape between the covers of a thriller. You'll have to focus on the pleasure writing gives you and on what motivates you. And if your daily process doesn't allow you to finish and still have a life, you'll have to create another schedule.

You have inflated, unrealistic notions about the amount you can accomplish in a day, so you double the time you think this project will take. You map out the territory you want to cover, the number of pages to aim for. You divide the work into parts. On the calendar, you mark deadlines and specifics for each stage. Every few days you'll reassess the work, reschedule tasks. You turn away from the rippling silk of the sea and head home. You are now una gallina culeca sitting on your eggs. You begin to brood. You nurture the idea by ignoring it, sit on your eggs until the tension begs to be written off.

When you wake, up you're still between realities, in "nepantla," a Nahuatl word for the space in-between, un lugar/no-lugar or tierra de un medio. Via nepantla you tap "el cenote," the archetypal inner stream of consciousness, dream pool or reservoir of unconscious images and feelings stored as iconic imagery. El cenote is a mental network of subterranean rivers of information that converge and well up to the surface, like a sinkhole or an opening to the womb of the Earth (see figure 5.1). The Maya in Chichén Itzá dedicated el cenote to el dios de la lluvia. Into their sacred well they threw their most precious possessions: turquoise, clay pottery, copal, virgins, and their children. Those who didn't die were supposed to bring back the rain god's promise for a good or bad year. You stand before la boca del poso sacrado, the great Pacific Ocean, and make your offering. Dreaming awake, you go deep, listen, and watch; you attend to the imaginal with the goal of translating it on paper.

Accessing the ocean of uncanny signs is one of the great mysterious acts of human imagination—for you, an act of pleasure. The creative rush of ideas, the sudden flash of an "other" reality rising out of the sea is exhilarating. Always, it renews tu espíritu. Unlike the rest, this aspect of writing is effortless. But the deep dives scare you—there's always a monster in the cave; the deeper you go, the sharper its fangs. If you don't find a way in, it will find a way out.

The next morning you stay in bed. Eyes closed, you lie quietly. With blankets and pillows, you make a womb-cave of night, entreating the moon to keep the daylight at bay. The moon lifts the veil between inner and outer worlds and you cross over. Protected by darkness, you descend into the warm, velvet underground cave. Rivulets of water sluice around you, swirling, eddying. Images rise up accompanied by

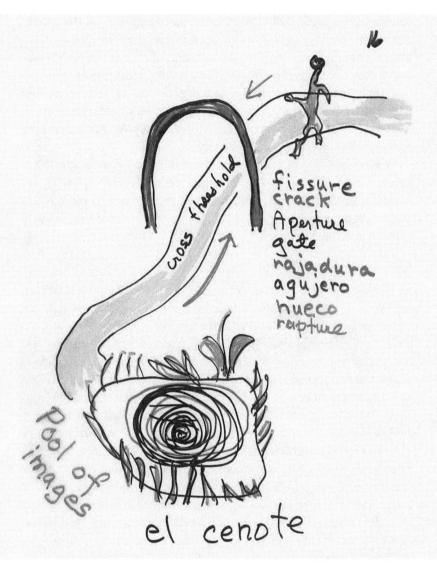

5.1 | El Cenote

sensations so brief that if you're not paying attention, they won't register. If they slip past you—you dream up others on the spot, one image spawning another. A visual, aural, or olfactory memory of some trivial incident triggers a stream of images. Subliminal events in your body or sensations provoked by its organs appear and vanish like fleeting fish, leaving behind a flash of el cuerpo's knowledge. At times a drama in Technicolor—complete with setting, dialogue, action, and soundtrack—unreels from el cenote.

The images spin out for hours. Soon, however, you must quit the cavernous theater of dreams to begin the work of deciphering the images, mining them for their symbolic meanings and manifesting them in language. You put the images en la olla (cauldron) of your historia and let them cook.

As soon as you wake, the familiar pressure is there: Should you write or not? Yes, no, maybe. You heave your body out of bed, prick your finger, and squeeze a drop of blood onto the glucose meter. You shoot insulin into your stomach, eat, go for a walk. You concentrate on your feet touching the ground, on the blue stretch of sky, the roar of crashing waves, the pungent odor of guano. You listen to the environment as Don Juan urged Castaneda to do. Searching for analogies to your budding ideas, you scan cypress trees with twisted trunks, a flock of pelicans flying low over the water, breakers shooting up the cliff walls like geysers.

You spent your childhood en ranchos in South Texas, watching cattle and horses graze, ruminate, and chew. Like them you graze the environment, assigning ideas to images, asking what reality has to do with your creative process, what the larger focus and purpose should be. Following the bay's edge, the wind gusting around you, you let nature help you create symbols for the story's ideas, help you develop ideas for its symbols, help you invent theories. Watching for signs, you look at the emerald waves marbled with white. They remind you of the network of vessels on the whites of the eye. This morning, when you looked at the mirror you saw two blood spots like red cactus tunas in your eye. When capillaries bleed you see floaters and pulsating lights—everything gets blurry. Híjole, your worst nightmare: if you can't see to write and read, there goes your life.

You hurry home y te recojes en el asiento de la ventana. A blanket across your lap and pre-draft at the ready, you search the field of bones for una seña of the root metaphor, the umbilicus to which all elements of la historia connect, a literary equivalent to chaos theory's strange attractor. You look for an image-pattern that will point to a framework that could contain the organized whole. When you find the conducting thread, llegas a la historia como llegar a un templo, exaltada, temblando. You bask in the artist's high, which may be why you're moved by designs in nature—the imprint of waves on sand, the shifting shadows of windblown trees.

As you write, the rhythm of words and the flow of images evolve a structure and act as catalysts for combining information in a new way. It's not always this easy. Some days you rack your brain, stretching over the surface chaos page after page before you discern a shape. But now you're flowing. You are the watcher con ojos de águila, alerta y vigilante, scrutinizing and processing every sensory experience. You become aware of a supernatural being. It shares with you a language that speaks of what is other; a language shared with the spirits of trees, sea, wind, and birds; a language that you'll spend many of your writing hours trying to translate into words. Walking between realities—one strange, another familiar—you experience the shock of recognition, the pleasure it gives you. A deep sounding from the landscape resonates through your bodymind. You get a hint of the ground of writing and a few tenuous tendrils groping for a trellis. You begin working the soil.

At the edge of the foaming sea you ask: How and from what point of view shall I tell this story? What mood do I want to evoke and sustain? What emotion does it arouse in me? What emotion do I want to arouse in the reader? How much of myself should I put in the text? Certainly, include your frustrations and elation, your fears and satisfactions, and, above all, the mystery. You take out your notebook and begin listing what this metaphysical observation of writing has taught you about yourself, about your process.

The sky darkens. Another storm is on its way. As you slosh through the field, floundering on sodden soil, you look for a container—a form or frame or womb—for the story, one that will collect the scattered images, connect the symbols, and unfold layers of meaning. This idea-generating dreaming writes the narrative as you move through your day. While vacuuming, it pulls the story through your body. Favoring interiority, it quickens en el terreno de sueños in the silence of night.

Now it's time to start composing the next pre-draft.[2] Anticipation and mild dread course through your body. You walk from desk to files to shelves, looking for something, a lost note, to anchor your attention. A part of you wants to write and a part of you doesn't—there's always a conflict as to which of you is running the writing. The part representing internalized goals and a personal standard of perfection has grandiose plans for your career, wants the story to be a work of art. Your controlling authoritarian spirit wants you to apply willpower and discipline; it wants you to produce and to be efficient about it. The rebel doesn't like to be forced and absolutely balks at any discipline. It hates iron-clad schedules and routines set for specific hours and, when left on its own, will sabotage the clock. Your struggle to find a methodology, a way of working, is constant. Balancing these aspects of spirit isn't easy. Writing is like pulling miles of entrails through your mouth.

Why the resistance? Because you're scared that you won't do it justice. Because it'll take time, and there's no guarantee that you'll be able to pull it off. Because it's stressful and exhausting. A veces pierdes el nervio, y Saca Vueltas tempts you to play coward and procrastinate, to do more reading and research or to work on another story. After all, writing is not only the physical act of drafting and revising. It also involves feeding the muse books on mythology and Aztec nagualismo (shamanism), reading voraciously in all disciplines, and taking notes. Writing also involves envisioning and conceptualizing the work and dreaming the story into a virtual reality. The different stages in embodying the story are not clearly demarcated, sequential, or linear; they overlap, shift back and forth, take place simultaneously.

You light copal incense, hoping the scent and the ritual will coax you into the writing. You stare at the fluttering flame of the Virgen de Guadalupe novena candle and invoke the memory de tus muertos, your dead, tus mamagrandes y tu papá who persevered and persisted and who walk between realities. You brew some chai tea, find music to accompany your visionary scape, to shift consciousness from beta toward alpha. Tex-Mex? Ambient? Enigma? Lourdes Pérez? The cavernous cello sounds of Yo-Yo Ma playing the Bach suites it is. You do a five-minute meditation observing your mind streaming, say your writer's prayer, and begin to compose.[3] At this point, your task is to re-member, translate into language the images arising from your body, the sea, the theater of dreams—allowing them to surface at will and capturing them in your net of words.

After a stint at the computer you walk around the house and yard, limbering a stiff back. Like an aching tooth, you suck on the problem of how to embody the story. Which genre: memoir, personal essay, or a combination? Memoir is a difficult genre. It's harder to manipulate the raw material of your own life than the details of an invented story. The problem is how to distinguish between you, the actual writer, and you, the narrative persona. The problem is how to improvise the self you create as you compose, how to make that self immediate and alive without falling into self-indulgence, sentimentality, or grandstanding. The problem is deciding which chunks of your inner struggle and pain to cannibalize and incorporate into the text.

What about the style—the particular way of saying things, the imprint of self you leave on the page? Style brings up the politics of utterance—who says what, how, to whom, and on whose behalf. When you use a particular language register to re-create particular realities, you include certain groups of people and exclude others. Style brings up issues of loyalty and ethics. You wonder whether you are unknowingly reproducing the dominant ideology along with its literary conventions. You weigh the benefits and the detriments of using a rhetoric different from dominant practices, of mixing a discursive style with a poetic one.

At this point, your concern is premature. Mostly una historia chooses its own form and style without your conscious guidance. Your task is to block the ego's insistence that you write "better," that you use the methodology of the head. But when you try to write like a writer, the language comes out stilted and abstract. You sit on your eggs and continue brooding. For days you continue to confuse the ego and feed la musa bruja with large doses of chaos theory, the poetry of Rosario Castellanos, and reruns of *The Outer Limits*.

From your aerie high up in the loft you listen to the wind howl and the sea lions bark. Through the skylight you watch the moon, Coyolxauhqui, suspended in the sky. You favor the night when things whisper. While the town sleeps you go through your electronic notebooks, cutting snippets and pasting them into the story file. Surfing from notebook to notebook, you gather every pertinent scrap or image you can find. You group similar ideas, order them in a semi-logical sequence, shuffle the clumps of semi-developed concepts into a loose order, and divide them into sections. At the pre-draft stage your anxiety fixates on how to organize the information. You take a break to squeeze a drop of blood, take your insulin shot, and grab a quick snack. Fingers back on the keyboard, you stare at the screen. You need to start drafting. Now.

Composing is an osseous process, the formation of bone, though at times it feels like sweating blood. You conjure up el cenote, throw yourself in and swim among images and memories of other writing times. You freewrite five to six pages at warp speed. You do not focus on form. You don't consider technical problems yet. You keep the critical, editing voice at bay. You go from tightly focused writing to brief pauses where you allow your attention to dart here and there. Keying in the words, you're scribe, medium channeling the story, and conductor orchestrating the process.

Besides being pleasurable, the work of putting down words engenders its own kind of trance; the physical act of writing is another kind of dreaming. Once you get into a working rhythm, you hate to interrupt it or leave it. Sure enough—your insulin shot was due hours ago.

At the end of the day, before sleep, you program yourself—yet another type of dreaming. Concentrating on feelings of contentment, delight, and satisfaction, you put yourself through a virtual reality of the next day's activities. While waiting for sleep to kick in, you suggest to your subconscious that it dream up another part of the story and surprise you in the morning.

You listen to the falling rain, to the sump pump sucking water out of the backyard, to the humming of the computer. You stare at the framed portrait of your naguala on the wall, flash back to when your queer comadre Randy painted your portrait twenty-three years ago. Every few minutes he would tilt your head. Squinting his eyes, he looked from your face to the sketchbook. When he finished, you got up and peered over his shoulder. It looked like some sort of wereanimal with fur-like feathers—exactly how you'd seen yourself in the mirror whenever you dropped angel dust. How did he know? He made two holes in the mask for eyes and strung a piece of elastic from ear to ear. Out of bits and pieces of cloth he created a costume. That Halloween night you were both the animal in you and your animal companion, yourself and other—naguala. You felt powerful, otherworldly, and privy to a secret knowledge. For the first time you felt at home in your body. To talk about the work of embodying consciousness, you appropriate the word "naguala" from your ancestors, the indigenous Mexicans, who believed that certain humans could turn into animals.

Now you stare at the sketch of la naguala, arch your back on the typing chair, and slowly exhale through your mouth. As the tension eases out, la bruja naguala takes over. La naguala is the dreaming body, a mode of consciousness that's emotionally complex, diverse, dense, deep, violent, and rich, one with a love of physicality and the ability to switch bodies and their expressive codes instantly. You invoke this sentience to help you, not to transcend but to more passionately embrace the physical. You metamorphose into someone else—a fictional character, a species of alter ego, a persona from your dramatic mask. You become an internal experience, a particular emotional state or mood; you give life to tumultuous feeling, to raging anger. You become the crashing waves, the lighthouse with its beacon.

A hyperempathic perception fuses you with your surroundings; you become what you observe: a face bulging out of the wall like in the sci-fi film, the woman lurking behind the wallpaper. Shifting and fluid, the boundaries of self-identity blur. You accommodate all identities. In naguala you alternate between this hyperempathy and excessive detachment, a seamless change from one form to another.

Where does the work of naguala take place? In the body. All emotions and ideas pass through it; writing is nothing if not a bodily act. An image produces a physiological reaction experienced in strong feelings (desire, hate, fear) and manifests itself in neuromuscular, respiratory, cardiovascular, hormonal, and other bodily changes. In other words, an image produces emotion. You can't have an emotion without a corresponding sensory image—and vice versa. The unconscious and the physical body do not distinguish between what is really happening and what is imagined or envisioned. Both are equally real. Once fed blood, once fleshed, the bones of inert and abstract ideas become embodied, become mental and emotional realities living inside your skin. Writer, then text, then reader become possessed by naguala.

After letting the pre-draft gestate for a few days, you pick it up again. You read the hard copy standing at the kitchen counter while you eat. In your study you ignore the answering machine's red blinking light and continue flipping through the pages, reacquainting yourself with its overall shape, pinpointing the major sections and subsections. Identifying each part with a subtitle (which you later get rid of after your comadre Randy tells you they fragment the piece), you integrate and merge some sections while shifting others.[4] Your goal is to raise a temporary skeleton. You're aiming not for a linear, logical structure of ideas but, instead, for an architectural body that supports and allows access to its innards.

Fresh copy in hand, you do several more flip-throughs, your first complete read-through, and yet another rearrangement of parts. As you're inputting changes, the lights in your study are blinking and then go out. You look out the window. Rain is falling in sheets; wind is lashing the trees. You walk from room to room checking the windows, then wait for the power to come back on.

Tonight's your writing date with Irene, one of your writing comadres. You go to a local coffeehouse, get a table by a wall outlet, and plug in your laptops. You discuss your projects and encourage each other. Before leaving the coffeehouse, you decide what you're going to do tomorrow, thus giving your unconscious something to work on. Next day you'll transit into the writing without having to jump-start it cold.

The moment of reckoning is at hand; it is time to write the first draft. You read over the pre-draft. It's an uncoordinated mass of information, a pile of bones. You start assembling los huesos in a way you hope will connect all the story's elements while adding add up to more than the sum of the bones. In school you had to memorize the bones in the body, more than two hundred. A story possesses a body: Its skeleton is the framework; the bones, its armature. All the bones are connected to the backbone, a single linchpin that holds the story's tension and contains the crucial threads running throughout the work. The story's ideas—including the most important organ, the heart—are held, encased, and protected by the skeleton.

You use transitioning devices (the ligaments, tendons, muscles, and skin of writing) to join the bones and bind nerves and organs: mood, description, plot, characterization, and dialogue. The sheer magnitude of the time and the stamina required to get all los huesos in order is overwhelming. To help organize the interaction of images and words into an eight-thousand-word essay and keep yourself from going completely crazy, you turn to a colored pen sketch you made of la Coyolxauhqui and invoke her. In Aztec mythology, Coyolxauhqui is the moon goddess, a warrior woman. Making her the first human sacrifice, her brother Huitzilopochtli, the war god, decapitated her, dismembered her body, and scattered her limbs. Organizing the parts into a unified whole and drafting a full version of el cuento is the act of putting Coyolxauhqui back together again.

Next day you read the first draft to find that overnight it has become a Frankenstein-like monster. The Coyolxauhqui you put together is a grotesque figure with arms sticking out of her back, her skull hanging between her legs. She has eye sockets for knees. You pull your hair and snarl at the screen. You will have to take the text apart bone by bone, again go through psychic dismemberment, fly apart, implode, splinter once more. This stage of the writing feels violent y siempre te desmadra. This stage reminds you of helping your mother desgranar (shuck) corn, scattering the hard kernels and then waiting for them to sprout. The second time you re-member the bones, Coyolxauhqui emerges less malformed. The text begins taking comely shape, begins discovering its own grace, its own organic force.

During the whole componiendo y des-componiendo drafting phase you're in a state of extreme unease. To reduce the intolerable pressure, you remind yourself that confusion is a necessary stage of creating, that the disequilibrium brought on by disorganization and chaos forces you to use your imagination to right the balance and compose in a better order. You're trying to teach yourself, as Clarice Lispector put it, "to bear the frustrating discomfort of disorder."[5]

Maybe a walk by the ocean will help you pull yourself together. When you are halfway to Natural Bridges, a surfer crashes against the rocks, his board breaking into pieces.

You return home from your walk and continue dreaming parts of the story as you putter about in your kitchen, opening and sorting through the mail, listening to the radio and the storm raging outside your window; you talk on the phone, monitoring what's going on inside your body. In a state of nepantla, you switch from one perception channel to another, channels reflecting the same information in different ways. The cacophony that comes from being open to multiple channels can feel like watching half a dozen TV stations at once—confusing, maddening, frustrating—until nepantla creates a wider space in your mind, allowing you to make the connections, allowing the various scenarios to merge and come into focus.

Creativity requires profound shifts of consciousness and a scattered kind of attention that goes against habits of thinking. Nepantla is your symbol for the transitional process, both conscious and unconscious, that bridges different kinds of activities by moving between and among different parts of the brain. The work of nepantla is a mysterious type of dreaming or perception that registers the workings of all states of consciousness. Shaman-like nepantla moves from rational to visionary states, from logistics to poetics, from focused to unfocused perception, from inner world to outer. Nepantla is the twilight landscape between the self and the world, between imagination's imagery and reality's harsh light.

Nepantla operates in the cracks between the worlds, in the liminal spaces. It navigates the razor edge of this rajadura, always teetering, about to fall either on the side of overly ordered organization or the side of bacchanalian chaos, always attempting to join the two in a seamless web. Rational consciousness sets goals and schedules. The imaginal consciousness, the dreaming naguala, seizes the symbols and metaphors that el cenote renders and turns them into sentient worlds, while nepantla interlaces those worlds into a coherent whole.

Your head is full of spiders, all weaving their glistening webs. Nepantla tries to marshal the field where images, words, feelings, and mind-sets vie for a place in the story. Nepantla averigua el conflicto. It provides associations and connective tissue. Performing mental, psychic, and spiritual gymnastics, nepantla interweaves multiple, superimposed strands of thought. Suddenly your writing is flowing smoothly as you ride with nepantla. If only you could ride this writer's high forever.

You've sat on the second draft for a couple of days, and now it's time to revise it. You take a deep breath and pick it up: 14,810 words, 314 paragraphs, and 56 pages. You need to eliminate more than half. Then you need to redesign. You groan—this constant destruction-reconstruction process is wearying. What if you don't get la historia to breathe, much less dance, by the deadline less than two weeks away? Qué le hace, it doesn't matter—today's writing must get done.

By now it's the middle of the night, and the whole pueblo sleeps. Night is a fecund terrain for you—eres más hija de la Coyolxauhqui y de la noche que del sol. The foghorn's mournful sounds and the rain drumming on the roof accompany the pecking of fingers on keyboard. You reacquaint yourself with the text's overall structure, pinpoint the major renovations, examine the linchpin holding it together. Your questions at this stage are: Does the piece possess coordination among parts, a balanced proportion and a varying pace that maintains interest? Will the reader find pleasure in the imagery and language and be satisfied by the form? Is spending time in your company worth the reader's time?

After re-envisioning la historia—and finding out what it's really about—you draw up a rough timetable for the next revision stage, list the sections and specifics of what you're to do. You do the first read-through silently. You work the large chunks, saving the detailed work for later revisions. You cut and rearrange, shape and focus the material repeatedly. You input the changes and tackle the repetitions and abstractions (your major literary vices). You throw out whole sections, paragraphs, sentences, and expand others. You look at the tone and ask: Does it reflect my feelings about my writing process? Is this story more than just a personal record of my process—that is, have I placed it in the context of the world and some of its social, political realities?

Next day your body is wiped out, but by evening you're riding the creative high tide again. You read through the draft, merging sections, reordering, knitting the connective tissue. You help the story say what it intends to say. Todavía no baila; that requires a wide-awake energy you don't have right now, an energy that's necessary to be totally present and engaged with the work. You know that working long sessions is counterproductive, but you keep slogging away, working like an automaton. As the sun begins to rise and burn off the fog along the coast, you print out the third draft.

You pull Coyolxauhqui apart again in the fourth draft. Again naguala shape-changes, compelling a rearrangement of parts. Nepantla reassembles the fragments around a different emerging center. Months later you're on draft number ten.[6] Just a couple more drafts and you'll be done, but you're feeling a lot of resistance. Why do you always run into a stone wall when bringing the work to its final completion?

Reading the tenth draft is like walking on a field of dead bones, and you wince at the dull, heavy-handed sentences. The thing rings hollow, its heartbeat silenced by dead wood. Not a breath of poetry to be found anywhere. Its narrative mode and first-person voice puts your ego in the text too much.[7] Not only does the story say nothing new; it says it badly. Más claro canta el gallo. And worst of all, it doesn't engage the reader emotionally. Doubts about your ability to pull it off by the deadline (an extended deadline negotiated months ago) gnaw your insides like rats.

To be innovative and subversive, a writer must write what readers haven't been taught to read yet—a different and unfamiliar literary form—present an experience not yet articulated or portray a familiar one from a radically different perspective. Not only must you outdo those who have come before, but you must also outdo yourself; each successive work of art must be different from your prior work. You have failed to do all this. No has dejado huellas nuevas.

The pressure and urge to speak in new ways, to say something different, to push genre boundaries without losing the reader is as constant as gravity. You're assailed with the angst peculiar to writers—namely, that this piece is the worst you've ever written. After a prolonged labor, you have nothing to show for it. You feel that you have betrayed the piece by not writing it up to your expectations. A profound depression sweeps you under.

You don't want to work on it anymore. Maybe you've run into the endurance wall, a marathon runner finding yourself drained six miles before the finish line. Maybe you need to protect it from the harsh outer world's weather until it's more developed. Maybe you did not allow enough time for the silence needed to attend to all the symbols in the story. When pressured to publish too soon, the last stage gets short-changed. The ideas and feelings seeking expression, seeking embodiment, have not yet been worked over, have not been kneaded enough; they are only partially digested. You have ordered it too soon; you have not borne the chaos, not worked the raw materials long enough. You forced a premature birth because you did not let the ideas grow all their fingers and toes. You did not wait long enough for the imaginative self to completely render up its treasures.

You hate having incompletes hovering over you—the all-but-dissertation doctoral degree, the projects promised—but what you hate most is passing something off as finished when you feel it isn't, when it hasn't lived up to its potential. Disgusted with yourself, you look around your study. Every surface is covered with folders, faxes, requests for submissions and letters of recommendation, manuscripts sent by friends and strangers who want you to write introductions or blurbs for the cover or take a few days out of your life to critique their five-hundred-page masterpieces. You're angry at your own internal demands that you should be able to do everything. You resent the pressure—your own and that of editors, publishers, and readers—to produce.

Stuck on an edge you can't get past, toda la mañana le sacas vueltas. You pace like a caged animal, wanting only to fling yourself against the wall. You wash the dishes; water sometimes gets you into the writing, but today not even the floodwater in your backyard could help. Naguala transforms itself into una bestia sombra, and, like the Creature from the Black Lagoon, rises up from the depths, grabs you, drags you into the deep waters of the cave. You have no immunities and few defenses against the monster's unscheduled visits. A writer can't afford to hide from herself. You must face the desconocimientos that you don't want to see. Possessed by your inner demon (the antagonist within, the part of you whose desire is in opposition to yours) and frustrated with the deadline, you feel hurried, pressured, and harassed. You can't deny, can't hide, from the shadow side of writing.

Just as the story's success depends on a deeper integration of all the pieces and a balance between order and chaos, you know that the solution to your depression lies en esa cueva oscura and a deeper integration of your psyche. Until you admit that the interior shadow is a part of you, is you, is your own irrationality, you may not survive (in your present form) to emerge with the message from the source. But you don't have time to brood in the cave. You have a deadline.

It's too much. Throwing up your hands, you head for the beach again. The gusting wind pushes you along West Cliff. The foaming surf is churning, and the breakers crashing against the bluffs are deafening. You can't see the lighthouse beacon. Out at sea the familiar blue boat and its Mackintoshed figure ride the rough swells. Doesn't the fool know enough to come out of the storm?

On your way home, with dark clouds hovering overhead and howling winds buffeting your body, you slog through the field that months of rain have turned into marsh. Two tall trees have been uprooted. They lie on their sides, huge patches of sod still clinging to their roots. When rain starts pouring down, you glory en la tempestad. Later, on the eleven o'clock news, you hear that two people have been swept away from the rocks on West Cliff and drowned.

The more time elapses, the more resistance and dread tighten the tension. The longer the story lies untouched on your desk, the more ansia you feel. You go through some of your other anti-block strategies—deep breathing, chanting your mantra. You use whatever you can get your hands on as a battering ram against the granite rock block. No le hace, nothing works. Every day it gets harder to stay rooted in the reality of calendar and clock.[8]

Hechas maldiciónes, you curse the text, barely resisting the urge to rip the misbegotten thing into little pieces and flush it down the toilet with the rest of the caca. Writing always calls your basic self-worth into question: You're a coward for not venturing far enough into yourself. You haven't gone all the way. You haven't pulled out all the stops. You haven't questioned values and beliefs deeply enough because doing so makes you tense and vulnerable. To write is to expose yourself, to let down the protective walls—a given that comes with the territory. Today estas cansada; you're too tired to face your flawed criatura.

Face it: You've fallen out of love with it; you can't stand the sight of it. You toss the text back on the desk, feeling a sense of relief at giving up, shucking the work, and putting it away indefinitely. By burying it deep you hope that your unconscious will do the work of integration. In the black hole of depression, sofocando gritos como una llorona mourning her loss, you also bury yourself away from society like the unclean or dead. For days you binge read through your depression.

Your friends try to comfort you. "You're not an ice cream machine," Liliana, a comadre who's a visual artist, tells you on the phone. "Producing art is not like producing ice cream." When your writing comadre Carmen comes to your house for your weekly session, you tell her that you feel like you're being tested. The beam holding up the second floor is rotting and needs to be replaced; the deck needs to be shored up; your backyard's flooded, despite the sump pump going day and night; the roof leaks in three places, and water is seeping up through the floor and warping the parquet in the living room; and people keep bugging you. You've been doing the writing, but not on this particular piece. In fact, you're blocked. You tell her that you're afraid you won't make this piece dance by the deadline.

"Sure, you can do it," she says. "It takes courage and a lot of hard work to delve into your process and to expose it honestly. Don't be so hard on yourself. The kind of work you're doing is not something light." Talking to your comadres about writing and receiving encouraging feedback always reaffirms you and the trabajo. You rely on your comadres to tell you what works and what doesn't, to help you to say what you're trying to express, and to keep you on track. Writing is a shared act of creation, an act of the imagination for both writer and reader.

After Carmen leaves, you hope that you're only suffering from performance anxiety and not a creative block. Telling yourself that toiling in the muck is fun, you summon enough energy to take up the draft once more. You transform a few abstract ideas into sensory images. You vary the sentences from simplicity to complexity and examine its rhythmic patterns, balancing syntactical elements, repeating key words and motifs. You stop. You realize that you've fooled yourself into treating a symptom rather than tackling the huge underlying problem, fooled yourself into unraveling a single thread rather than the whole skein. But you refuse to dismember the story again.

Foot thumps on the roof. The sounds of a drill and hammer. Michele, the carpenter, is replacing the damaged downspouts and gutters. Three inches of rain fell yesterday, and another storm system's moving in tomorrow, but today's a day of respite after months of rain. You decide that you need a respite from the stillborn corpse of the story that you've been dragging from room to room all week. Time is the only line of defense left. Time to let the piece ferment in the imagination's dark caves until you're ready to work on it again. Time to let the scattered pieces turn over and over in the unconscious until they reformulate. But time is a commodity you've run out of.

You trudge along West Cliff. The path is barricaded with sawhorses held down by sandbags and cordoned off with yellow caution tape and orange plastic wire. Pavement, iron rails, and boulders have collapsed, forming a sinkhole. As you peer into the depths of the crater, water shoots up along its walls like a geyser, drenching you. You gasp at the shock of cold, in a burst of light as a new awareness floods you. You realize that writer's block may be a condition you have manufactured as grist for the mill, the silent brooding dark intelligence of the shadow beast sitting on its eggs. The block is the struggle that grants meaning even in failure. When you start a new project you want to write painlessly, swiftly, to produce a good work. When this doesn't happen by the deadline, you convince yourself that you're blocked. If you've invented this block, you can un-invent it.

Relief courses through your body.

To dismantle your block, you must change your behavior. To change your behavior, you must change your attitude. To change your attitude, you must change some basic beliefs about yourself, your writing habits, and your ability to do the work. To make these changes, you must be aware: What notion about writing or about this stage in particular is holding you up? That you should be able to whip out these historias faster? This is your monster—the myth that real writing comes out perfect in a few drafts.

You know that to become unblocked something must give, something must die—your ambition, your obsession with perfection. You have to let go of the illusion that the writer exerts full conscious control over her writing process.

After honoring the dark cave with time, three and a half months later you pick up the story, go over the marks on the cave walls.[9] You empty yourself so that your serpent spirit can enter and re-dream the metaphors. Then, to analyze the text, you shift from the creative right to the critical left brain. You pay attention to the meaning of words, to their tempo, cadence, and pulse. You read aloud as you revise, toying with word order, repetition, sentence construction, sentence length, and parallelism to create rhythm and texture. You want to increase the story's internal order, its self-organization, to get every part into synchronization with every other part, to polish, make clear and strong, and, if you can, to improve on your initial conception. As soon as you tackle the first section, nepantla kicks in. Nepantla, as a syncretistic faculty, watches the unconscious struggle between several possible readings. It finds and recognizes what belongs together and facilitates interaction between ambiguity and control, between undifferentiated confusion and defined clarity.

One scene attracts a fragment that in turn attracts another that matches its resonance. You rework the material until alignment and balance occur. Then you try to get each section to lock into sync with every other section, lock and pulse together with the undercurrent rhythm of the whole piece. When it becomes an animated, live thing, comiensa a bailar—it starts to dance. Something alive is more than the configuration of components in a whole—living things continue to develop and evolve.

What you've learned from your body and chronic illness that you can apply to the creative process is that change in one part or organ triggers adjustments in all the other parts. A minor change in the text causes reverberations throughout. You've become aware that being out of control (of your blood sugars) and in extreme disequilibrium prompts self-organization and a return to balance. You've learned that writing about writing is more about life than it is about writing; that writing mirrors the struggle in your own life, from denial to recognition and change; that writing illumines your fears and dreams. All these insights are precious because you wrestled them out of the granite walls of your creative block.

You put your faith on this: that some mysterious ordering faculty ultimately refines the piece or that the components of the piece, the symbols, attract the necessary parts and the whole rearranges itself, that writing is an alchemical process demanding dissolution so that the transmutation of images and emotions into words may occur. If you've done your job, the reader will also undergo an alchemical process.

The lighthouse draws you toward the horizon. When you arrive, you watch water sluicing over the rough edges of a round rock, slowly paring it down and sculpting it. You wonder if it's smoothing the rock or if it's making pits on its glistening surface. Maybe it's time to stop diddling with the text. According to Kenneth Atchity, "the concept of 'finishing your work' is a contradiction in terms so blatant and so dangerous that it can lead to nervous breakdowns—because it puts the pressure on the wrong places in your mind and habits."[10] To get past this last wall, you must change your assumptions about what finishing means. Whenever you read any of your published work, you think it needs more revisions. There is never a final "fin," just a lot of small ones. You have to accept the imperfections of your work, accept its partial incoherence, accept the fact that it will never attain the surface of a water-smoothed stone. Like a person's life, all art is a work in progress.

Your faith y tu larga espera have finally paid off, your tenacity rewarded. Head hanging low, a runner at the end of the race, you watch each page emerge from the printer crisp and clean and almost perfectly composed, almost like a water-smoothed stone. Something tangible has emerged out of the chaos and raw material of your life. You hope that one day, after many more revisions, this Coyolxauhqui will finally emerge from the cave's cauldron and maybe, just maybe, gain artistic immortality through the elixir of "The Art." But for now you put the "unfinished" story in an envelope, stick it in your mailbox, and offer it to the world.

As you walk along the cliff, you stare down into the waves washing over the rocks, incessantly, persistently, until the end of time. You watch the sun, looking like a perfect golden stone, slowly swallowed up by the ocean. You watch the small blue boat in the bay return to the mainland.[11] Dreaming another story, comiensas a empollar otro huevo. You head back home. Largo camino te queda.

an offering

As you walk across Lighthouse Field, a glistening black ribbon undulates in the grass, crossing your path from right to left. You swallow air, your primal senses flare open. From the middle of your forehead, a reptilian eye blinks, surveys the terrain. This visual intuitive sense, like the intellect of heart and gut, reveals a discourse of signs, images, feelings, words that, once decoded, carry the power to startle you out of tunnel vision and habitual patterns of thought. The snake is a symbol of awakening consciousness—the potential of knowing within, an awareness and intelligence not grasped by logical thought. Often nature provokes un "aja," or "conocimiento," one that guides your feet along the path, gives you el ánimo to dedicate yourself to transforming perceptions of reality, and thus the conditions of life.[1] Llevas la presencia de éste conocimiento contigo. You experience nature as ensouled, as sacred. Éste saber, this knowledge, urges you to cast una ofrenda of images and words across the page como granos de maize, like kernels of corn. By redeeming your most painful experiences, you transform them into something valuable, algo para "compartir" or share with others so they, too, may be empowered. You stop in the middle of the field and, under your breath, ask the spirits—animals, plants, y tus muertos—to help you string together a bridge of words. What follows is your attempt to give back to nature, los espíritus, and others a gift wrested from the events in your life, a bridge home to the self.

THE JOURNEY: PATH OF CONOCIMIENTO

You struggle each day to know the world you live in, to come to grips with the problems of life. Motivated by the need to understand, you crave to be what and who you are. A spiritual hunger rumbles deep in your belly, the yearning to live up to your potential. You question the doctrines claiming to be the only right way to live. These ways no longer accommodate the person you are or the life you're living. They no longer help you with your central task: to determine what your life means, to catch a glimpse of the cosmic order and your part in that cosmovisión, and to translate these into artistic forms. Tu camino de conocimiento requires that you encounter your shadow side and confront what you've programmed yourself (and have been programmed by your cultures) to avoid (desconocer), to confront the traits and habits distorting how you see reality and inhibiting the full use of your facultades.

At the crack of change between millennia, you and the rest of humanity are undergoing profound transformations and shifts in perception. All, including the planet and every species, are caught between cultures and bleed-throughs among different worlds—each with its own version of reality. We are experiencing a personal, global identity crisis in a disintegrating social order that possesses little heart and functions to oppress people by organizing them into hierarchies of commerce and power—a collusion of government, transnational industry, business, and the military, all linked by a pragmatic technology and science voracious for money and control. This system and its hierarchies affect people's lives in concrete and devastating ways and justify a sliding scale of human worth used to keep humankind divided. It condones the mind theft, spirit murder, exploitation, and genocide de los otros. We are collectively conditioned not to know that every comfort of our lives is acquired with the blood of conquered, subjugated, enslaved, or exterminated people, an exploitation that continues today. We are completely dependent on consumerism, the culture of the dollar, and the colossal powers that sustain our lifestyles.

We stand at a major threshold in the extension of consciousness, caught in the remolinos (vortices) of systemic change across all fields of knowledge. The binaries of colored/white, female/male, mind/body are collapsing. Living in nepantla, the overlapping space between different perceptions and belief systems, you are aware of the change-ability of racial, gender, sexual, and other categories rendering the conventional labelings obsolete.[2] Though these markings are outworn and inaccurate, those in power continue using them to single out and negate those who are "different" because of color, language, notions of reality, or other diversity. You know that the new paradigm must come from outside as well as within the system.

Many are witnessing a major cultural shift in their understanding of what knowledge consists of and how we come to know, a shift from the kinds of knowledge valued now to the kinds that will be desired in the twenty-first century, a shift away from knowledge contributing both to military and corporate technologies and to the colonization of our lives by television and the Internet, to the inner exploration of the meaning and purpose of life. You attribute this shift to the feminization of knowledge, one beyond the subject-object divide, a way of knowing and acting on ese saber you call "conocimiento." Skeptical of reason and rationality, conocimiento questions conventional knowledge's current categories, classifications, and contents.

Those who carry conocimiento refuse to accept spirituality as a devalued form of knowledge and instead elevate it to the same level occupied by science and rationality. A form of spiritual inquiry, con-ocimiento is reached via creative acts—writing, art-making, danc-ing, healing, teaching, meditation, and spiritual activism—both mental and somatic (the body, too, is a form as well as site of creativ-ity). Through creative engagements, you embed your experiences in a larger frame of reference, connecting your personal struggles with those of other beings on the planet, with the struggles of the Earth itself. To understand the greater reality that lies behind your personal perceptions, you view these struggles as spiritual undertakings. Your identity is a filtering screen limiting your awareness to a fraction of your reality. What you or your cultures believe to be true is provisional and depends on a specific perspective. What your eyes, ears, and other physical senses perceive is not the whole picture but one determined by your core beliefs and prevailing societal assumptions. What you live through and the knowledge you infer from experience is subjective.

Intuitive knowing, unmediated by mental constructs—what inner eye, heart, and gut tell you—is the closest you come to direct knowledge (gnosis) of the world, and this experience of reality is partial, too.

Conocimiento comes from opening all your senses, consciously inhabiting your body and decoding its symptoms—that persistent itch in your scalp, not caused by lice or dry skin, may be a thought trying to snare your attention. Attention is multileveled and includes your surroundings, bodily sensations and responses, intuitive takes, emotional reactions to other people and theirs to you, and, most important, the images your imagination creates—images connecting all tiers of information and their data. Breaking out of your mental and emotional prison and deepening the range of perception enables you to link inner reflection and vision—the mental, emotional, instinctive, imaginal, spiritual, and subtle bodily awareness—with social, political action and lived experiences to generate subversive knowledges. These conocimientos challenge official and conventional ways of looking at the world, ways set up by those who benefit from such constructions.

Information your sense organs register and your rational mind organizes coupled with imaginal knowings derived from viewing life through the third eye, the reptilian eye looking inward and outward simultaneously, along with the perceptions of the shape-shifting naguala, the perceiver of shifts, results in conocimiento.[3] According to Christianity and other spiritual traditions, the evil that lies at the root of the human condition is the desire to know—which translates into aspiring to conocimiento (reflective consciousness). Your reflective mind's mirror throws back all your options, making you aware of your freedom to choose. You don't need to obey the reigning gods' laws (popular culture, commerce, science) and accept fate as decreed by church and culture. To further the self, you choose to accept the guidance and information provided by symbology systems such as the Tarot, I Ching, dowsing (pendulum), astrology, and numerology.

Throughout millennia, those seeking alternative forms of knowledge have been demonized. In the pursuit of knowledge, including carnal knowledge (symbolized by the serpent), some female origin figures "disobeyed." Casting aside the status quo of Edenic conditions and unconscious "being," they took a bite of awareness—the first human to take agency. Xochiquetzal, a Mexican indigenous deity, ascends to the upper world to seek knowledge from "el árbol sagrado," the tree of life, que florecía en Tamoanchan.[4] In another Garden of Eden, Eve snatches the fruit (the treasure of forbidden knowledge) from the serpent's mouth and "invents" consciousness—the sense of self in the act of knowing.[5] Serpent Woman, known as Cihuacoatl, the goddess of origins, whom you think of as la Llorona and sketch as a half-coiled snake with the head of a woman, represents not the root of all evil but instinctual knowledge and other alternative ways of knowing that fuel transformation.[6]

These females are expelled from "paradise" for eating the fruit from the tree of knowledge of good and evil and for taking individual agency. Their "original sin" precipitates the myth of the fall of human-kind, for which women have been blamed and punished. The passion to know, to deepen awareness, to perceive reality in a different way, to see and experience more of life—in short, the desire to expand consciousness—and the freedom to choose, drove Xochiquetzal, Eve, and Cihuacoatl to deepen awareness. You, too, are driven by the desire to understand, know, y saber how human and other beings know. Beneath your desire for knowledge writhes the hunger to understand and love yourself.

seven stages of conocimiento

You're strolling downtown. Suddenly the sidewalk buckles and rises before you. Bricks fly through the air. Your thigh muscles tense to run, but shock holds you in check. Dust rains down all around you, dimming your sight, clogging your nostrils, coating your throat. In front of you the second story of a building caves into the ground floor. Just as suddenly, the Earth stops trembling. People with pallid faces gather before the collapsed building. Near your feet a hand sticks out of the rubble. The body of a woman attached to that hand is pulled from the debris. A bloody gash runs down one side of her face, and one arm sticks out unnaturally. As they place her on the sidewalk, her skirt rides up to her waist, exposing a plump thigh. You fight the urge to pull her skirt down, protect her from all eyes.

The first aftershock hits. Fear ripples down your spine, frightening your soul out of your body. You pick your way through the rubble, dodging bricks, and reach your car; except for a few dents on the hood, it's still in one piece. Coasting over the cracked bridge and pits in the pavement, you drive home at five miles an hour. One street over from your apartment, a fire spews smoke and flames into the sky. You unlock the door of your home, but the door won't budge. Putting shoulder to wood you shove back books, plants, dirt, and broken pottery the earthquake has flung to the floor.

Every few minutes an aftershock rattles the windows, drying the spit in your mouth. Each time the walls sway, you run to a doorway, brace yourself under its frame, holding your breath and willing your house not to fall on top of you. The apartment manager comes to check and tells you, "No te puedes quedar aquí. You have to evacuate. The gas lines are not secure; there's no electricity; and the water's contaminated." You want to salvage your books, your computer, and three years' worth of writing. "I'm staying home," you reply as you watch your neighbors gather sleeping bags, blankets, and food and head for the sports field nearby. Soon most of the city and county keep vigil from makeshift tents.

You boil water, sweep up the broken cups and plates. Just when you think the ground beneath your feet is stable, the two plates again grind together along the San Andreas Fault. The seismic rupture moves the Monterey Peninsula three inches north. It shifts you into the crack between the worlds, shattering the mythology that grounds you. You strive for leverage in the fissures, but Tonan, la madre tierra, keeps stirring beneath you. In the midst of this physical crisis, an emotional bottom falls out from under you, forcing you to confront your fear of others breaching the emotional walls you've built around yourself. If you don't work through your fear, playing it safe could bury you.

Éste arrebato, the earthquake, jerks you from the familiar and safe terrain and catapults you into nepantla, the second stage. In this liminal, transitional space, suspended between shifts, you're two people, split between before and after. Nepantla, where the outer boundaries of the mind's inner life meet the outer world of reality, is a zone of possibility. You experience reality as fluid, expanding and contracting. In nepantla you are exposed, open to other perspectives, more readily able to access knowledge derived from inner feelings, imaginal states, and outer events, and to "see through" them with a mindful, holistic awareness. Seeing through human acts both individual and collective allows you to examine the ways you construct knowledge, identity, and reality, and explore how some of your/others' constructions violate other people's ways of knowing and living.[7]

When overwhelmed by the chaos caused by living between stories, you break down, descend into the third space, the Coatlicue depths of despair, self-loathing, and hopelessness. Your refusal to move paralyzes you, making you dysfunctional for weeks. In the fourth space, a call to action pulls you out of your depression. You break free from your habitual coping strategies of escaping from realities you're reluctant to face, reconnect with spirit, and undergo a conversion.

In the fifth space, your desire for order and meaning prompts you to track the ongoing circumstances of your life; to sift, sort, and symbolize your experiences and try to arrange them into a pattern and story that speak to your reality. You scan your inner landscape, books, movies, philosophies, mythologies, and the modern sciences for bits of lore you can patch together to create a new narrative articulating your personal reality. You scrutinize and question dominant and ethnic ideologies and the mind-sets their cultures induce in others. And putting all the pieces together, you re-envision the map of the known world, creating a new description of reality and scripting a new story.

In the sixth space, you take your story out into the world, testing it. When you or the world fail to live up to your ideals, your edifice collapses like a house of cards, casting you into conflict with self and others in a war between realities. Disappointed with self and others, angry and then terrified at the depth of your anger, you swallow your emotions, hold them in. Blocked from your own power, you're unable to activate the inner resources that could mobilize you. In the seventh space, the critical turning point of transformation, you shift realities; develop an ethical, compassionate strategy with which to negotiate conflict and difference within self and between others; and find common ground by forming holistic alliances. You include these practices in your daily life, act on your vision—enacting spiritual activism.

The stages of conocimiento illustrate the four directions (south, west, north, east), below and above, and seventh, the center. They symbolize los siete "ojos de luz," or seven chakras of the energetic, dream body, spirit body (counterpart of the physical body), the seven planes of reality,[8] the four stages of the alchemical process (nigredo, albedo, citrinitas, and rubedo), and the four elements: air, fire, water, and earth. In all seven spaces you struggle with the shadow, the unwanted aspects of the self. Together, the seven stages open the senses and enlarge the breadth and depth of consciousness, causing internal shifts and external changes. All seven are present within each stage, and they occur concurrently, chronologically or not. Zigzagging from igno-rance (desconocimiento) to awareness (conocimiento), you may in a day's time go through all seven stages, though you may dwell in one for months. You're never only in one space, but partially in one, partially in another, with nepantla occurring most often—as its own space and as the transition between each of the others. Together, these stations comprise a meditation on the rites of passage, the transitions of life from birth to death, and all the daily births and deaths in between. Bits of your self die and are reborn in each step.

1. el arrebato . . . rupture, fragmentation . . . an ending, a beginning
The assailant's hands squeeze your throat. Gasping for breath, your scream eeks out as a mewling sound. You kick and scratch him as he drags you across the Waller Creek bridge. He shoves you against the rail. Heart in your throat, you peer at the wet rocks below lapped by the gurgling stream. If he throws you off the bridge, bones will break, maybe your neck. He finally wrestles your bag from you and sprints away. Anger pulses through you. You snatch up a big rock and run after him. You survive este arrebato and witness his capture, but every night for months when safe in your bed his snarl echoes in your head, "I'm going to get you, bitch." Footsteps behind you, people's sudden movements, stop your breath, and your body responds as though he's attacking you again. Your relationship to the world is irrevoca-bly changed: You're aware of your vulnerability, wary of men, and no longer trust the universe.[9]

   This event pulled the linchpin that held your reality/story together, and you cast your mind to find a symbol to represent this dislocation. In 1992 you first saw the huge round stone of the dismembered moon goddess Coyolxauhqui in Mexico City. She's lived in your imaginal life since then, and this arrebato embeds her and her story deeper in your flesh. When Coyolxauhqui tried to kill her mother, Coatlicue, her brother Huitzilopochtli, the war god, sprang out from the womb fully armed. He decapitated Coyolxauhqui and flung her down the temple, scattering her body parts in all directions, making her the first sac-rificial victim. Coyolxauhqui is your symbol for both the process of emotional psychical dismemberment, splitting body/mind/spirit/soul, and the creative work of putting all the pieces together in a new form, a partially unconscious work done in the night by the light of the moon, a labor of re-visioning and re-membering. Seven years after the attack, a psychic gives you a reading, telling you to find the scattered, missing parts of yourself and put them back together.

Every arrebato—a violent attack, rift with a loved one, illness, death in the family, betrayal, systematic racism, and marginalization—rips you from your familiar "home," casting you out of your personal Eden, showing that something is lacking in your queendom. Cada arrebatada (snatching) turns your world upside down and cracks the walls of your reality, resulting in a great sense of loss, grief, and emptiness, leaving behind dreams, hopes, and goals. You are no longer who you used to be. As you move from past presuppositions and frames of reference, letting go of former positions, you feel like an orphan, abandoned by all that's familiar. Exposed, naked, disoriented, wounded, uncertain, confused, and conflicted, you're forced to live en la orilla—a razor-sharp edge that fragments you.

The upheaval jars you out of the cultural trance and the spell of the collective mind-set, what Don Miguel Ruiz calls the collective dream and Charles Tart calls consensus reality.[10] When two or more opposing accounts, perspectives, or belief systems appear side by side or inter-twined, a kind of double or multiple "seeing" results, forcing you into continuous dialectical encounters with these different stories, situations, and people. Trying to understand these convergences compels you to critique your own perspective and assumptions. It leads to re-interpreting the story you imagined yourself living, bringing it to a dramatic end and initiating one of turmoil, being swallowed by your fears, and passing through a threshold. Seeing through your culture separates you from the herd, exiles you from the tribe, wounds you psychologically and spiritually. Cada arrebatamiento is an awakening that causes you to question who you are, what the world is about. The urgency to know what you're experiencing awakens la facultad, the ability to shift attention and see through the surface of things and situations.

With each arrebatamiento you suffer un "susto," a shock that knocks one of your souls out of your body, causing estrangement.[11] With the loss of the familiar and the unknown ahead, you struggle to regain your balance, reintegrate yourself (put Coyolxauhqui together), and repair the damage. You must, like the shaman, find a way to call your spirit home. Every paroxysm has the potential to initiate you to something new, giving you a chance to reconstruct yourself, forcing you to rework your description of self, world, and your place in it (reality). Every morning in ritual you turn on the gas stove, watch the flame, and, as you wait for the teapot to boil, ask Spirit for increased awareness. You honor what has ended, say good-bye to the old way of being, commit yourself to look for the "something new," and picture yourself embracing this new life. But before that can happen, you plunge into the ambiguity of the transition phase, undergo another rite of passage, and negotiate another identity crisis.

2. *nepantla* . . . . .*torn between ways*

> Pero, ay, como Sor Juana, como los transterrados españoles, como tantos mexicanos no repuestos aún de la conquista, yo vivía nepantla—un aislamiento espíritual.
>
> [But, oh, like Sor Juana, like the land-crossing Spanish, like so many Mexicans who have not recovered from the conquest, I lived nepantla—a spiritual isolation. [trans. GEA]]
> ROSARIO CASTELLANOS

There's only one other Chicana in your doctoral program at the University of Texas, Austin, in a state heavily populated with Chicanos, and you're never in the same class. The professors dislike the practice of putting yourself in the texts, insisting that your papers are too subjective. They frown on your unorthodox perspectives and ways of thinking. They reject your dissertation topic, claiming Chicana/o literature illegitimate and feminist theory too radical.

Leaving home has cast you adrift in the liminal space between home and school, bereft of your former frame of reference. In class you feel you're on a rack, body prone across the equator between the diverse notions and nations that compose you. Remolinos (whirlwinds) sweep you off your feet, pulling you here and there. While home, family, and ethnic culture tug you back to the tribe, to the chicana indígena you were before, the anglo world sucks you toward an assimilated, homogenized, whitewashed identity. Each separate reality and its belief system vies with others to convert you to its worldview. Each exhorts you to turn your back on other interpretations, other tribes. You face divisions within your cultures—divisions of class, gender, sexuality, nationality, and ethnicity. You face both entrenched institutions and the oppositional movements of working-class women, people of color, and queers. Pulled between opposing realities, you feel torn between "white" ways and Mexican ways, between Chicano nationalists and conservative Hispanics. Suspended between traditional values and feminist ideas, you don't know whether to assimilate, separate, or isolate.

The vortices and their cacophonies continuously bombard you with new ideas and perceptions of self and world. Vulnerable to spiritual anxiety and isolation, suspended on the bridge between rewind and fast-forward, swinging between elation and despair, anger and forgiveness, you think, feel, and react in extremes. Now you flounder in the chaos, now feel cradled en la calma. In the transition space of nepantla you reflect critically, and as you move from one symbol system to another, self-identity becomes your central concern. While the opposing forces struggle for expression, an inner impasse blocks you. According to Jung, if you hold opposites long enough without taking sides, a new identity emerges. As you make your way through life, nepantla itself becomes the place you live in most of the time—home. Nepantla is the site of transformation, the place where different perspectives come into conflict and where you question the basic ideas, tenets, and identities inherited from your family, your education, and your different cultures. Nepantla is the zone between changes where you struggle to find equilibrium between the outer expression of change and your inner relationship to it.

Living between cultures results in "seeing" double, first from the perspective of one culture, then from the perspective of another. Seeing from two or more perspectives simultaneously renders those cultures transparent. Removed from that culture's center, you glimpse the sea in which you've been immersed but to which you were oblivious, no longer seeing the world the way you were enculturated to see it. From the in-between place of nepantla you see through the fiction of the monoculture, the myth of the superiority of the white races. And eventually you begin seeing through your ethnic culture's myth of the inferiority of mujeres. As you struggle to form a new identity, a demythologization of race occurs. You begin to see race as an experience of reality from a particular perspective and a specific time and place (history), not as a fixed feature of personality or identity.

According to nagualismo, perceiving something from two different angles creates a split in awareness. This split engenders the ability to control perception. You will yourself to ground this doble saber (double knowing) in your body's ear and soul's eye, always alerta y vigilante of how you are aware. Staying despierta becomes a survival tool. In your journal you doodle an image of a double-headed, double-faced woman, una cara in profile and the other looking ahead. The twin-faced pat-lache of your indigenous queer heritage is also the symbol of la otra tu, the double or dream body (energetic body). La naguala connects you to these others and to unconscious and invisible forces. In nepantla you sense more keenly the overlap between the material and spiritual worlds; you're in both places simultaneously—you glimpse el espíritu—see the body as inspirited. Nepantla is the point of contact where the "mundane" and the "numinous" converge, where you're in full aware-ness of the present moment.

You can't stand living according to the old terms—yesterday's mode of consciousness pinches like an outgrown shoe. Craving change, you yearn to open yourself and honor the space/time between transi-tions. Coyolxauhqui's light in the night ignites your longing to engage with the world beyond the horizon you've grown accustomed to. Fear keeps you exiled between repulsion and propulsion, mourning the loss, obsessed with retrieving a lost homeland that may never have existed. Even as you listen to the old consciousness's death rattle, you continue defending its mythology of who you were and what your world looked like. To and fro you go, and just when you're ready to move, you find yourself resisting the changes. Though your head and heart decry the mind/body dichotomy, the conflict in your mind makes your body a battlefield where beliefs fight each other.

3. the Coatlicue state . . . desconocimiento and the cost of knowing

> There is an underbelly of terror to all life. It is suffering, it is hurt.
> MING-DAO

Three weeks after the doctor confirms your self-diagnosis, you cross the trestle bridge near the wharf, your shortcut to downtown Santa Cruz. As you listen to your footsteps echoing on the timber, the reality of having a disease that could cost you your feet . . . your eyes . . . your creativity . . . the life of the writer you've worked so hard to build . . . life itself . . . finally penetrates, arresting you in the middle del puente (bridge). You're furious with your body for limiting your artistic activi-ties, for its slow crawl toward the grave. You're infuriated with your-self for not living up to your expectations, not living your life fully. You realize that you use the whip of your ideals to flagellate yourself, and the masochist in you gets pleasure from your suffering. Tormented by self-contempt you reproach yourself constantly and despair. Guilt and bitterness gnaw your insides and, blocked by your own grand expectations, you're unable to function. You double over. Clinging to the rail you look down. Con tus otros ojos you see the black hole of anger sucking you into the abode of the shadow. Qué desgracia.

Tú, la consentida, the special one, thought yourself exempt from living like ordinary people. Self-pity swamps you, que suerte maldita! Self-absorbed, you're unable to climb out of the pit that's yourself. Feeling helpless, you draft the script of victimization and retreat from the world, withdraw from your body, losing kinesthetic consciousness. You count the bars of your cage, refusing to name your demons. You repel intrusions, rout off friends and family by withholding attention. When stress is overwhelming, you shut down your feelings, plummet into depression and unremitting sorrow. Consciousness diminished, your body descends into itself, pulled by the weight, mass, and gravity of your desconocimientos. To escape emotional pain (most of it self-imposed), you indulge in addictions. These respites from reality allow you to feel at one with yourself and the world, gaining you brief sojourns in Tamoanchan (paradise). When you surface to the present, your unrelenting consciousness shrieks, "Stop resisting the truth of what's really happening, face your reality." But salvation is illusive, like the scent of a dim memory. De éste lugar de muerte viva the promise of sunlight is unreachable. Though you want deliverance, you cling to your misery.

You look around, hoping some person or thing will alleviate the pain. Pero virgen santísima, you've purposely cut yourself off from those who could help—you've no desire to reconnect with community. Separated from all your tribes, estás en exilio en un destierro, forced to confront your own desconocimiento. Though you choose to face the beast depression alone, you have no tools to deal with it. Overwhelmed, you shield yourself with ignorance, blanking out what you don't want to see. Yet you feel you're incubating some knowledge that could spring into life like a childhood monster if you paid it the slightest attention. The last thing you want is to meditate on your condition, bring awareness to the fore, but you've set it up so that you must face reality. Still, you resist. You close your eyes to the ravening light waiting to burst through the cracks. Once again you embrace desconocimientos' comfort in willful unawareness. Behind your isolation is its opposite—a smoldering desire for love and connection. You pour ice water on that fire.

Last night cramps in your legs jerked you awake every few minutes. The lightest touch of the sheet burned your legs and feet. Finally you fell asleep, only to be roused out of your dreams by a hypo, a hypoglycemic incident—not enough sugar in the blood. Heart pounding, dripping sweat, confused, you couldn't remember what to do. Listing from side to side, you staggered to the kitchen and gulped down orange juice with two teaspoons of sugar. The thought of one night sleeping through a hypo and slipping into a coma te espanta.

Now you sag against the bridge rail and stare at the railroad tracks below. You swallow, tasting the fear of your own death. You can no longer deny your own mortality, no longer escape into your head—your body's illness has taken residence in all your thoughts, catapulting you into the Coatlicue state, the hellish third phase of your journey. You listen to the wind howling like la Llorona on a moonless night. Mourning the loss, you sink like a stone into a deep depression, brooding darkly in the lunar landscape of your inner world. In the night mind of the night world, abandoned to a maelstrom of chaos, you dream of your own darkness, a surrealist sueño of disintegration.

Beating your breast like a gothic heroine you burst into the melodramatic histrionics of the victim. Cast adrift from all that's familiar, you huddle deep in the womb cave, a stone repelling light. In the void of your own nothingness, you lie in a fetal curl clutching the fragmented pieces and bits of yourself you've disowned. As you listen to the distant waves slapping the cliffs, your shadow beast rises from its dark corner and mounts you, punishing you with isolation. Eres cuentista con manos amarradas, poeta sin saliva sin palabra sin pluma. Escondida en tu cueva no puedes levantar cabeza, estás cansada y decepcionada. Los días vuelan como hojas en el viento. Impaled bats infest your dreams and dark clouds move through your soul like shadows. You wallow in the ruins of your life—pobre de ti—until you can't stand the stench that's yourself.

On the edge of awareness, you seek comfort by blanking out reality and retreating into fantasies. You succumb to your addiction of choice—binge reading. During these gray foggy endless days and nights, you lose yourself in Lucha Corpi mysteries. Sucked into Laurell Hamilton's stories of Anita Blake killing and loving vampires and werewolves, you turn página after page to drown out la Llorona's voice, the voice of your musa bruja. Pero el viento keeps blowing and your black angelos (daimon) whispering, "Why aren't you writing?" But you have no energy to feed the writing. Getting out of bed is a Sisyphean task. Like the ghost woman, you become a pale shade of your former self, a victim of the internalized ideals you've failed to live up to.

When first diagnosed with diabetes, your response was denial. This couldn't be happening; hadn't your body paid its dues? Why now, when you had the time and means to do good work? Digging in your heels you refused the reality—always your first line of defense to emotional pain. But the reality intruded: Your body had betrayed you. You no longer had the agility to climb up to the roof to check the leak over the living room. Were you being punished for having been found wanting? No, it is you, not an external force, punishing yourself.

Back on the timber bridge, the wind shifts, whipping your hair away from your eyes. La Llorona's wail rises, urging you to pay heed. All seven ojos de luz blink "on." Your body trembles as a new knowing slithers up like a snake, stirring you out of your stupor. You raise your head and look around. Following the railroad tracks to the horizon, you note the stages of your life, the turning points, the rips in your life's fabric. Gradually the pain and grief force you to face your situation, the daily issues of living laid bare by the event that has split your world apart. You can't change the reality, but you can change your attitude toward it, your interpretation of it. If you can't get rid of your disease, you must learn to live with it. As your perception shifts, your emotions shift—you gain a new understanding of your negative feelings. By seeing your symptoms not as signs of sickness and disintegration but as signals of growth, you're able to rise from depression's slow suicide. By using these feelings as tools or grist for the mill, you move through fear, anxiety, and anger, and blast into another reality. But transforming habitual feelings is the hardest thing you've ever attempted.

As you begin to know and accept the self uncovered by the trauma, you pull the blinders off, take in the new landscape in brief glances. Gradually you arouse the agent in this drama, begin to act, to dis-identify with the fear and the isolation. You sit quietly and meditate, trance into an altered state of consciousness, temporarily suspending your usual frames of reference and beliefs while your creative self seeks a solution to your problem by being receptive to new patterns of association. You observe how stimuli trigger responses from your body and how these reactions function. You urge yourself to cooperate with the body instead of sabotaging its self-healing. You draw a map of where you've been, how you've lived, where you're going. Sorting and re-sorting, you go through the trauma's images, feelings, sensations. While an internal transformation tries to keep pace with each rift, each reenactment shifts your ground again.

A paradox: The knowledge that exposes your fears can also remove them. Seeing through these cracks makes you uncomfortable because it reveals aspects of yourself (shadow beasts) you don't want to own. Admitting your darker aspects allows you to break out of your self-imposed prison. But it will cost you. When you woo el oscuro, digging into it, sooner or later you pay the consequences—the pain of personal growth. Conocimiento will not let you forget the shadow self, greedy, gluttonous, and indifferent; will not let you lock the cold "bitch" in the basement anymore. Though modern therapies exhort you to act against your passions (compulsions), claiming health and integration lies in that direction, you've learned that delving more fully into your pain, anger, despair, depression will move you through them to the other side, where you can use their energy to heal. Depression is useful—it signals that you need to make changes in your life, it challenges your tendency to withdraw, it reminds you to take action. To reclaim body consciousness tienes que moverte—go for walks, salir a conocer mundo, engage with the world.

Periods of being lost in chaos occur when you're between "stories," before you shift from one set of perceptions and beliefs to another, from one mood to another. By realizing that it's negative thoughts (your reactions to events) that rouse the beast and not something "real" or unchangeable out there in the outer world, you avert being hijacked by past trauma and the demons of self-pity and doomsday ruminations. But you also know that grief and depression may originate in the outside world. You still grieve for this country's original trauma—the most massive act of genocide in the world's history, the mass murder of indigenous peoples. Before the European colonizers came to the "new world," there were five million to seven-and-a-half million Indians in the territory between Mexico and Canada. By 1900, there were only 250,000 left. You descended from the world's oldest "races," thirty thousand or forty thousand years old, and you cry out at the injustice, the waste. You mourn the devastation that the slave trade cost Africa and the United States. You lament the loss of connection to the Earth, a conscious being that keens through you for all the trees felled, air poisoned, water polluted, animals slaughtered into extinction.

Above, Coyolxauhqui's luz pulls you from the pit of your grief. Realizing that you always use the same tactics, repeat the same behavior in each stage, breaks your paralysis. What you most desire is a way up, a way out. You know that you've fallen off a metaphorical bridge and into the depths. You look up toward la luna casting light in the darkness. Its bouncing light filters through the water. You want to heal; you want to be transformed. You begin the slow ascent and as you rise feel as though you're passing through the birth canal, the threshold nepantla. Only when you emerge from the dead with soul intact can you honor the visions you dreamed in the depths. In the deep fecund cave of gestation lies not only the source of your woundedness and your passion, but also the promise of inner knowledge, healing, and spiritual rebirth (the hidden treasures), waiting for you to bear them to the surface.

During the Coatlicue phase you thought you'd wandered off the path of conocimiento, but this detour is part of the path. Your body-mindsoul is the hermetic vessel where transformation takes place. The shift must be more than intellectual. Escaping the illusion of isolation, you prod yourself to get out of bed, clean your house, then yourself. You light la Virgen de Guadalupe candle and copal and, with a bundle of yierbitas (ruda y yerba buena), brush the smoke down your body, sweeping away the pain, grief, and fear of the past that's been stalking you, severing the cords binding you to it.

You realize you've severed mind from body and reversed the dichotomy—in the beginning you blamed the body for betraying you; now you blame your mind. Affirming they're not separate, you begin to own the bits of yourself you've disowned, take back the projections you've cast onto others, and relinquish your victim identity. Esta limpia unclogs your ears, enabling you to hear the rustling of los espíritus; it loosens the constriction in your throat, allowing you to talk with them. Claiming the creative powers and processes of the unconscious (Coyolxauhqui), you thank your soul for the intense emotions y los desconocimientos that wrung consciousness from you. Though you try to thank the universe for your illness, emotional trauma, and habits that interfere with living fully, you still can't accept these, may never be fully present with the pain, never fully embrace the parts of self you ousted from consciousness, may never forgive the unconscious for turning hostile. Though you know change will happen when you stop resisting the dark side of your reality, still you resist. But despite the dread and spiritual emptying, the work you do in the world is not ready to release you.

4. *the call . . . el compromiso . . . the crossing and conversion*

At four in the morning, the pounding of your heart wakes you. It's banging so hard, you're afraid it'll crack your ribs. You sit up gasping for air, fumble for the bed light, and pull the switch. Your arms are livid and swollen like sausages. Your face feels puffy and so hot it scorches your fingertips. Something slithers and swooshes against the inside walls. Bile rises, your stomach heaves. It feels like you've giving birth to a huge stone. Something pops out. You fall back onto the mattress in blessed relief. Is this what it feels like to die?

Cool and light as a feather, you float near the ceiling looking down at your body spread-eagle on the bed, a bed that's in the wrong place and reversed—the room is oddly elongated, the walls curved, the floor sloped. Though it's deep night and the light's off—but didn't you just turn it on?—you see everything like it was high noon in the desert. As you float overhead you bob into a white light—the lightbulb or the sun? You could glide out the window and never return. The instant you think this, you swoop back into the body. The reentry feels like squeezing ten pounds of chorizo through a keyhole.

You get out of bed, stretch cramped limbs, and stumble across the room like an arthritic patient. Soon energy zings up tu cuerpo (body) in an ecstasy so intense it can't be contained. You twirl around, hugging yourself, picking up speed and kicking the walls. Later you wonder whether you made up an out-of-body story in an attempt to explain the inexplicable. It dawns on you that *you're not contained by your skin—* you exist outside your body and outside your dream body, as well. If the body is energy, is spirit—it doesn't have boundaries. What if you experienced your body expanding to the size of the room, not your soul leaving your body. What if freedom from categories occurs by widening the psyche/body's borders, widening the consciousness that senses self (the body is the basis for the conscious sense of self, the representation of self in the mind). It follows that if you're not contained by your race, class, gender, or sexual identity, the body must be more than the categories that mark you.

Leaving the body reinforces the mind/body, matter/spirit dichotomy that you're trying to show does not exist in reality. The last thing you want to uphold is the Cartesian split, but thus far you haven't a clue how to unknot el nudo de cuerpo/mente/alma, despite having just had an experience that intellectually unknots it. If el conocimiento that body is both spirit and matter intertwined is the solution, it's one that's difficult to live out, requiring that this knowledge be lived daily in embodied ways. Only then may the split be healed.[12]

What pulled you out of your body? Was the Seven and Seven you drank at the party still in your system when you took the Percodan? You know that mixing booze with drugs can end in death, so why did you do it? So that el jaguar, tu doble, que vigila por la noche could come from the south to stalk you, to pull you de tu cuerpo so you could experience . . . what, a different kind of knowledge? In the deepest part of night you followed the jaguar through the transparent wall between the worlds. Shapes shifted. Did you assume another pair of eyes, another pair of ears, another body, another dream body? Maybe you took your physical body, and in this other place it metamorphosed into a jaguar.

Acts of self-abuse may lead to insight—or so you rationalize your experimenting with mind-expanding drugs. Insight originates from the light of the moon (Coyolxauhqui consciousness), enabling you to see through your identifications, through the walls that your ethnic cultural traditions and religious beliefs have erected. The lechuza eyes of your naguala open, rousing you from the trance of hyper-rationality induced by higher education.[13] An image flickers—nonverbal, brief, and subtle—signaling otro conocimiento: besides the mortal body you have a trans-temporal, immortal one. This knowing prompts you to shift into a new perception of yourself and the world. Nothing is fixed. The pulse of existence, the heart of the universe, is fluid. Identity, like a river, is always changing, always in transition, always in nepantla. Like the river downstream, you're not the same person you were upstream. You begin to define yourself in terms of who you are becoming, not who you have been.

These states of awareness, while vital, don't last. Yet they provide the faith that enables you to continue la lucha. When you feel low, the longing for your potential self is an ache deep within. Something within flutters its feathers, stretches toward the sky. You try to listen more closely, bringing all your faculties to bear on transforming your condition. Using these insights to alter your current thoughts and behavior, you reinterpret their meanings. As you learn from the different stages you pass through, your reactions to past events change. You re-member your experiences in a new arrangement. Your responses to the challenges of daily life also adjust. As you continually reinterpret your past, you reshape your present. Instead of walking your habitual routes you forge new ones. The changes affect your biology. The cells in your brain shift and, in turn, create new pathways, rewiring your brain.

On the path ahead you see otro puente, a footbridge with missing planks, broken rails. You walk toward it, step onto the threshold, and freeze, right hand clutching the past, left hand stretching toward the unknown. Behind, the world admonishes you to stick to the old-and-tried dominant paradigm, the secure relationships within it. "Adelante," la Llorona whispers. "You have a task, a calling. Only you can bring forth your potential." You yearn to know what that ever present inner watcher is asking of you. Loosening your grip on the known and reaching for the future requires that you stretch beyond self- and culturally-imposed limits. By now you've found remnants of a community—people on a similar quest/path. To transform yourself, you need the help (the written or spoken words) of those who have crossed before you. You want them to describe las puertas, to hold your hand while crossing. You want them to mentor your work within the Chicana, queer, artistic, feminist, spiritual, and other communities.

To learn what to transform into you ask, "How can I contribute?" You open yourself and listen to la naguala and the images, sensations, and dreams she presents. (La naguala's presence is so subtle and fleeting it barely registers unless tracked by your attention's radar.) Your inner voice reveals your core passion, which will point to your sense of purpose, urging you to seek a vision, devise a plan. Your passion motivates you to discover resources within yourself and in the world. It prompts you to take responsibility for consciously creating your life and becoming a fully functioning human being, a contributing member of all your communities, one worthy of self-respect and love. You want to pursue your mission with integrity, to honor yourself and to be honored. Holding these realizations in mind, you stand at the brink and reconsider the crossing.

Are you sure you're ready to face the shadow beast guarding the threshold—that part of yourself holding your failures and inadequacies, the negativities you've internalized, and those aspects of gender and class you want to disown? Recognizing and coming to terms with the manipulative, vindictive, secretive shadow beast within will take the heaviest toll. Maybe this bridge shouldn't be crossed. Once crossed, it can't be uncrossed. To pass over the bridge to something else, you'll have to give up partial organizations of self, erroneous bits of knowledge, outmoded beliefs of who you are, your comfortable identities (your story of self, tu autohistoria).[14] You'll have to leave parts of yourself behind.

The bridge (boundary between the world you've just left and the one ahead) is both a barrier and a point of transformation. By crossing, you invite a turning point, initiate a change. And change is never comfortable, easy, or neat. It'll overturn all your relationships; leave behind lover, parent, friend who, not wanting to disturb the status quo or lose you, try to keep you from changing. OK, so cambio is hard. Tough it out, you tell yourself. Doesn't life consist of crossing a series of thresholds? Conocimiento hurts, but not as much as desconocimiento. In the final reckoning, it comes down to a matter of faith, trusting that your inner authority will carry you across the critical threshold. You must make the leap alone and of your own will. Having only partial knowledge of the consequences of crossing, you offer la Llorona, who regulates the passage, a token. You pray, repeat affirmations, take a deep breath, and step through the gate. Immediately, a knowing cracks the façade of your former self and its entrenched beliefs: You are not alone; those of the invisible realm walk with you; there are ghosts on every bridge.

You stand on tierra sagrada—nature is alive and conscious; the world is ensouled. You lift your head to the sky, to the wingspread of pelicans, the stark green of trees, the wind sighing through their branches. You discern faces in the rocks and allow them to see you. You become reacquainted with a reality called spirit, a presence, force, power, and energy within and without. Spirit infuses all that exists— organic and inorganic—transcending the categories and concepts that govern your perception of material reality. Spirit speaks through your mouth, listens through your ears, sees through your eyes, touches with your hands. At times the sacred takes you unaware; the desire to change prompts it and then discipline allows it to happen.

With awe and wonder you look around, recognizing the preciousness of the earth, the sanctity of every human being on the planet, the ultimate unity and interdependence of all beings—somos todos un paíz. Love swells in your chest and shoots out of your heart chakra, linking you to everyone/everything—the aboriginal in Australia, the crow in the forest, the vast Pacific Ocean. You share a category of identity wider than any social position or racial label. This conocimiento motivates you to work actively to see that no harm comes to people, animals, ocean—to take up spiritual activism and the work of healing. Te entregas a tu promesa to help your various cultures create new paradigms, new narratives.

Knowing that something in you, or of you, must die before something else can be born, you throw your old self onto the ritual pyre, a passage by fire. In relinquishing your old self, you realize that some aspects of who you are—identities people have imposed on you as a woman of color and that you have internalized—are also made up. Identity becomes a cage you reinforce and double-lock yourself into. The life you thought inevitable, unalterable, and fixed in some foundational reality is smoke, a mental construction, fabrication. So, you reason, if it's all made up, you can compose it anew and differently.

5. putting Coyolxauhqui together . . . new personal and collective "stories"
Returning from the land of the dead, you wake up in the hospital bed minus your ovaries and uterus. Scattered around you en pedazos is the old story's corpse with its perceptions of who you used to be.[15] Como luciérnaga a light crosses your dark inner landscape awakening un saber (a knowing). You've passed a turning point—decided not to drag the dead self into the present and future just to preserve your history. Instead, you've chosen to compose a new history and self—to rewrite your autohistoria. You want to be transformed again; you want a keener mind, a stronger spirit, a wiser soul. Your ailing body is no longer a hindrance but an asset, witnessing pain, speaking to you, demanding touch. Es tu cuerpo que busca conocimiento; along with dreams your body is the royal road to consciousness.

Before rewriting the disintegrating, often destructive "stories" of self constructed by psychology, sociology, anthropology, biology, and religion, you must first recognize their faulty pronouncements, scrutinize the fruit they've borne, and then ritually disengage from them. Reflexive awareness and other aspects of conocimiento, if practiced daily, overrule external instructions transmitted by your ethnic and dominant cultures, override the internal mandates of your genes and personal ego. Knowing the beliefs and directives your spiritual self generates empowers you to shift perceptions, te capacita a soñar otros modos of conducting your life, revise the scripts of your various identities, and use these new narratives to intervene in the cultures' existing dehumanizing stories.

After examining the old self's stance on life/death, misma/otra, individual/collective consciousness, you shift the axis/structure of reference by reversing the polarities, erasing the slash between them, then adding new aspects of yourself. To make meaning from your experiences you look through an archetypal psycho-mytho-spiritual lens, charting the various shifts of consciousness as they play out in your daily activities. You use your imagination in mediating between inner and outer experience. By writing about the always-in-progress, transformational processes and the constant, ongoing reconstruction of the way you view your world, you name and ritualize the moments/processes of transition, inserting them into the collective fabric, bringing into play personal history and fashioning a story greater than yourself.

You shed your former bodymind and its outworn story like a snake its skin. Releasing traumas of the past frees up energy, allowing you to be receptive to the soul's voice and guidance. Taking a deep breath, you close your eyes and call back tu alma—from people, ideas, perceptions, and events you've surrendered it to. You sense parts of your soul return to your body. Another inhalation, more tendrils of spirit reenter the places where it went missing. The lost pieces draw to you like filaments to a magnet. With a tender newly formed sense of self you stand, wobbly. Sensing los espíritus all around, you face east, the direction of the visionary, offering a dream of the possible. Challenging the old self's orthodoxy is never enough; you must submit a sketch of an alternative self. As a modern-day Coyolxauhqui, you search for an account that encapsulates your life, and finding no ready-made story, you trust her light in the darkness to help you bring forth (from remnants of the old personal/collective autohistoria) a new personal myth.

After dismantling the body/self, you recompose it—the fifth stage of the journey, though reconstruction takes place in all stages. When creating a personal narrative, you also co-create the group/cultural story. You examine the description handed to you of the world, picking holes in the paradigms currently constructing reality. You doubt that traditional western science is the best knowledge system, the only true, impartial arbiter of reality. You question its definition of progress, whose manifest destiny imperializes other peoples' energies and snuffs out their realities and hopes of a better life. You now see the western story as one of patriarchal, hierarchical control; fear and hatred of women; dominion over nature; science/technology's promise of expanding power; seduction of commerce; and to be fair, a celebration of individual rights—freedom, creativity, and ingenuity. You turn the established narrative on its head, seeing through, resisting, and subverting its assumptions. Again, it's not enough to denounce the culture's old account—you must provide new narratives that embody alternative potentials. You're sure of one thing: the consciousness that's created our social ills (dualistic and misogynist) cannot solve them—we need a more expansive conocimiento. The new stories must partially come from outside the system of ruling powers.

You examine the contentions accompanying the old cultural narratives: Your ethnic tribe wants you to isolate, insisting that you remain within race and class boundaries. The dominant culture prefers that you abandon your roots and assimilate, insisting that you leave your Indianness behind and seek shelter under the Hispanic or Latino umbrella. The temptation to succumb to these assimilationist tactics and escape the stigma of being Mexican stalls you on the bridge between isolation and assimilation. But both are debilitating. How can you step outside ethnic and other labels while cleaving to your root identity? Your identity has roots you share with all people and other beings—spirit, feeling, and body constitute a greater identity category. The body is rooted in the earth, la tierra itself. You meet ensoulment in trees, in woods, in streams. The roots del árbol de la vida of all planetary beings are nature, soul, body.

Reframing the old story points to another option besides assimilation and separation—a "new tribalism."[16] An image of your tío's dying orange tree comes to mind, one still possessed of a strong root system and trunk. Tu tío grafted a sturdier variety of orange to it, creating a more vigorous tree. In similar fashion, you "grow into" an identity of mestizaje you call the new tribalism by propagating other worldviews, spiritual traditions, and cultures to your árbol de la vida. You pick and choose views, cultures with transformational potential—a partially conscious selection, not a mestizaje imposed on you, but one whose process you can control. (You distinguish this mestizaje from acts of hybridization such as genetically engineering and modifying live organisms without their consent or consideration of their existence as integrated beings, or from acts resulting in cyborgian animal/machine hybrids.) A retribalizing mestizaje becomes your coping mechanism, your strategy of resistance to both acculturating and enculturating pressures.

Tussling con remolinos (whirlwinds) of different belief systems builds the muscles of mestiza consciousness, enabling it to stretch. Being Chicana (indigenous, Mexican, Basque, Spanish, Berber Arab, Gypsy) is no longer enough; being female, woman of color, patlache (queer) no longer suffices. Your resistance to identity boxes leads you to a different tribe, a different story (of mestizaje), enabling you to rethink yourself in more global-spiritual terms instead of conventional categories of color, class, career. It calls you to retribalize your identity to a more inclusive one, redefining what it means to be una mexicana de este lado, an American in the U.S., a citizen of the world, classifications reflecting an emerging planetary culture. In this narrative, national boundaries dividing us from the "others" (nos/otras) are porous, and the cracks between worlds serve as gateways.

At first, la nueva historia resembles Frankenstein's monster—mismatched parts pieced together artificially—but soon the new rendition fuels your drive to seek alternative and emerging knowledges. It motivates you to expose oppressive cultural beliefs, such as all women are traicioneras (betrayers), queers are abnormal, whites are superior, and sparing the rod spoils the child, and replace these notions with new ones. It inspires you to engage both inner and outer resources to make changes on multiple fronts: inner/spiritual/personal, social/collective/material.

The new stories explore aspects of reality—consciousness, hope, intention, prayer—that traditional science has ignored, deeming these nonexistent, as they cannot be tested in a lab. In the new stories, postmodern science shifts its orientation, no longer holding itself to what can be validated empirically by the five senses. It acknowledges nonphysical reality, inner subjective experiences, and spirit. The world, from the depth of the sea to the highest mountain, is alive, intelligent, ensouled. In the fourth stage del camino de conocimiento you caught glimmers of this holistic story—a paradigm that's always served indigenous cultures. Beliefs and values from the wisdom of past spiritual traditions of diverse cultures, coupled with current scientific knowledge, is the basis of the new synthesis. The emerging narratives are multicultural. They not only insist on analyzing and combatting oppressive power systems; but also advocate the need to collaborate and capacitar (empower) in realizing common goals.

The new accounts trace the process of shifting from old ways of viewing reality to new perceptions. They depict your struggles, recount your losses, reignite your hope for recovery, and celebrate the workings of the soul that nourish us with visions. They articulate unnamed, unvoiced, and repressed experiences and realities. The new versions of reality they offer demand that you employ alternative ways of knowing and rewire your ways of seeing, thinking, feeling, and expressing. By using information derived from multiple channels and different systems of knowing you collectively create new societies. Together you attempt to reverse the Cartesian split that turned the world into an "other," distancing humans from it. Though your body is still la otra and though pensamientos dualisticos still keep you from embracing and uniting corporally con esa otra, you dream of the possibility of wholeness. Collectively, you rewrite the story of "the fall" and the story of western progress—two opposing versions of the evolution of human consciousness.[17] Collectively you note the emergence of the new gatekeepers of the earth's wisdom.

Led by the light of the moon (Coyolxauhqui consciousness) you take the fifth step and see through the illusion of permanence—the fantasy that you can pull yourself together once and for all and live happily ever after. You again suffer otro espanto, and another dislocation. Surrendering the self, sacrificing a certain way of being, you go through the whole process again, repeating all seven stages of the cycle. Your inability to live with your old self is also a bodily function and not merely a mind thing—every seven years your body sheds its cells completely as it regenerates new cells. When the latest story/self/body ceases to be credible or is not developing the way you want, you reinterpret the story you imagine yourself to be living. Tu autohistoria is not carved in stone but drawn on sand and subject to shifting winds. Forced to rework your story, you invent new notions of yourself and reality—increasingly multidimensional versions where body, mind, and spirit interpenetrate in more complex ways.

In struggling with adversity and noting your reactions to it, you observe how thoughts direct perceptions of reality. You realize that personal/collective reality is created (often unconsciously) and that you're the artist scripting the new story of this house/self/identity/essay under construction. You realize it's the process that's valuable and not the end product, not the new you, as that will change often throughout your life. Connecting the disparate parts of information from a new perspective, you re-member Coyolxauhqui in a new composition, temporarily restoring your balance and wounded psyche. Your story's one of la búsqueda de conocimiento, of seeking experiences that'll give you purpose, give your life meaning, give you a sense of belonging. It's a quest story of ordeal and distress, cyclical life stages, and identity transformations. Like the heroine in a myth or fairy tale, after an arduous struggle in the dark woods, you return bringing new knowledge to share with others in your communities.

Coyolxauhqui personifies the wish to repair and heal, as well as rewrite the stories of loss and recovery, exile and homecoming, disinheritance and recuperation, stories that lead out of passivity and into agency, out of devalued into valued lives. Coyolxauhqui represents the search for new metaphors to tell you what you need to know, how to connect and use the information gained, and, with intelligence, imagination, and grace, solve your problems and create intercultural communities.

6. the blow-up . . . a clash of realities

> New knowledge occurs through tension, difficulties, mistakes and chaos.
> RISA D'ANGELES

You fly in from another speaking gig on the East Coast, arriving at the feminist academic conference late. Hayas un desmadre. A racist incident has unleashed flames of anger held in check for decades. In postures of defiance, enraged women of color protest their exclusion from the organization's decision-making processes; "white" middle-class women stand, arms crossed, refusing to alter the policies. When they continue conducting business as usual, las mujeres de color walk out.

The urgency compelling every woman to give testimony to her views is so thick you can almost taste it. Caras reflejan angustia and blanched looks of shock; eyes glint with hostility; feelings of disgust, bitterness, disillusionment, and betrayal clash, spatter, and scatter in all directions. These emotions flare through your body as you turn from one group to another like a weathervane. You lose yourself in the maelstrom, no longer able to find the calm place within as everything collapses into unresolvable conflict. You know that in the heart of the conflagration lies its solution, but your own anguish clouds true perception. Catching your co-presenter's eye, you both grimace in recognition. Though for years you've felt the tectonic bedrock of feminism shifting under your feet, you never imagined that the seismic crack would be so devastating, the blow-out so scorching. El mar de coraje (anger) se te viene encima—you recoil from its heat. Trying to be objective, you distance yourself until you feel as though you're in an airplane observing safely from above.

Like most feminist conferences, this one begins as a bridge, a place of mutual access where thousands crisscross, network, share ideas, and struggle together to resolve women's issues. After fifteen years of struggle, of putting their trust on this common space, of waiting for the organization to deal with racism as it's promised, the women of color and some Jewish, working-class, and progressive white allies feel betrayed by their white middle-class sisters. Seething in frustration they cancel their panels and workshops, quejandose que las feministas anglas do not allow their intellectual, emotional, and spiritual realities into this academic setting. They're tired of being treated as outsiders. They feel that whites still view issues of racism as the concern of women of color alone, anti-Semitism, the concern only of Jewish women; homophobia, the concern of lesbians; and class, the concern of working-class and poor women. They accuse whites of reinscribing the imperialist tradition of dominance and call them on their white privilege.

White women accuse women of color and their allies of emotionalism—after all, this is the academy. Feeling unjustly attacked, they adamantly proclaim they're not racist but just following the organization's policies. Though their intentions—making "common ground"—are good, they don't realize que su base de acuerdo may be different or too narrow from el terreno comunal de otras mujeres and not really common at all. They ignore the input of mujeres de color in defining common ground.

You view most white women's racism as covert and always cloaked. An insidious desconocimiento, it refuses to allow emotional awareness and its threat into their consciousness. They deny their recognition of the situation, then forget having denied this recognition. This forgetting of having forgotten their denial (repression) is at the core of desconocimiento. Though most white feminists intellectually acknowledge racism, they distance themselves from personal responsibility, often acting as though their reality and ways of knowing are universal, not culturally determined. They assume feminist racialized "others" share the same values and goals. Some view gender and race oppression as interchangeable. As members of a colonized gender, they believe they're experts on oppression and can define all its forms; thus, they don't have to listen/learn from racial others. They herd women of color under the banner of their brand of feminism and impose their experiences and interpretations of reality, especially of academic life, on them—all racist acts.

The refusal to think about race (itself a form of racism) is a "white" privilege. The white women who do think about race rarely delve beyond the surface: they allude to the category, cite a few women-of-color texts, tack on a token book to their syllabi, and assume they've dealt with race. Though many understand the racism perpetrated by white individuals, most do not understand the racism inherent in their identities, in their cultures' stories. They can't see that racism harms them as well as people of color, itself a racially superior attitude. Those who see don't feel prepared to deal with race, though they do "feel bad" about it, suffering the monkey on their backs—survivor guilt, the guilt of privilege that, when unacknowledged, breeds greater guilt.

When their racism is exposed, they claim they're the victims of attacks and are outraged at being "mauled" by these pit-bullish others. They use white privilege to coax women of color to toe the line. When that doesn't work, they pull rank. They fail to meet the women of color halfway, don't bother negotiating the give-and-take between "majority" culture and "minority." Though they may pay lip service to diversity issues, most don't shift from positions of power. The privilege of whiteness allows them to evade questions of complicity with those in power; it gives leave to disrespect other people's realities and types of knowledge—"race" and "soul" remain four-letter words. Their socialization does not allow women-of-color consciousness to transform their thinking. Afraid of losing material and psychological privilege, they drown others' voices with white noise.

Con nudo en la garganta, you look at your hermanas de color, challenged warriors, who try to stop being victims, only to fall into the trap of claiming moral higher ground, using skin color as license for judging a whole category of people. They're forced to belabor the point because most white women won't listen. Leading with their wounds focuses their energy on the role of victim: Oh, poor me, I'm so oppressed. Though inadvertently at times, you, too, assume this attitude, you have little sympathy for it. Buying into victimhood forces you/them to compete for the coveted prize of the walking wounded. Many are driven to use the truth of their ill treatment as a stick to beat whites into waking up; they are the experts on oppression and thus don't have to listen/learn from whites. Some women of color—las meras meras—strut around with macha in-your-face aggressiveness. Hiding their vulnerabilities behind clenched fists and a "que se chinguen" attitude, they overlook the wounds bonding them to the other and instead focus on las herridas (wounds) that divide. As a writer, one of your tasks is to expose the dualistic nature of the debate between whites and people of color, the false idealized pictures and other desconocimientos each group has but would rather ignore, and promote a more holistic perspective.

Seeing women from both camps throw words at each other like stones gives you stomach cramps. Apedradas (pelted with stones), each woman tries to regain her ground. Weaving her experience into a storyline where she's the one who has been put upon, she incites her allies to torch the bridge with inflammatory rhetoric. Pitting herself against the other (the enemy), she feeds las llamas her energy and repressed shadow parts, turning the conference into a militarized zone where desconocimiento runs rampant. In full-frontal attack, each camp adopts an "us-versus-them" model that assumes a winner and loser, a wrong and right—the prevailing conflict resolution paradigm of our times, one we continue to use despite the recognition that confrontational tactics rarely settle disputes for the long run.

You watch some women react to psychological violence in instinctive knee-jerk ways or in ways they've programmed themselves or have been programmed to respond. The usual tactics for dealing with conflict and threat are fighting, fleeing, freezing, or submitting. Those who fight or flee shut their ears and assume a hypervigilant guard mode to help them attack or escape. Those who freeze separate their awareness from the reality of what's happening—they dissociate. Those who submit surrender their ground to more aggressive forces. All struggle to burrow back into their past histories, former skins, familiar racial and class enclaves, even though these may be rife with discomfort and disillusionment and no longer feel like "home."

Caught in the middle of the power struggle, you're forced to take sides, forced to negotiate another identity crisis. Being coerced to turn your back on one group/person and favor the other feels like a knife to the heart. It reminds you of the 1970s, when other lesbians reprimanded you and urged you to abandon your friendships with men. Women of color will brand you disloyal if you don't walk out with them. Nationalistic fence maintainers will label you malinchista; lesbians will think you not queer enough. You retreat from your feelings, take refuge in your head, priding yourself on equanimity, an objectivity detached from the biases of personal fear, anger, anxiety. As you observe others, pitying their misguided actions, you catch yourself feeling superior because you don't let your emotions take over. Not you, you've achieved spiritual and emotional equilibrium. You'd like to believe that detachment is always a strength, that remaining emotionally distant allows you to bring a sense of balance to conflicted situations. But instead of attaining spiritual non-attachment, you've withdrawn from painful feelings—a detachment that cuts you off from your body and its feelings.

What takes a bashing is not so much you as the idea/picture of who you think you are, an illusion you're hell bent on protecting and preserving at all costs. You overlook the fact that your self-image and history (autohistoria) are not carved in stone but drawn on sand and subject to the winds. A threat to your identifications and interpretations of reality enrages your shadow beast, who views the new knowledge as an attack on your bodily integrity. And it is a death threat—to the belief that posits the self as local and limited to a physical body, a body perceived as a container separating the self from other people and other forms of knowledge. New conocimientos (insights) threaten your sense of what's "real" when it's up against what's "real" to the other. But it's precisely this threat that triggers transformation.

You think you've made progress, gained a new awareness, found a new version of reality, created a workable story, fulfilled an obligation, and followed your own conscience. But when you cast to the world what you've created and put your ideals into action, the contradictions explode in your face. Your story fails the reality test. But is the failure due to flaws in your story—based on the tenuous nature of relationship between you and the whole—or is it due to all-too-human and therefore imperfect members of the community?

The bridge buckles under the weight of these feminist factions, and as in the Russian tale of "Two Goats on the Bridge,"[18] the different groups butt each other off. With other in-betweeners (nepantleras) from both sides of the divide, you navigate entre tres aguas, trying to sustain some sort of dialogue among the groups. Pronto llegas a un crucero—you have to decide whether to walk off or remain on the bridge and try to facilitate passage. Though you've always been a bridge, not a separatist, es difícil decidir. From the eye of the storm you choose to hold fast to the bridge and witness for all camps. With only half the participants present at the roundtable, you use the forum to discuss the causes of the blowup and possible strategies to resolve the conflict.

Often in the following days, you and other nepantleras feel frustrated, tempted to walk out as the bridge undergoes more tremors. Negotiating cuesta trabajo. Las nepantleras must alter their mode of interaction—make it more inclusive, open. In a to-and-fro motion, they shift from their customary position to the reality of first one group then the other. Though tempted to retreat behind racial lines and hide behind simplistic walls of identity, las nepantleras know their work lies in positioning themselves—exposed and raw—in the crack between these worlds, and in revealing current categories as unworkable. Saben que las herridas (wounds) that separate and those that bond arise from the same source. Besides fighting, fleeing, freezing, or submitting las nepantleras usan otra media—they employ a fifth tactic.

Recognizing that the basic human hunger to be heard, understood, and accepted is not being met, las nepantleras listen to members of both camps. By attending to what the other is not saying, what she's not doing, what isn't happening, and by looking for the opposite, unacknowledged emotion—the opposite of anger is fear, of self-righteousness is guilt, of hate is love—las nepantleras attempt to see through the other's situation to her underlying unconscious desire. Accepting doubts and ambiguity, the nepantleras reframe the conflict and shift the point of view. Sitting face to-face with all parties, they identify common bonds, name reciprocities and connections, and finally draft a mutually agreeable contract.

When perpetual conflict erodes a sense of connectedness and wholeness la nepantlera calls on the "connectionist" faculty to show the deep common ground and interwoven kinship among all things and people.[19] This faculty, one of less structured thoughts, less rigid categorizations, and thinner boundaries, allows us to picture—via reverie, dreaming, and artistic creativity—similarities instead of solid divisions. In gatherings where people luxuriate in their power to prevent change instead of using it to cause transformation, where they spew verbal abuse in a war of words and do not leave space for others to save face, where feelings are easily bruised or too intense to be controlled by will alone—la nepantlera proposes individual and group rituals to contain volatile feelings and channel them into acts of conocimiento.

In gatherings where people feel powerless, la nepantlera offers rituals to say good-bye to old ways of relating; prayers to thank life for making us face loss, anger, guilt, fear, and separation; rezos to acknowledge our individual wounds; and commitments to not give up on others just because they hurt us. In gatherings where we've forgotten that the object of conflict is peace, la nepantlera proposes spiritual techniques (mindfulness, openness, receptivity) along with activist tactics. Where before we saw only separateness, differences, and polarities, our connectionist sense of spirit recognizes nurturance and reciprocity and encourages alliances among groups working to transform communities. In gatherings where we feel our dreams have been sucked out of us, la nepantlera leads us in celebrating la comunidad soñada, reminding us that spirit connects the irreconcilable warring parts para que todo el mundo se haga un paíz, so that the whole world may become un pueblo.

7. shifting realities . . . . acting out the vision or spiritual activism

The bridge will hold me up.
GABRIELLE IN XENA: WARRIOR PRINCESS

You're three years old and standing by the kitchen table staring at the bright orange globe. You can almost taste its tart sweetness. You'll just die if you don't have it. You reach for it, but your arms are too short.

Body quivering, you stretch again, willing yourself to get the fruit. Your arms elongate until your small hands clasp the orange. You sense you're more than one body—each superimposed on the others like sheaths of corn. Years later, after a few more experiences of bilocation, you describe it as a yoga of the body.[20] The ability to recognize and endow meaning to daily experience (spirituality) furthers the ability to shift and transform.

When and how does transformation happen? When a change occurs, your consciousness (awareness of your sense of self and your response to self, others, and surroundings) becomes cognizant that it has a point of view and the ability to act from choice. This knowing/knower is always with you but is displaced by the ego and its perspective. This knower has several functions. You call the function that arouses the awareness that beneath individual separateness lies a deeper interrelatedness, "la naguala."

When you shift attention from your customary point of view (the ego) to that of la naguala, and from there move your awareness to an inner-held representation of an experience, person, thing, or world, la naguala and the object observed merge. When you include the complexity of feeling two or more ways about a person/issue, when you empathize and try to see her circumstances from her position, you accommodate the other's perspective, achieving un conocimiento that allows you to shift toward a less defensive, more inclusive identity. When you relate to others, not as parts, problems, or useful commodities, but from a connectionist view, compassion triggers transformation. This shift occurs when you give up investment in your point of view and recognize the real situation free of projections—not filtered through your habitual defensive preoccupations.[21] Moving back and forth from the situation to la naguala's view, you glean a new description of the world (reality)—a Toltec interpretation. When you're in the place between worldviews (nepantla), you're able to slip between realities to a neutral perception. A decision made in the in-between place becomes a turning point initiating psychological and spiritual transformations, making other kinds of experiences possible.

Core beliefs command the focus of your senses. By changing some of these convictions you change the mental/emotional channel (the reality). In the Coatlicue state, an intensely negative channel, you're caged in a private hell; you feel angry, fearful, hopeless, and depressed, blaming yourself as inadequate. In the more optimistic space cultivated by las nepantleras you feel love, peace, happiness, and the desire to grow. Forgiving yourself and others, you connect with more aspects of yourself and others.

Orienting yourself to the environment and your relationship to it enables you to read and garner insight from whatever situation you find yourself in. This conocimiento gives you the flexibility to swing from your intense feelings to those of the other without being hijacked by either. When confronted with the other's fear, you note her emotional arousal, allow her feelings/words to enter your body; then you shift to the neutral place of la naguala. You detach so those feelings won't inhabit your body for long. You listen with respect, attend to the other as a whole being, not as an object, even when she opposes you.[22] To avoid miscommunication, you frequently check your understanding of the other's meaning, responding with, "Yes, I hear you. Let me repeat your words to make sure I'm reading you right." When an experience evokes similar feelings in both, you feel momentarily in sync. Like consciousness, conocimiento is about relatedness—to self, others, world.

When troubled, conocimiento prompts you to take a deep breath, shift your attention away from what's causing pain and fear, and call on a power deeper and freer than that of your ego, such as la naguala y los espíritus, for guidance. Direction may also come from an inner impression, dream, meditation, I Ching, Tarot cards. You use these spiritual tools to deal with various problems, large and small. Power comes from being in touch with your body, soul, and spirit and letting their wisdom lead you.

By moving from a militarized zone to a roundtable, nepantleras acknowledge an unmapped common ground: the humanity of the other. We are the other, the other is us—a concept AnaLouise Keating calls "re(con)ceiving the other."[23] Honoring people's otherness, las nepantleras advocate a "nos/otras" position—an alliance between "us" and "others." In nos/otras, the "us" is divided in two, the slash in the middle representing the bridge—the best mutuality we can hope for at the moment. Las nepantleras envision a time when the bridge will no longer be needed—we'll have shifted to a seamless nosotras. This move requires a different way of thinking and relating to others; it requires that we act on our interconnectivity, a mode of connecting similar to hypertexts' multiple links—it includes diverse others and does not depend on traditional categories or sameness. It enacts a retribalization by recognizing that some members of a racial or ethnic group do not necessarily stay with the consciousness and conditioning of the group they're born into but shift momentarily or permanently. For example, some whites embody a woman-of-color consciousness, and some people of color embody a "white" consciousness.

Conocimiento of our interconnectivity encourages white women to examine and deconstruct racism and "whiteness." But perhaps, as Keating suggests, "white" women who are totally invested in this privileged identity can't be nepantleras: "I really think that 'whiteness' is a state of mind—dualistic, supremacist, separatist, hierarchical . . . all the things we're working to transform; I'm still not sure how this concept of 'whiteness' as an oppressive/oppressing mind-set corresponds to light-skinned bodies, but I do believe the two are not synonymous."[24]

This move to a roundtable—generated by such concepts as nos/otras and retribalization—incites women of color to speak out and eventually refuse the role of victim. Though most identify with their mestizaje, you wonder how much of a mestiza a person must become before racial categories dissolve and new ones develop, before committing to social concerns that move beyond personal group or nation, before an inclusive community forms. You wonder when others will, like las nepantleras, hand themselves to a larger vision, a less defended identity.

This is your new vision, a story of how conocimiento manifests, but one with a flaw: It doesn't work with things that are insurmountable or with all people at all times (we haven't evolved to that stage yet), and it doesn't always bring about immediate change. But it works with las nepantleras, boundary crossers, thresholders who initiate others in rites of passage, activistas who, from a listening, receptive, spiritual stance, rise to their own visions and shift into acting them out, haciendo mundo nuevo (introducing change). Las nepantleras walk through fire on many bridges (not just the conference one) by turning the flames into a radiance of awareness that orients, guides, and supports those who cannot cross over on their own. Inhabiting the liminal spaces where change occurs, las nepantleras encourage others to ground themselves to their own bodies and connect to their own internal resources, thus empowering themselves. Empowerment is the bodily feeling of being able to connect with inner voices/resources (images, symbols, beliefs, memories) during periods of stillness, silence, and deep listening or with kindred others in collective actions. This alchemy of connection provides the knowledge, strength, and energy to persist and be resilient in pursuing goals. Éste modo de capacitar comes from accepting your own authority to direct rather than letting others run you.

Not long ago your mother gave you un milagro, a tiny silver hand with a heart in its palm, never knowing that for years this image has resonated with your concept of El Mundo Zurdo amplified here into the model of conocimiento; la mano zurda with a heart in its palm is for engaging with self, others, world. The hand represents acting out and daily implementing an idea or vision, as opposed to merely theorizing about it. The heart es un corazón con razón, with intelligence, passion, and purpose, a "mind-full" heart with ears for listening, eyes for seeing, a mouth with tongue narrowing to a pen tip for speaking/writing. The left hand is not a fist pero una mano abierta raised with others in struggle, celebration, and song. Conocimiento es otro mode de conectar across colors and other differences to allies also trying to negotiate racial contradictions, survive the stresses and traumas of daily life, and develop a spiritual-imaginal-political vision together. Conocimiento shares a sense of affinity with all things and advocates mobilizing, organizing, sharing information, knowledge, insights, and resources with other groups.

Although all your cultures reject the idea that you can know the other, you believe that besides love, pain might open this closed passage by reaching through the wound to connect. Wounds cause you to shift consciousness—they either open you to the greater reality normally blocked by your habitual point of view or else shut you down, pushing you out of your body and into desconocimiento. Like love, pain might trigger compassion—if you're tender with yourself, you can be tender to others. Using wounds as openings to become vulnerable and available (present) to others means staying in your body. Excessive dwelling on your wounds means leaving your body to live in your thoughts where you reenact your past hurts, a form of desconocimiento that gives energy to the past where it's held ransom. As victim you don't have to take responsibility for making changes. But the cost of victimhood is that nothing in your life changes, especially not your attitudes and beliefs. Instead, why not use pain as a conduit to recognizing another's suffering, even that of the one who inflicted the pain. In all the great stories, says Jean Houston, wounding is the entrance to the sacred.[25] Openings to the sacred can also be triggered by joyful experiences—for example, meditation, epiphanies, communion with nature, sexual ecstasy, and desire, as in your childhood experience of reaching for the orange. Because most of you are wounded, negative emotions provide easier access to the sacred than positive emotions.

You reflect on experiences that caused you, at critical points of transformation, to adopt spiritual activism. When you started traveling and doing speaking gigs, the harried, hectic, frenzied pace of the activist stressed you out, subjecting you to a pervasive form of modern violence that Thomas Merton attributes to the rush of continual doing. To deal with personal concerns while also confronting larger issues in the public arena, you began using spiritual tools to cope with racial and gender oppression and other modern maldades—not so much the seven deadly sins but the small acts of desconocimientos: ignorance, frustrations, tendencies toward self-destructiveness, feelings of betrayal and powerlessness, and poverty of spirit and imagination. The spiritual practice of conocimiento, such as praying, breathing deeply, meditating, writing—dropping down into yourself, through the skin and muscles and tendons, down deep into the bones' marrow where your soul is ballast—enabled you to defuse the negative energy of putdowns, complaints, excessive talk, and verbal attacks, as well as other killers of the spirit. Spirituality became a port you moor to in all storms.

This work of spiritual activism and the contract of holistic alliances allows conflict to dissolve through reflective dialogue. It permits an expansive awareness that finds the best instead of the worst in the other, enabling you to think of la otra in a compassionate way. Accepting the other as an equal in a joint endeavor, you respect and are fully present for her. You form an intimate connection that fosters the empowerment of both (nos/otras) to transform conflict into an opportunity to resolve an issue, to change negativities into strengths, and to heal the traumas of racism and other systemic desconocimientos. You look beyond the illusion of separate interests to a shared interest—you're in this together, no one's an isolated unit. You dedicate yourself, not to surface solutions that benefit only one group, but to a more informed service to humanity.

Relating to others by recognizing commonalities does not always serve you. The person/group with conflicting desires may continuously attack you, no matter how understanding you are. Can you assume that all of us, Ku Klux Klan and holistic alliance members, are in it together just because we're all human? If consciousness is as fundamental to the universe as matter and energy, if consciousness is not local, not contained in separate vessels/bodies, but is like air and water, energy and matter, then we *are* all in it together.[26] When one person steps into conocimiento, the whole of humanity witnesses that step and eventually steps into consciousness. It's like Rupert Sheldrake's concept of morphic resonance: when rats in a laboratory maze learn the way out, as time goes on rats in other mazes all over the world do it more and more quickly because of morphic resonance from previous members that have learned the hard way.[27] Before holistic alliances can happen, many people must yearn for a solution to our shared problems.

But sometimes you need to block the other from your body, mind, and soul. You need to ignore certain voices to respect yourself—as when in an abusive relationship. It's impossible to be open and respectful to all views and voices. Though las nepantleras witness as impartially as they can to prevent being imprisoned by the other's point of view, they acknowledge the need for psychological armor (picture un nopal) to protect their open, vulnerable selves from negative forces while engaging in the world. For attempting the best possible outcome not just for her own group but for the other—the enemy—la nepantlera runs the risk of being stoned for this heresy, a case of killing the messenger. She realizes that to make changes in society and transform the system, she must make time for her needs; the activist must survive burnout. When the self is part of the vision, a strong sense of personal meaning helps in identity and culture construction. By developing and maintaining spiritual beliefs and values, la nepantlera gives the group hope, purpose, identity.

You hear la Llorona/Cihuacoatl wailing. Your picture of her coiled serpent body with the head of a woman, shedding its skin, regenerating itself reminds you of the snake story in Genesis. A hunger to know and to build on your knowledge sweeps over you. You recommit to a regime of meditation, reflection, exercise. These everyday acts contain the sacred, lending meaning to your daily life.

Through the act of writing you call, like the ancient chamana, the scattered pieces of your soul back to your body. You commence the arduous task of rebuilding yourself, composing a story that more accurately expresses your new identity. You seek out allies and, together, begin building spiritual/political communities that struggle for personal growth and social justice. By compartiendo historias, ideas, las nepantleras forge bonds across race, gender, and other lines, thus creating a new tribalism. Éste quehacer—internal work coupled with commitment to struggle for social transformation—changes your relationship to your body and, in turn, to other bodies and to the world. And when that happens, you change the world.

For you, writing is an archetypal journey home to the self, un proceso de crear puentes (bridges) to the next phase, next place, next culture, next reality. The thrust toward spiritual realization, health, freedom, and justice propels you to help rebuild the bridge to the world when you return "home." You realize that "home" is that bridge, the in-between place of nepantla and constant transition, the most unsafe of all spaces. You remove the old bridge from your back, and though afraid, allow diverse groups to collectively rebuild it, to buttress it with new steel plates, girders, cable bracing, and trusses. You distend this more inclusive puente to unknown corners—you don't build bridges to safe and familiar territories; you have to risk making mundo nuevo, have to risk the uncertainty of change. And nepantla is the only space where change happens. Change requires more than words on a page: It takes perseverance, creative ingenuity, and acts of love. In gratitude and in the spirit of your Mamagrande Ramona y Mamagrande Locha, despachas éstas palabras y imágenes as giveaways to the cosmos.

RITUAL . . . PRAYER . . . BLESSING . . . FOR TRANSFORMATION

Every day you visit the sea, walk along Yemayá's glistening shores. You want her to know you, to sense your presence as you sense hers. You know deep down that she's not independent of humans, not indifferent, not set apart. At the lips del mar you begin your ritual/prayer: with the heel of your left foot you draw a circle in the sand, then walk its circumference, stand at the center, and voice your intention: to increase awareness of Spirit, recognize our interrelatedness, and work for transformation.

Then with feather, bone, incense, and water you attend the spirits' presence:

Spirit embodying yourself as rock, tree, bird, human, past, present,
and future,
you of many names, diosas antiguas, ancestors,
we embrace you as we would a lover.

You face **east**, feel the wind comb your hair, stretch your hands toward
the rising sun and its orange filaments, breathe its rays into your
body, on the outbreath send your soul up to el sol,[28] say:

Aire, with each breath may we remember our interrelatedness
see fibers of spirit extend out from our bodies
creating us, creating sky, seaweed, serpent, y toda la gente.
"El alma prende fuego,"[29] burns holes in the walls
separating us
renders them porous and passable, pierces through
posturing and pretenses,
may we seek and attain wisdom.

Moving sunwise you turn to the **south**:
Fuego, inspire and energize us to do the necessary work,
and to honor it
as we walk through the flames of transformation.
May we seize the arrogance to create
outrageously
soñar wildly—for the world becomes as
we dream it.

Facing **west** you send your consciousness skimming over the waves
toward the horizon, seamless sea and sky. Slipping your hands into el
ojo del agua you speak to the spirit dwelling here en éste mar:

Agua, may we honor other people's feelings,
respect their anger, sadness, grief, joy as we do our own.
Though we tremble before uncertain futures
may we meet illness, death, and adversity
with strength
may we dance in the face of our fears.

You pivot toward the **north**, squat, scoop sand into your hands:

Madre tierra, you who are our body, who bear us into life, swallow
us in death

forgive us for poisoning your lands, guide us to wiser ways
of caring for you.
May we possess the steadfastness of trees
the quiet serenity of dawn
the brilliance of a flashing star
the fluidity of fish in our element
Earth, you who dream us, te damos las gracias.

Completing the circle, retornas al **centro**, look down to the
underworld: '

May the roaring force of our collective creativity
heal the wounds of hate, ignorance, indifference
dissolve the divisions creating chasms between us
open our throats so we who fear speaking out raise our
voices
by our witnessing, find connections through our
passions
pay homage to those whose backs served as bridges.
We remember our dead:
Pat Parker, Audre Lorde, Toni Cade Bambara, Barbara
Cameron, y tantas otras.

You raise your head to the **sky:**

May the words and the spirit of this book, our "giveaway" to the
world,
take root in our bodies, grow, sprout ears that listen
may it harm no one, exclude none
sabemos que podemos transformar este mundo
filled with hunger, pain, and war
into a sanctuary of beauty, redemption, and possibility
may the fires of compassion ignite our hands
sending energy out into the universe
where it might best be of service
may the love we share inspire others to act.

You walk back along the circle, erase the lines en la arena, leave a
tortilla to symbolize feeding the ancestors, feeding ourselves, and the
nurturing shared in this book.

Qué éste libro gather in our tribe—all our tribes—y alce
nuestras voces en canto.
Oh, Spirit—wind sun sea earth sky—inside us, all
around us, enlivening all
we honor tu presencia and celebrate the spirit of
this book.
We are ready for change.
Let us link hands and hearts
together find a path through the dark woods
step through the doorways between worlds
leaving huellas for others to follow,
build bridges, cross them with grace, and claim these
puentes our "home";
si se puede, que así sea, so be it,
estamos listas, vámonos.
Now let us shift.

contigo,
gloria

AGRADECIMIENTOS | ACKNOWLEDGMENTS

Les agradezco todo el apoyo espiritual que me dieron. Yo se que no lo hice sola, sino con la fuerza que mis seres queridas/os me dieron y me dan siempre. The coffehouses where my comadres and I motivated each other and where we held our writing dates: Lulu Carpenter's, Java House, Caffe Pergolesi, and Coffeetopia. To my naguala (daimon or guiding spirit). To nature for inspiring me, Lighthouse Field, the Guadalupe tree on West Cliff. The music I played around the clock: Enya, Robbie Robertson, Jennifer Berens, Llasa, Leonard Cohen, Lila Downs.

Muchisimas gracias a mis "comadres in writing," AnaLouise Keating, Carmen Morones, Irene Reti, Randy Conner, Irene Lara, Yolanda Venegas, y Kit Quan por sus comentarios. This book is richer for your criticisms, support, encouragement, and faith in my work. A special thanks to my literary assistants/interns: Vicki Alcoset, Audrey Berlowitz, Jaime Lee Evans, Alisa Huerta, Melissa Moreno, Rosalinda Ramírez, Claire Riccardi, Dianna Williamson.

I thank Betsy Wootten, Barbara Lee, and the staff and faculty of Kresge College, and Nicolette Czarrunchick, Women's Studies, UCSC. This book started in Donna Haraway's Feminist Theory class in fall 1988 as notes for a paper that would be written the following quarter. I had returned to graduate school, this time in Santa Cruz, to have a community in which I could do my research and writing and get feedback.

Especialmente les agradezco a Helene Moglen, Donna Haraway, José Saldívar, and Norma Alarcón who sat on my orals committee and to Rob Wilson for his encouragement. I am especially grateful to my dissertation committee Helene Moglen, Donna Haraway, and Aída Hurtado. Thanks to the Feminist Studies Focused Research Activity (FRA) and the UCSC Literature Board for small grants for travel and research. I am grateful to the many conferences, colleges, universities, Women's Centers, and community places/organizations where I presented aspects of my work in progress.

Editor's Acknowledgments

This book would not have been published without the support of the Anzaldúa family—especially Hilda Anzaldúa, whose commitment to this project and to the future of her sister's work more generally has been crucial. (I also thank Miranda Garza for allowing me to check in periodically.) I am indebted to Sonia Saldívar-Hull, whose encouragement, insights, advice, and other forms of support have been invaluable throughout this project. Suzanne Bost and the anonymous readers of earlier versions of the proposal and this manuscript made suggestions that greatly improved the finished product—especially my introduction. Thanks to Betsy Dahms, Robyn Henderson-Espinoza, and Kelli Zaytoun for feedback on earlier versions of my introduction. Thanks to Christian Kelleher and the staff at the Nettie Lee Benson Latin American Collection for assistance with archival material. Thanks to Donna Haraway, Aída Hurtado, Helene Moglen, and José David Saldívar for so promptly replying to my e-mails and Facebook messages; I appreciate your willingness to discuss your memories of working with Gloria during her time at UCSC. Thanks to Claire Joysmith for sharing with me the original call for papers for the 9/11 project that led to chapter 1; thanks to Irene Lara for sharing memories of Anzaldúa's participation in las comadritas; thanks to Randy Conner for sharing feedback on Anzaldúa's fourth chapter; and thanks to Betsy Dahms, Gabriel Hartley, Irene Lara, Malea Powell, and Max Wolf Valerio for help with last-minute questions and concerns. It's been great working with Duke University Press. I very much appreciate Gisela Fosado's excitement about this project, as well as her ongoing encouragement and advice; I'm grateful to Lorien Olive and Sara Leone for assistance with artwork, formatting, and other manuscript-related items. Thanks to Santa Barraza for allowing us to use her images.

At Texas Woman's University, I am grateful to Provost Robert Neely for granting me a faculty development leave in spring 2014; the time away from the classroom and administrative work lifted a huge burden and greatly facilitated my editorial process. I thank Claire L. Sahlin, department chair, for her support over the years; Gail Orlando, whose assistance saved me many hours; and Jimmie Lyn Harris, Faculty Information and Research Support Team (FIRST) librarian, for hunting down all sorts of reference material. I'm grateful to the students in my graduate Anzaldúa seminar for their passionate energy and excitement. And, closest to home, I thank my family: my parents for their support over the years; my nuclear family, Eddy Lynton and Jamitrice KreChelle Keating-Lynton for their understanding, encouragement, generosity, and all-around awesomeness. I'm incredibly fortunate to be sharing life with you. Over the years, Gloria Anzaldúa has been a presence in our lives, and you have had to share me—first with Gloria, my friend, the flesh-and-blood person, and now with her writings and writing projects. In my obsession to finish this latest project (like so many others over the years), I have been an absent presence, at times. You have bolstered my heart and energized me, and I lack the words to truly express my gratitude. Finally, I thank the orishas, espíritus, and ancestors (including, now, "la Gloria") for guidance, encouragement, inspiration, and support.

Appendix 1 | *Lloronas* Dissertation Material

(Proposal, Table of Contents, and Chapter Outline)

Draft of *Lloronas* Dissertation Proposal

[The *Lloronas* dissertation proposal exists in multiple forms. I have selected this version, rather than any other, because Anzaldúa viewed it as the most recent iteration of her 1990s dissertation topic. She included it in her dissertation computer folder "08h diss, biblio," in the subfolder "old diss prospectus, biblio." Anzaldúa last saved this document, titled "descrip of diss-lloronas," on April 20, 2002.]

Description: Lloronas—Women Who Wail: (Self)Representation and the Production of Writing, Knowledge, and Identity

The work is an investigation of self-representation and the production of writing, knowledge, memory, imagination, consciousness, identities, and the political resistance and agency of the female postcolonial cultural Other (particularly the Chicana/mestiza). It is about the position of the writing postcolonial subject and the process of "negotiating" discursive spaces from which to speak. It asks such questions as who has voice and who does not, who represents, and for what and for whom and how does it represent. It explores the relationship of self-representation to the referent—the body, gender and history—and to language, fantasy and the desire to write. It questions the constitution of the narrative "I," its interlocutors and its audience; and it explores reader response theory.

The book looks at some of the repressive social, linguistic and literary mechanisms that neo-colonize ethnic/Other female writers and women whose subjectivities have been formed under the stresses of conquest in the past and neo-colonization in the present.

Central to the book in theorizing mythic and historical aspects of identity for mestizas/Chicanas/mejicanas is the cultural figure and narratives of la Llorona (the weeping woman whose antecedent was the Aztec Cihuacoatl, Serpent Woman). I use the metaphor of la Llorona to track how certain mythic components of identity have become part of the cultural language of the mestiza/Chicana and to link the various aspects of identity. Lloronas explores transgressive aspects of identity—identity formation and dissolution in the complex crossroads of multiple and seemingly contradictory subject positions: racial, ethnic, cultural, lesbian, feminist, ideological, political, historical, sexual, social, geographic, artistic, intellectual, and academic. Blending theoretical discourse with personal history, it examines the forces and discourses that have shaped the identities of racial/ethnic Others, the effect colonialism has had on them, and how they combat racial oppression as artists and cultural activists. It addresses how they were constructed by colonialism and are constrained by neo-colonialism and how they constitute themselves as subjects and objects. Exploring the problematic of subjectivity of the cultural Other necessitates interrogating, from cultural and feminist perspectives, the ideology of "femininity," "woman," "lesbian," "mestiza," and "Chicana."

The work explores its own modes of conceptualization, rhetorical devices, and narrative strategies while at the same time reflecting on the author's development as a feminist, as a writer, and as a lesbian. It incorporates interdisciplinary methodological approaches such as literary analysis, structural anthropology, and folklore, as well as psychoanalytic theory, cultural anthropology, cultural criticism, history, folklore, and contemporary Chicana and Mexican women's literature and personal historias to explore how various identities are constructed by these different discourses; to explore the reconstruction of Chicana/mestiza subjectivities and the implicated historical, political, and theoretical processes; and to formulate a theory of the formation of the racial ethnic/Other and her positionings.

It further explores the origin, nature, methods, and limits of knowledge—especially how debates about race, class, sexuality, and colonialism are staged in the production of knowledge in feminist, ethnic, cultural, and literary studies. It explores the politics of emotions and questions Western academic theories of emotion. Intellectuals of color are struggling not to get seduced into replicating dominant patterns of discourse and their specialized languages, which dominate. Those that have been slowly, insidiously, and unconsciously forced to make dominant discourse their tool are trying to break out of this prism of language.

Helene Moglen _____   Date _____
Dissertation Adviser

José David Saldívar _____   Date _____
Donna Haraway _____   Date _____
Norma Alarcón _____   Date _____

Lloronas Table of Contents and Chapter Outline

[This document, named "table chap outlines–lloronas 4," was last saved on May 20, 2002, although Anzaldúa wrote it in the early 1990s. It is located on Anzaldúa's hard drive, in the folder "08h diss, biblio," subfolder "old diss prospectus, biblio." Anzaldúa's bracketed numbering system refers to the location of various notes and drafts that she intended to insert.]

Lloronas—Writing, Reading, Speaking, Dreaming

Dedication & Acknowledgments [8g]
Abstract/Prospectus
Preface or Introduction

1. Gig: traveling, speaking; cuerpaso: passing through the body; images of the collective self; conference as community/the museums as community; dreaming 1; rampas de entrada—intro;

2. I.D.; (A) a work in progress; under construction; Symbolic environment; USF: reimagining id; the laws of genes, cultures, and personal self; ideal self; transcendent self; the self as information; money

   (B) [8g]; shape-shifting subjects, extra-modern mestizas and transgressive identities, internal exile; derramando, desarollo [8e];

mujeres que escapan de jaulas, barred witness: intellectual captivity, literary/artistic creations and class identities [8g] multiculturism; nos/otras—patlache sexual identities [8f]; carta a colón-nialism: surpassing the tongue: nos/otras tenemos manos: 500 years of struggle to reclaim América

3. Compositioning: theories of composition; creativity; writing and reading; the woman who writes—the writing and reading subject; ellas se escriben [8e, 8g]; the woman who writes me, postcolonial writing subject y escribiendo el ser de nos/otras [8g]; the woman who reads (me): the writer as reader; the electronic page.

4. Autobiography: mujeres que cuentan vidas: writing personal & collective histories/autobiographies and problematizing assumptions about autohistorias-teorías, identity and representation in nos/otras [8g]

5. Poet Philosopher: producing knowledge; Consciousness and identity, conocimiento; intelligence; la mujer piensa; the poet is critic/the poet is theorist: intellectual identities, aesthetics and the production of knowledge and culture [8e]; Chicana theory

6. Llorona: noche y su nidada; the woman who haunts (me); el cuerpo y las paciones de la Llorona; monsters and mother lloronas; politics of emotions [8f] coping mechanisms—escape into rage

7. Dreaming—rampas de entrada—intro. [8f]; facultad of paying attention; Facultad awareness; spiritual skills; Nepantla, spiritual mestisaje; altars; alone with nature; internalizing landscape

8. SIC: depression—rampas de salida—exit ramps [8f]

9. Movimiento macha; theorizing Nepantla, the artist and the community; activism [8e] ally; multiculturalism; planetary citizen, remolinos—complexity of modern life; virtual communities; power, new forms of domination and of resistence; a theory of agency; Bibliography [8g]

Chapter Outlines

Chicana/Colored Creativity and Critical Thought inside Enemy Territory, Speaking in Tongues Letter Two

I. Personally Positioned—vagamundiando
- Acts of Self-Writing and Self-Reading
- Through the Eyes of a Stranger/Familiar
- Consumed by Soledad in Privileged Positions
- Colonized Consciousness: The Appropriation

II. Writing on the Edge of Stress
- No Safety Factor
- Desde la orilla of the Precipice
- El desmadre
- Making Space(s) to W(rite)
- The Reader as Voyeur
- (Be)laboring the Writing de este trabajo
- In Psychic Exile, the Writer
- Metaphors in the Tradition of the Shaman

The Poet Is Critic/The Poet Is Theorist, Speaking in Tongues, Carta Tres

I. Theorizing Mestiza Style
- How I "Do" Theory
- Fictive and Theorizing Processes—One and the Same

II. We Have Always Theorized
- Neo-colonizing Discourses/Violated by "High" Theory
- The Post Modern Mestiza Subject
- Movidas of the Mestiza: Teorías to Save Our Lives

Narrative and History in Ethnic Autohistorias, Speaking in Tongues Quarta Carta

I. Remembering and Subverting in the "Historias" of Chicanas & Women of Color
- The Writing of Historias: Personal Narrative and History in Ethnic Autobiographies
- Quest for the Lost Object
- Busqueda de Identidad/Quest for Origins/Quest for Symbols
- How a Writer Comes to Write That Which Wants to Come Out

II. New Knowledges
- The Marks of Race
- Literature/Aesthetics: An Ahistorical Space

Appendix 2 | Anzaldúa's Health

[As a genre, e-mail can offer an immediacy and intimacy that goes beyond that of Anzaldúa's heavily revised autohistorias. The following three e-mails from Anzaldúa provide intimate glimpses into some of the health-related struggles she experienced in the last years of her life. Addressing her writing comadres, Anzaldúa lets down her guard and speaks personally and frankly.]

Date: Thu, 28 Feb 2002 15:36:37
Subject: been sick
From: Gloria Anzaldúa
To: analouise keating

hi al,
Sorry i haven't gotten back to you this week as i'd planned—my eyes are still strained & light sensitive. also i've been sick & depressed. I'm struggling to shift out of feeling depressed & overwhelmed. sometimes by using my imagination i'll shift out of it but then hypos will drag me down, again. i think this time my depression is partly chemical & partly psychological. if i overcompensate with food & sugar my blood sugar will shoot into the other extreme. i also think that i let myself get too exhausted, spiritually & emotionally drained & now

i'm paying for it. i sure wish i could learn to manage my life/work better.

how are you doing?
contigo, g

Date: Sun, 18 Aug 2002 03:36
Subject: how i'm doing; a poem
From: Gloria Anzaldua
To: analouise keating

querida comadre,
i can't seem to get my spirits up. i'm cradled in the arms of Coyol-xauhqui, dwelling in the depth of night consciousness. it feels like this is where i need to be for now. need to honor darkness.
here's a poem i just now wrote—the shitty first draft:

Healing Wounds
I have been ripped wide open
by a word, a look, a gesture—
from self, kin, and stranger.
My soul jumps out
scurries into hiding
i hobble here and there
seeking solace
trying to coax it back home
but the me that's home
has become alien without it.
Wailing, i pull my hair
suck snot back and swallow it
place both hands over the wound
but after all these years
it still bleeds
never realizing that to heal
there must be wounds
to repair there must be damage
for light there must be darkness.

kit was scheduled to come down this weekend. i called her to reschedule. i also don't feel like going to irene's housewarming later today. in fact i'd rather not see anyone for a while & may cancel my critiquing date with Carmen as well. in the meantime the dirty dishes continue to pile up, i don't feel like cleaning up.

Date: Wed, 26 Feb 2003 19:02:28 -0800
Subject: health/devotional & writing matters
From: Gloria Anzaldua
To: las comadritas

queridas comadritas,
my meditation/prayer/devotional practice is slowly becoming more consistent.
the prayers—i do them 3-4 times a day—are solid.
the meditations—i do the spiral counter-clockwise/clockwise—are sporadic & short. am trying to do a couple a day, some days i do none or only once, other days twice. i exercise for about 1-1/2 hours every day on my health rider, 1/2 more than in the past, & manage to get some walks in.

my physical health:
i had laser surgery on my right eye three weeks ago and last week i had laser treatment on the left one. i had my teeth checked & my perio-dontist (or whatever the gum doctor is called) said i was doing a great job keeping the gum problem down (had surgery on my gums some years back). i also had to get my health insurance to re-process a claim for depth shoes inserts & shoes that they had refused to pay. i get so tired of dealing with all this health bureacracy (sp?). all the members of National Writers Union were going to lose our insurance by March 1, but we just got word that we have it until the end of this June, so i'm trying to get in all the health care i can manage in the next few week[s] & months. i do not look forward to converting my insurance out of group insurance into individual insurance (which [is] much more costly). comoquiera, i'll probably have to find another insurance. i hate having to take the time but i have to grin & bear it & try to keep a positive attitude.

my emotional health: my depression has lifted a little bit. i have plans for getting acupuncture & therapy for it & other health related stuff, but it looks like i'll have to pay for $80–$105 treatment sessions out of pocket.

i got my blood work done at the lab finally after a couple of tries. i have to fast for 12 hour[s], ingesting nothing but water during that time. with no food for 12 hours my sugar level got way down. the day i was supposed to go to the lab my blood sugar level was 45 which means get some sugar & food pronto or go into a hypo. without the sugar my vision got blurred—kept me from driving to Unilab. even if i'd found a friend to drive me (most of them work) i would have had to sit in the waiting room for god knows how long until i was called. in the time it takes me to get there & wait my turn, I would probably have lost consciousness.

i went over the lab results with primary care doctor. not good. my blood sugar levels are too high despite all my efforts to control them, yet when i increase the NPH, Regular & Ultralente insulin i get hypos. i've had 5 hypos in the last 3 days. hypos mess up my ability to think & work, affect my vision & bring doomsday feelings down on me.

so i'm making changes in my intensive-insulin therapy. i'm going to try out a new insulin called Lantus which has a 24-hour basal line with no peak periods. i'll still have to take Regular insulin (which acts between 2 & 4 hours) "bolus" shots before meals, so i'll still be doing 4 injections a day & drawing blood 3–4 times a day. but because Lantus does not peak like NPH & lasts 24 hours (NPH only lasts 14.5 hours) hopefully it will eliminate some of the hypos i've been having. i'll have to go through a trial-by-error period, gradually increasing the dosage, & monitor the change-over. i know this will stress out my body but maybe it won't be so bad.

my thyroid results were not good. so we're doubling the dosage. the kidney & hypertension results were not good either—i have to take more medication of what i was already taking plus a new medicine, HCTZ [hydrochlorothiazide], which again will put stress on my body.

for the first time ever my LDL ("bad") cholesterol is too high (223), I'll have to take a new med. called Lovastatin & try to bring the fat in my blood down to 100. my blood pressure is too high, too. it's 160 over 90 & should be around 120 over 80. she wants me to take an aspirin a day but because i have retinopathy (eye complication) the aspirin may thin my blood, esp. of the eyes, too much. so i have to consult with my ophthalmologist about the aspirin.

and i'm anemic.

my primary care doc wants to see me more often. if it was just her i had to see i wouldn't mind but there's all those other doctors to visit. and i want to add an acupuncturist & a therapist to the list. i must be nuts.

the good news: i've lost weight, but want to clean out my system more. irene & i are both just starting on the fat flush plan by Ann Louise Gittleman. her plan allows more protein, more fat, 2 eggs a day, unsweetened cranberry juice, ground up flaxseeds, etc. below is some info on it. you can find out about it at www.iVillage.com site.

work on dissertation:
I'm working on the nos/otras essay. right now it's about the length of "now let us shift." i've made major changes/additions on. it's coming along a bit faster than turtle pace (considering my vision problems). i need to give it to the editors by march 1st. i think i'll have time to revise while the editors finalize the book. keep your fingers crossed that i'll have revision time.

i don't know if you want me to go into so much detail over my health problems. writing about them allows me to sort it all out— putting it all into words does help me, but it may waste your time. if i'm taking too much space let me know.

see you on March 15th at 10:30 AM.

con mucho cariño, g

Appendix 3 | Unfinished Sections and Additional Notes from Chapter 2

[The following material is drawn from the file "essay flights of imaginal-2," the most recent draft of chapter 2, on Anzaldúa's hard drive in the folder "diss chapters," subfolder "2. flights of imagin." Although the document was last saved on April 4, 2004, the material itself was probably written before that date. I include these partial sections in the appendix rather than simply deleting them for two reasons: (1) their presence in the most recent chapter manuscript indicates their importance to Anzaldúa; (2) the material offers readers additional insights into Anzaldúa's work.]

A. *Soul and image work: Distinguishing soul from spirit*

In distinguishing soul from spirit, Tenzin Gyatso, 14th-Century Dalai Lama of Tibet, said, "I call the high and light aspects of my being Spirit and the dark and heavy aspects soul." To [James] Hillman, spirit favors detached abstractness, purity, and unity—all characteristics that transcend earth and body, while soul thrives on attachments and imaginings, the concrete and sensual, emphasizing the multiplicity and imperfection that cling to earth and body ("Peaks and Vales"). According to Thomas Moore, the soul seeks connection; the spirit, enlightenment (*The Soul's Religion*).

"Anima" is Latin for soul; "psyche" is Greek for soul. According to Hillman, the word "soul" refers to "that unknown component which makes meaning possible, turns events into experiences, is communicated in love, and has a religious concern." He offers three meanings: "First, 'soul' refers to the *deepening* of events into experiences; second, the significance soul makes possible, whether in love or in religious concern, derives from its special *relation with death*. And third, by 'soul' I mean the imaginative possibility in our natures, the experiencing through reflective speculation, dream, image, and *fantasy*—that mode which recognizes all realities as primarily symbolic or metaphorical" (*Re-Visioning Psychology*, x).

B. Acts of reading, writing, storytelling, and self-making

To this mix of nagualismo, or indigenous worldview, and the imaginal activity that precedes the reconstruction, re-visioning, rewriting, re-imagining that accompanies significant and often traumatic events in life, I add the process that occurs in acts of reading, writing, storytelling, self-making, and other creative acts. Storytelling and reading and listening to stories is not only how we make sense of ourselves, our lives, and our place in the world, and how we make the Self. Storytelling is healing when it expands the autohistorias (self-narratives) of the tellers and the listeners, when it broadens the person that we are.

Reading puts you into a trance. The skills required in reading are to empathize with characters, to imagine or play in your mind the scenery, get involved.

Reading, writing, and art making are processes of processing information.

The well of imagination (el cenote) is full of subterranean rivers, expansive caves and grottos. The architecture of the imagination, the labyrinth of the imagination.

The reality of mental imagery. Reality cannot be linked to physical phenomena perceived through/by the senses nor that represented by the rational intellect. Henry Corbin articulates a world between these two, a median and mediating place, the **mundus imaginalis** (the world of images). The snares of literalism—not to interpret literally. Are spirits literally present or are they imaginally present? They are both. Fantasy is not just a coping with reality, a correction of reality, or a supplement to reality. A dream/fantasy frees you from the confines of daily time and space, from your habitual identity.

C. *Glifo de la lengua: Serpent's tongue*

La lengua de culebra es el glifo de la lengua, de habla. The serpent's tongue is the hieroglyph of language, sprouting bones against the edge con la vírgula de palabra. Sugún la teoría (according to theory), language co-constitutes reality. Language, says Linda Hogan in "A-Different Yield," is more than a set of signs and symbols that communicate meanings: "We read one another via gesture, stance, facial expression, scent" (*Dwellings*, 5–7). We read minute changes in breathing, the angles of brow and lips—an unconscious leakage.

You start a work with an intention: to bring other, nonverbal kinds of perception to the center of awareness. A work of art represents and reveals. Because it brings about a new interrogation that goes against the existing order, art is revolutionary. Art has a political purpose: to push the world in a certain direction, to change others' ideas of reality, and to tell them what reality to strive for. Art helps you to realize yourself spiritually. Prayer is a technique I use to prepare myself to write.

The imagination is a powerful generative force, a transformative genius, a genius that transforms the self. In assembling, ordering, and constructing, I myself am assembled, ordered, and constructed. The Latin *ars* is the root of the English "art" and "artist." Contemplation, from the Latin *contemplari*, is the ability to see things as they really are. Imaginary reality. The artist as culture-bearer.

La luna, coyolxauhqui, silvery-white crescent moon cyclical menstrual movement embodies fertility and transformative energy and creativity.

D. *Creating reality*

In the French edition of *Crash*, [J. G.] Ballard writes,

> We live in a world ruled by fictions of every kind—mass merchandizing, advertising, politics conducted as a branch of advertising, the instant translation of sciences and technology into popular imagery, the increasing blurring and intermingling of identities within the real of consumer goods. . . . We live in an enormous novel. For the writer in particular it is less and less necessary for him to invent the fictional context of his novel. The fiction is already there. The writer's task is to invent the reality.

The creation of a work of art is the bringing together of a new combination of elements—in other words, making new connections or making connections more broadly. Arthur Koestler's term "bissociation" refers to the bringing together of two different lines of thought—in other words, making new connections. The successful work of art must connect with the emotional state of the reader/viewer, as well as that of its creator.

E. Anzaldúa's Additional Notes for "How real is reality?"

Outer reality is not real. It is a dream from which you can't escape, but you can change this existential delusion. The inner reality is not real, either. You can refute both realities. If all life is illusory and your life is also illusory, use those illusions. Read the present moment; whatever you need to learn about life is written there. You just need to decode the messages. Once you decode them, you can re-encode them. Problem solving requires a paradigm shift, requires that you see into the problem differently.

Truth is relative. Different cultures believe different things. I object to one people/group claiming that they possess the "real" truth and using their claim to dominate others. Psychological destruction results in loss of identity, and identity loss means psychic extinction. Loss of self-esteem, self-authority, and authenticity leads to alienation.

As a people you understand yourselves through your stories, your communities, your cultures, and your nation. Your stories provide you with social purpose and ethical guidance. They tell you what you need to know, what kinds of information you need, and what kinds you don't need.

Appendix 4 | Alternative Opening, Chapter 4

[The following excerpts are from Anzaldúa's penultimate draft of this chapter, "geo of selves_nosotras," last saved March 23, 2003. Given Anzaldúa's penchant for ongoing revision, as well as her indecision about this chapter, it's impossible to know whether she would have reinserted some or all of this material into the "final" version of chapter 4. The draft is located on Anzaldúa's hard drive in the folder "diss chapters," subfolder "4. geo of selves."]

GEOGRAPHIES OF THE SELF—REIMAGINING IDENTITY: NOS/OTRAS (US/OTHER) AND THE NEW TRIBALISM

Thirty years ago, Raza students across the U.S. demonstrated in high schools and on university campuses. During the late 1960s, they criticized public schools and universities for being complicit with the system of white supremacy. They demanded educational self-determination and sought to give students and teachers normally silenced a voice in learning institutions. Via sit-ins, speak-outs, and walkouts, they empowered students and connected with community struggles. Their activism precipitated the birth of Chicano studies, Raza, ethnic studies, women's [studies], and, later, Latino studies. Thirty years ago tomaron el compromiso, they committed to transform not only the entire educational system but also society.

Raza studies today

Today, thirty years later, that struggle y ese compromiso continues for third millennium Raza, or, as a *Newsweek* article called this group, "Generation Ñ" (those between 18 and 35). We share with esos que lucharon in previous generations las ganas and the guts to keep on struggling, despite the hardship. Today Raza studies still struggles to transform the racist educational system, still commits itself a ésta lucha. It's still pioneering interdisciplinary scholarship for and by people of color; still fighting for autonomy to set our own educational standards, hire faculty, and admit students; still supporting student and community organizing; still trying to connect curriculum to community struggles and issues. Today ethnic studies and its radical agenda is still seen as a threat and is feared, is still castigated as a bastion of self-imposed isolation, shoddy scholarship, and unqualified professors. Along with Native American studies, the various Raza studies are being forced to submit to academia's dominant-culture elitist leaders, rules, rewards, and punishments. We now more than ever recognize that the purpose of education is not only to fight against oppression but to heal the wounds that oppression inflicts and to cultivate individual and collective growth—laying the foundation for justice and balance. (Oppression is an extreme state of imbalance.)

We must continue to address the crises of Raza and Raza studies. We must explore unexamined connections of the Raza legacies we rely upon. Today we must engage discussions of how Raza feminisms, through various generations, contribute to trans-categorical conversations and collaborations and inform the needs of nuestros pueblos. To transform curriculum and education we must practice what *This Bridge Called My Back* calls theory in the flesh, which sees practice as a form of theorizing and theorizing as a form of practice. Today we must bridge the chasm between campus political activity and grassroots activism, women and men, us and others (of whatever race or culture they may be). Through our scholarship and creative expression we must be willing to translate across (mis)perceived differences instead of highlighting our separate worlds, be willing to facilitate rather than obstruct dialogue and collaboration. Today we are poised on the brink of our own flowering. We need to increase our capacity for awareness, vision, presence, and compassion and integrate reflective and contemplative practices into daily professional routines. For this, our moment in history, we need to clarify collective and personal identities and visions.

The ground from which I speak

Soy de rancho. I speak and write from what grounds me at any given moment and that hub of core identity—my physical body, the body of a female, a Chicana tejana, embedded in an indigenous Mexicana culture rich in symbols and metaphors, a body immersed in many cultures, a queer body. My struggle, like yours, is an anticolonial one against cultural imperialism, intellectual piracy, and mental colonialism, while dealing with my complicity in being positioned as an "internal exile." I am not an academic (having done a three-month stint in 1988 and three months in 2001, a total of six months in the last eighteen years). But via the lecture circuit and participation in conferences, I circulate on the fringes of women's, ethnic, Chicana/o, Latino, composition, and American studies and other disciplines where my work is taught.

Here I attempt to map identity both "outside" (world) and "inside" (mental activity, genes) the body and to chart it in both inner and outer communities. I discuss the internal struggles and cracks among the women and men of la Raza and those between the different Latino ethnic groups. I present some ideas for expanding awareness and working together to create a new "story" and a new agenda. I write from the position of being an other-sider, half way between a complete outsider and an insider. My chief forms of orientation to the world are feminism, soul work, and devotion to spirituality. My struggle has always been to combine the inner work of the soul with outer service in the world.

What follow are my identity stories. I place the form of narrative over "identity" or "reality" or any other theme to organize and order them. It is through narrative that you come to understand and know your self and make sense of the world. Through narrative, we formulate our identities by unconsciously locating ourselves in social narratives not of our own making. I'm compelled to tell my stories/theories using my own consciousness as a guinea pig. I invite the reader to enter the text emotionally, not just intellectually.

My struggle, like yours, is always to be fully who and what I am, to act out of that potential, to strive for wholeness, and to understand both the fragments and the whole of my being. Like you, I struggle to come to grips with the stresses, traumas, problems, and challenges I encounter. Our struggle is simultaneously to cope with the messy changing conditions and disturbances in our lives and to live with our obstacles if we can't overcome them. The crises we face daily, and have [faced] for generations, are how to deal with the traumas of racism—marginalization, delegitimation, disenfranchisement, and other violations. The legacy that racism and other accompanying violations have bequeathed us is post-traumatic [stress] syndrome and various dysfunctions.

We cope by changing our attitudes about others, about reality, and about identity while trying to change other peoples' ideas of reality and of the world. Because all cultures and their pictures of reality are resistant and slow to change, it's up to the individual to initiate change. Making éstos cambios (changes) are the hardest things we'll ever undertake.

It's important to reimagine our diverse struggles, especially our struggles with identity. What does it mean to be a Chicana or a Latina today, to be Raza? What are our common conditions, our different circumstances? What do all of us want, and what stands in our way of getting it? Some basic questions of identity we ask those who are subsumed under a racial identity, the Latino pan-ethnic umbrella (or any other broad category) are: Who are you? Where do you come from? Where are you going? What is your place in the world? How do you identify? What category boxes do you put yourself in? The intra- and interpersonal conflicts and misperceptions among Chicanas y Chicanos, Latinas y Latinos, Raza and non-Raza, queer and straight are basically struggles of identity. To bridge the fissures among us, I present several interconnected concepts of identity that may offer new perspectives and conocimientos.

PART 2 RE-IMAGINING IDENTITIES

I am often asked, "What's your primary identity? Is it Chicana, mexicana, Mexican American, Latina, or Hispanic? Is it being a woman, queer, working class, an elder, short; is it being a writer, diabetic, intellectual, spiritual activist, mystic, dreamer . . . ?" This question assumes that a person can be fragmented into pieces like Coyolxauhqui, and I answer, "All of me is my primary identity. I can't be cut up like a pie, with each wedge assigned a category of identity." Like the genetic code, all of me is in each cell, and every single little piece has all of me. I am all of the above, but also more.

Which "I" are you?

Each of us is a trinity: body, mind/soul/psyche, and spirit. The body and outward behavior are the objective dimension (what we show the outside world). Psyche/soul/mind is the subjective dimension of inner feelings, thoughts, sensations, desires, intuitions, and images. When at times you position yourself (the "I") in outside surroundings, you are aware of how hot or cold it is; through your senses, you are aware of sounds, smells, sights, and sensations. When you place the "I" in the subjective dimension of mind/soul/psyche, you are aware of your feelings, thoughts, meaningful associations, and images. Wherever you place your attention (your "I"), an observing self or watcher (distinct from the "I" that's attentive to the outside world or the inner dimensions) is looking on. This observer is able to switch from inner to outer or to be in both dimensions simultaneously. As you observe, you learn that the watcher is constant, which means that you are not the state or mood of mind; you are not the contents (thoughts) of consciousness; you are not the passing stream of psyche-body experience. You are the one who observes, reflects, and acts on these states, mood, contents. But neither are you separate from psyche-soma experiences. When you watch yourself and observe your mind at work, you find that behind all your identities is a state of awareness. When you are conscious of this, you can't get caught up in one identity, can't get completely lost in it. You see through it. You always have a central point of reference to the self (though you may not be aware of it) while the particulars and peripheries change.

So which "I" is really you, or more truly you? The observing self, because it transcends (goes beyond) all dimensions. The nature of the watcher is transcendent; it is both/and—a unity of body, soul, and spirit. The point of connection between you the person and your core center/core self or watcher (what some call the higher self) reflects the sense that you exist and are a unique and worthy person. Wounding disrupts that sense of self and disturbs that union, causing alienation from physical experience.

Wounds split body, soul, and spirit. For most of us, identity is a sense of a separate self; we experience ourselves as separate—as the nos/otras with the slash in the middle.

Identity is a composition of a composite

Identity is a framework for a complex composition that melds together disparate persons. It is an ongoing activity of constructing an ordered latticework of time, space, and emotional climate, of stringing together a series of scenes and experiences, and of holding all these together by memory. Memory is the adhesive and the myths of your tribes; what may be called the collective dream are the narratives that your fiction is embedded in. Each of us lives in a fiction of our own construction, one supported by consensual reality.

Identity is an embodiment of theories from various discourses. Identity is a composite of different sets of information, an embodiment of theories, markers, and bars on our human flesh. The personality is a composite of different systems of information, at times a layering one upon the other like an onion, at times converging like spokes in a wheel. Identity is a shifting, changing chameleon. You would think that so many frames and seismic shiftings would result in a fragmented, dislocated being, but this is not so. Such shiftings and fragmentations impel us to use our imaginations to figure out who we are and who and what we can become.

Identity is based, in part, on copying others. You create identity and your life by reading (observing) the people, the events around you, and yourself. You take in what you read and apply what you've learned to yourself, to your situation. Identity creation is an interaction with the world, a relational activity.

A field of "sub-personalities"

Identity is a field of relations. We reside in multiple realities. For Raza, being placed in tidy and simple boxes is no longer an option. None of us subsists in one box or two or even three. We are an interplay that allows the perspectives of many boxes to converge and collaborate. Each of us is populated by different puntos de vista whose sands are constantly shifting. Each consists of an inner multiplicity of various selves, often fighting among themselves. We become another person in response to different situations or social worlds—at home, at the job, and so on. Roberto Assagioli calls these different identities "sub-personalities."[1] When I visit my family en el Valle of South Texas, my child self is evoked by sibling rivalry or a smarting comment from my mother, and suddenly I, the competent adult, am eclipsed and a bratty kid makes her appearance, trapping me in the melodrama. It's as if I must be that sullen child persona with my mother. Where I position the "I" and which "I" takes center stage depends on who's in the room with me. In the course of a day, I move among various identifications. Identity is a composite image that shifts with setting (position) and the other people and things in the landscape.

Certain situations call forth certain identities. One way to reimagine identity is to look at it as a series of interchangeable roles. But around these temporary senses of self is there an eternal sense of self, a more permanent identity? Does a core or more constant identity lie behind all roles? I think this identity is connected to soul. When you watch yourself and observe your mind at work, you find that behind all your identities is a state of awareness. When you are conscious of this, you can't get caught up in one identity, can't get lost in it completely. You see through it. You always have a central point of reference to the self (though you may not be aware of it) while the particulars and peripheries change.

Identity is a social position

Identity is about repositioning yourself.[2] It's about willing to be moved from your social positions—your age, social class, gender, geographic area, race, and family history—all factors that frame your sense of self. Age is also an identity, a vital aspect of who, how, and what you are. Even if your circumstances may not change drastically (and change they will), you may experience your circumstances differently. Identity is always in process, in nepantla (between who we were yesterday and are yet to be tomorrow).

The role of imagination in identity formation

It is a human characteristic to define ourselves and our territories, but our identities and territories are also our prisons. When identities get in the way—when they limit you, when you pretend to be other than who you are, identity becomes a prison: each label (your sex, gender, class, etc.) is a bar of your cell.

To change or reinvent yourself, you engage the facultad of your imagination. You have to interrupt or suspend the conscious "I" that reminds you of your history because it ties you to a certain identity and behavior. You then insert the idea, with accompanying images, of the new you. To invent a self (image), you cultivate a pretend self and act as though you are this pretend self. Eventually, that self becomes the real you, at least until you change again.

In the past (and, to some extent, today) we depended on Chicano society (or whatever racial group we belong to) to confer an identity or role. In part, identities have their basis in ethnic background, the age one lives in, one's geographic location, the class one emerges from as well as the class one moves into, gender conditioning, sexual preference, vocation or career, and many other variables. Identities (of individuals and collective groups) are constructed on several sites: class, race, sexual preference, work vocation, geography, and historical period. But because shared communal meanings are constantly shifting and dissolving, today we depend on individual consciousness to confer identity. Such an identity is not just social but also individual/subjective, based on experiences and values.

Identity is often an identity of the ego (the persona or mask we show the world), a reassembling collection/selection of internalized images (often fictitious) from our encounters with the world. We wear mascaras to reveal true aspects of ourselves as well as false aspects. In the TV show *The Hitchhiker*, a protected witness demands facial surgery to seal his new identity—and gets it. The hitchhiker says, "Becoming another means more than changing your name or the way you look," implying that identity is a lifestyle adjustment and not mere pretending.

Virtual identities, pretend selves

Though statistically Raza surfs the Internet in smaller percentages than do whites and other groups of color, I see more and more Chicano and Latino websites. The Internet helps us in re-imagining identity beyond notions of nation, community, pueblos, gender, and sexual orientation. Today, computer technologies are affecting your sense of identity; shaping your identity; affecting the way you interact with family, friends, colleagues. Via shared virtual conference rooms, virtual communities, chat rooms, gaming sites, MUDs (multiuser dimensions), computer bulletin boards, and sexual encounters (cybersex), computers are extending your physical presence. Virtual communities allow you to generate online personas and relationships. They provide simulations into which you deploy your virtual selves. Online technology can be used to mask identity as well as to free it up. (The undercover cop who pretended to be a fourteen-year-old boy to trap a cyber-pedophile comes to mind.) In MUDs, gender lines are blurred as in "transpostites," people who pose as members of the opposite gender. Computers compel you to renegotiate old boundaries of all sorts.

Rapid communication enabled by computers has changed how we do activism. (The antiwar petition "Latinos Speak Out against War: An Action for Peace and Social Justice" circulated via e-mail during February 2003, providing a sense of solidarity. In the "virtual march" on Washington, DC, on February 26, 2003, more than two hundred thousand people signed up to call/fax their senators and the White House.)

Cyber-selves are constructed by language. With words you cultivate or project an image, you become that image, you become that new name. Some of us have two or more separate identities in cyberspace. Fluid rather than fixed conceptions of ourselves are derived in part through role playing, through going out of habitual character. The Internet provides space for you to explore aspects of yourself that are socially taboo. Online (and in your fantasies) you can act out other personalities, leaving in abeyance your habitual and perhaps inhibited selves. Exploring diverse identities in your imagination opens you to new self-constructions. Identity is limited only by your imagination.

As computer users, you are becoming increasingly comfortable with substituting representations of reality for the real. You go to computers for experiences that will change your ways of thinking and affect your social and emotional life. You log into a "community" where you have virtual friends and lovers. You explore simulation games and fantasy worlds.

Decolonizing identity

If reality is made up, then so, too, is identity. The imagination's shape-shifting power (what I call la naguala) enables you to shift identity. Now you are this type of person with these identification features; now you are that type with other distinguishing characteristics, making identity fluid not fixed. Decolonizing identity consists of unlearning identity labels; it means unlearning consensual "reality"; it means seeing through the roles and description of reality and of identity by what Don Juan calls acts of "not-doing." Something breaks down, one falls to pieces (dismembered), and one has to pull oneself together and reconstruct oneself (remembered) on another level. I call this the Coyolxauhqui process. In an instant of insight/conocimiento, your life and its dismembered parts get reconstituted. You enact a healing. The myth of our lives struggles to be heard. Each of us has a story within us; we can speak it through the various disguises and voices of our different personas.

Appendix 5 | Historical Notes on the Chapters' Development

[This appendix includes background information on Anzaldúa's writing process for each chapter, as well as information about where the drafts can be located.]

Preface. Gestures of the Body—Escribiendo para idear

Anzaldúa drafted this preface specifically for *Light in the Dark*. She began thinking about it in the summer of 2002 but did not seriously focus on it until 2003. Her notes indicate that she drew from her *La Prieta* story collection, dissertation proposal and chapters from the 1990s, and other writing notes, copying over and pasting in episodes and descriptions that explored body-soul connections to create her pre-draft. As she explained to me in conversation, she developed "Gestures of the Body" by looking through the book chapters to draw out "common threads." When she sought feedback on the chapter drafts, she asked me (and probably other writing comadres) to locate "key terms/concepts you find interesting in this essay & the ones you remember from the other essays." Material for this chapter is on Anzaldúa's hard drive, in the folder "08h diss, biblio," subfolder "diss chapters," sub-subfolder "o. toc_preface." This chapter, a file titled "pref-3," was last saved on April 13, 2004. Anzaldúa was also working with material in the following files, located in the "o. toc_preface" subfolder: "chap annotations" (last saved April 13, 2004); "ALKcomments-preface" (last saved January 4, 2004); and "pref-2 notes" (last saved December 9, 2003). For an earlier version of this preface, see the folder titled "drafts" (in diss 08) and the file titled "Intro-Re-Writing Reality-1" (last saved on June 28, 2002).

1. Let us be the healing of the wound: The Coyolxauhqui imperative—la sombra y el sueño

In some ways, it's ironic that this chapter has found its way into *Light in the Dark* and that it effectively sets up the book, functioning as the initial stage in Anzaldúa's chamanistic journey of conocimiento: susto, the fall, el arrabato. Originally, Anzaldúa did not plan to include it in *Light in the Dark*, although she was working on it simultaneously with her dissertation/book project. She wrote "Let us be the healing of the wound" at the invitation of Claire Joysmith and Clara Lomas ("the two Claras," as she described them to me), who were developing a book in response to the September 11, 2001 terrorist attack on the United States. As they envisioned it, the book would be a dialogue between Latina/Chicana-identified authors on both sides of the U.S.-Mexico border. Although Anzaldúa was involved in several other projects with pressing deadlines and was determined to complete her dissertation as soon as possible, she agreed to take part and began pre-drafting what she anticipated would be a short "testimonio statement." The first draft, titled "tiempo de la Llorona: Entremundos: between the shadow and the dream," was completed by December 6, 2001. (This draft is located on Anzaldúa's hard drive, in the folder "08de-drafts," subfolder "drafts-recent essays"; the draft is saved as "testimonio-o.") Anzaldúa produced two additional drafts in December and six more drafts the following month, reluctantly sending the editors the most recent version of her essay, which she felt needed further revision. (These drafts are in "08de-drafts," subfolder "drafts-recent essays.") When the editors contacted her in summer 2003, letting her know that the project was in its final stages and almost ready to go to press, Anzaldúa decided to pull her essay because it did not meet her rigorous standards for good writing. However, because the editors used her piece to develop the volume's title, they persuaded her to leave it in their book and gave her additional time to revise it. Even after she gave them a revised version in September 2003, she was dissatisfied with it, writing to me in an e-mail dated September 29, 2003: "The essay needs more work, at least one more pass but i had to get it off my work schedule"; around this time Anzaldúa decided to use the essay in the dissertation/book "as a prologue as it alludes to most of the ideas found in the other chapters."

In the same e-mail, Anzaldúa wrote, "i may just be prolonging the whole process by including these new things, but i feel that the project lacks cohesiveness, integrity of wholeness—something is missing & adding these two pieces+the preface might flesh it out, make it more of a complete 'entity.' right now the diss feels like it's a body missing some limbs." As this e-mail indicates, although Anzaldúa did not originally plan to include this piece in her dissertation/book project, she revised it (and the other chapters) to highlight key themes. (See appendix 6 for the original call for papers.) I underscore this chapter's origins in 9/11 to complicate future discussions of Anzaldúa's (post) nationalism. It seems important to consider how the editors' invitation that Anzaldúa speak specifically as a Chicana (i.e., as a woman of U.S. citizenship) might have shaped her discussion.

Material for this chapter, including the most recent draft, is on Anzaldúa's hard drive, in the folder "08h diss, biblio," subfolder "diss chapters," sub-subfolder "1. healing of wound." The chapter is the version titled "testimonio-8" (last saved September 25, 2003). Other drafts in this subfolder include "ALK critique of testimonio-4" (last saved January 17, 2002); "Notes-testimonio" (last saved September 25, 2003); "Sept 11 postings" (last saved December 4, 2001); "testimonios-Claire" (last saved January 15, 2002); "Word Work File D2" (last saved January 11, 2002); "Word Work File D3" (last saved January 14, 2002); and "Word Work File D4" (last saved September 5, 2003). Anzaldúa also saved ten more drafts of this essay in her folder "08de-drafts," in the subfolder "drafts-recent essays." The essay drafts are saved as follows: "lara testimonio-6 1_2" (last saved February 3, 2002); "testimonio alk-6" (last saved January 27, 2002); "testimonio-0 (last saved December 6, 2001); "testimonio-1" (last saved December 11, 2001); "testimonio-2" (last saved January 7, 2002): "testimonio-3" (last saved January 14, 2002); "testimonio-4" (last saved January 16, 2002); "testimonio-5" (last saved January 25, 2002); "testimonio-6" (last saved January 26, 2002); "testimonio-6 1_2" (last saved January 29, 2002); "testimonio-6 1_2 b" (last saved February 6, 2002).

2. Flights of the Imagination: Rereading/Rewriting Realities

Anzaldúa wrote this chapter specifically and exclusively for *Light in the Dark* and designed it to pull together the book's themes. It was the final chapter she wrote and (not surprisingly) more fragmented and incomplete than the other chapters in *Light in the Dark*. Fortunately, Anzaldúa wrote it in sections. Thus, while some parts of this chapter were extremely polished, others were not and existed only as notes and partial paragraphs. This pattern was useful when revising the manuscript for publication: I moved the unfinished sections to appendix 3 and inserted notes in the text directing readers to these fragments. Anzaldúa had numerous possible titles for this chapter, including the following: "Flights of Imagination," "Ensueños and the Dreaming Body: Re-Reading/Re-Writing Reality," "Flights of Imagining: Re-Reading and Re-Writing Reality," "Night Horse/Dream Horse: Ensueños and Re-Reading and Re-Writing Reality," and "Flights of the Imagination: Re-Reading/Re-Writing Realities." Had Anzaldúa lived to see the book published, she might have continued revising the title. Although I considered not including this chapter because of these partial sections, it offers significant insights into the development of Anzaldúa's thought, as well as her important information about her creative process and decolonial ontological project. Material for this chapter, including the most recent draft, is located on Anzaldúa's hard drive, in the folder "08h diss, biblio"; subfolder "diss chapters," sub-subfolder "2. flights of imagin." This chapter is the version from the file titled "essay flights of imaginal-2" (last saved on April 8, 2004). The other files in this sub-subfolder are: "add to shamanism" (last saved on June 30, 2002); "lengua" (last saved on July 4, 2002); "notes-flights of imaginal" (last saved on January 12, 2004); and "on writing" (last saved on June 16, 2002).

3. "Border Arte: Nepantla, el Lugar de la Frontera"

The original version of this chapter was first published in 1993, in *La Frontera/The Border: Art about the Mexico/United States Border Experience*, the catalogue for an exhibition curated by Patricio Chávez and Madeleine Grynsztejn and coordinated by Kathryn Kanjo at the Centro Cultural de la Raza and Museum of Contemporary Art in San Diego in 1993. It was later reprinted in the journal MACLA 27.1 under the title "Chicana Artists: Exploring nepantla, el lugar de la Frontera"; in *The Latino Studies Reader: Culture, Economy and Society*, edited by Antonia Darder and Rudolfo D. Torres; and in *The Gloria Anzaldúa Reader*. Anzaldúa revised it considerably for *Light in the Dark*, incorporating themes she was developing in the other chapters. According to her notes, she had also considered adding a section exploring "Non-Native appropriation of Native spirituality and culture." Material for this chapter, including the most recent draft, is on Anzaldúa's hard drive in the folder "o8h diss, biblio"; subfolder "diss chapters," sub-subfolder "3. border arte." This chapter is the file titled "b art-7" (last saved on June 30, 2002). The only other file in this subfolder is "notes-border arte" (last saved on October 1, 2002). Earlier versions of this chapter can be found elsewhere on Anzaldúa's hard drive. In the "o8h diss, biblio" folder, subfolder "drafts," are two files ("b art-5" [last saved on November 17, 2001] and "b art-6" [last saved on May 30, 2002]), and in the folder "o8drafts" are five files ("b art" [last saved July 24, 1992]; "b art-1" [last saved November 9, 1992]; "b art-2" [last saved November 9, 1992]; "b art-3" [last saved around October 24, 1992]; and "b art-3_" [last saved February 9, 1993]).

4. Geographies of Selves—Reimagining Identity: Nos/Otras, Las Nepantleras, and the New Tribalism

This chapter originated in the talk "Nos/otros: Us vs. Them, (Des) Conocimientos y Compromisos," which Anzaldúa delivered on October 29, 1999, at the Territories and Boundaries: Geographies of Latinidad conference organized by Matt García and Angharad Valdivia at the University of Illinois, Urbana-Champaign. Anzaldúa anticipated developing the lecture into a chapter for the conference organizers' proposed collection on Latinidad. She began with the lecture transcript, which was slightly under five thousand words, and developed it into an essay, completing the first draft on December 18, 2001. At this point, Anzaldúa did not plan to include it in her book, but she was open to the possibility, writing to me that "if this paper looks promising i'll substitute if for one of the four i earmarked for the dissertation." This chapter was the most challenging for Anzaldúa to write; it underwent more revisions and was viewed by more external readers than any other chapter, and Anzaldúa expressed great frustration with her attempts to complete it. (Despite these challenges, she was insistent about including this chapter in her book, perhaps because of the ways she developed the Coyolxauhqui imperative.) Anzaldúa did not work on the essay much, if at all, during 2002 but returned to it the following year. She retitled it at least seven times: "Nos/otros: Us vs. Them . . . (Des)Conocimientos y Compromisos" (December 2001); "Nos/otras: Us/Them . . . The New Tribalism and Re-Committing to la Lucha" (January 2002); "Nos/otras: Us/Them . . . Re-Imagining Identity: The New Tribalism and Renewing our Commitment to la Lucha" (January 2003); "Geographies of the Self—Re-Imagining Identity: Nos/otras (Us/Other) and the New Tribalism" (February 2003); "Geography of Selves—Re-Imagining Identity: Nos/otras (Us/Other), and the New Tribalism" (March 2003); "Geography of Selves—Re-Imagining Identity: Nos/otras (Us/Other), Las nepantleras, and the New Tribalism" (Fall 2003); and, ultimately, "Geographies of Selves—Re-Imagining Identities: Nos/otras (Us/Other), Las nepantleras and the New Tribalism" (2004). These titles point to a few of the changes in Anzaldúa's thinking. (For locations of these manuscripts, see below.)

Anzaldúa had been developing her theory of the geography of selves for at least half a decade; as she revised and expanded the transcript, she included notes and excerpts from other lectures and works in progress. At its largest, the draft grew to almost eighteen thousand words. As her e-mails and notes indicate, she felt that the essay was "too abstract"; she wanted to make the piece "more lyrical, imagistic, personal, in other words, *alive*" (her emphasis) and "extend the chief metaphors." There are many reasons for Anzaldúa's difficulty in finishing this piece, ranging from her declining health to the fact that, because she was writing it for a book focused specifically on Latinidad, she had to juggle her interests and changing ideas with the editors' expectations and the book's parameters. Anzaldúa's notes indicate that she would have made substantial revisions to this chapter. I have tried to follow Anzaldúa's editorial notes, but because I believe that her ideas might have changed further before deciding on a "final" version, I have also included material from several excised sections in appendix 4. Material for this chapter, including the most recent drafts, are on Anzaldúa's hard drive, in the folder "08h diss, biblio," subfolder "diss chapters," sub-subfolder "4. geo of selves." The chapter is the file titled "geo o selves_nosotras." Other files in the subfolder are "geo o selves_nosotras-8" (last saved March 23, 2003); "GeoOfSelv.ALK 3_03" (last saved March 3, 2003); "matt garcia.latinidad-intro" (last saved

May 22, 2003); "mat-geo of s-9" (last saved April 30, 2004); and "Notes 1" (last saved January 15, 2004). Additional drafts are in "08h diss, biblio," subfolder "drafts." These files are "GeoOfSelv.ALK 3_03" (last saved March 3, 2003); "GeoOfSelv" (last saved March 3, 2003); "matt-geo of s-2" (last saved May 18, 2003); "matt-geo of s-3" (last saved May 30, 2003); "matt-geo of s-4" (last saved July 16, 2003); "matt-geo of s-5" (last saved September 24, 2003); "matt-geo of s-6" (last saved October 17, 2003); "matt-geo of s-7" (last saved November 28, 2003); "matt-geo of s-8" (last saved February 9, 2004); "matt-geo of selves" (last saved March 16, 2003); "nos_otros urbana 1" (last saved December 17, 2001); "nos_otros urbana-0" (last saved December 17, 2001); "nos_otras urbana-4" (last saved November 10, 2002); "nos_otras urbana-5" (last saved January 21, 2003); "nos_otras urbana-6" (last saved February 5, 2003); "notes-Nos_otras" (last saved May 22, 2003); "notesOSU-geo of selves" (last saved April 21, 2003); "SonomaSU-nepantleras" (last saved May 12, 2003); "Trojan_selling raza_r st" (last saved March 19, 2003); and "Word Work File D 2950" (last saved April 2, 2004).

5. Putting Coyolxauhqui Together: A Creative Process

This chapter originated in an invitation from Marla Morris, Mary Aswell Doll, and William E. Pinar to contribute to their edited collection, *How We Work*, in which writers from a variety of academic disciplines "describe some of their working methods, offering hints and presenting personal quirks and reflections." The piece went through at least seventeen drafts between 1998 and 2003. Anzaldúa worked on it from January through March 1998, completing several pre-drafts and drafts numbered 1–10 during this time. These drafts were written in the first person (as was the original title, "Embodying the Story: How I Write"). Beginning with draft 11 (last modified June 25, 1998), Anzaldúa shifted from first- to second-person narration. Quite possibly, this shift enabled her to address a concern expressed in draft 10:

> I read the second draft and cringe at the dull, heavy-handed sentences, not a breath of poetry anywhere. I grandstand—the narrative mode I picked puts me and my ego in the text too much. The heartbeat of the story is silenced by the dead wood. Not only does the story not say anything new, it says it badly. Más claro canta el gallo. And the voice is the same old one. To be subversive a writer

writes what readers haven't been taught to read—a different and unfamiliar literary form, an experience never articulated before, or a new perspective on a familiar experience. And, I'm not surprising the reader with new ways of telling.

During spring 1998, as she continued drafting and revising the piece, she changed the title numerous times: "Embodying the Story: Writing Process and Habits"; "Embodying the Story: How I Write"; "Embodying the Story: My Process of Writing"; "Embodying la Historia: How I Write/My Process of Writing"; "Working the Story: Como escribes/How You Write"; "The Dance of Nepantla: Dreaming Naguala"; "Re-membering the Bones, Putting Coyolxauhqui Together." She did not decide on the final title, "Putting Coyolxauhqui Together: A Creative Process," until June 1998. (These drafts are on Anzaldúa's hard drive, in the folder "11c book-drafts.") Anzaldúa returned to the piece in January 2002, revising it for inclusion in *Light in the Dark*. Her revisions involved, in part, looking over earlier versions of the draft and selecting sections to revise and reinsert. (She had to cut the draft considerably to meet the edited collection's word count parameters.) Anzaldúa concludes her tenth draft with these words: "I leave you with one final caveat: Approach all meta-stances of referring to and reflecting on the self with suspicion. Like the real self, the writing self is fictitious—something I learned from Jorge Luis Borges. Every piece of writing is a work of fiction." Material for this chapter, including the most recent draft, is located on Anzaldúa's hard drive, in the folder "08h diss, biblio," subfolder "diss chapters," sub-subfolder "5. coyolxauhqui." The sub-subfolder contains the following files: "coyol-14" (last saved January 17, 2002); "coyol-14_" (last saved July 11, 1998); "Coyolxauhqui-1-poem" (last saved November 5, 1997); "elisa, coyol-14" (last saved November 17, 2001); and "irene, coyol-14" (last saved January 22, 2002).

6. now let us shift . . . conocimiento . . . inner work, public acts

Anzaldúa wrote this chapter both for her dissertation/book project and for our co-edited collection, *this bridge we call home: radical visions for transformation*—a multi-genre anthology exploring the legacy of the 1981 classic text, *This Bridge Called My Back: Writings by Radical*

Women of Color (which Anzaldúa had edited with Cherríe Moraga) and the current state of feminism and other social-justice movements. Even in the initial stages Anzaldúa viewed this piece as the "sister essay" to "Putting Coyolxauhqui Together" (chapter 5 in this volume). She began working on the chapter in 1999 and completed it in late 2001. Her goal was to offer an extensive discussion of her theory of conocimiento and an "[a]ttempt to 'queer' the conventional ways of knowing." In her annotations to this chapter, Anzaldúa writes:

> The aim of the essay is to transform my personal life into a narrative with mythological or archetypal threads, not in the confessional tone of a participant in the drama who is seeking another form of order. And to do it representing myself without victimization or sentimentality. Your state of discontent forces you to begin the journey. You want greater meaning. The first step is to choose a path, or allow one to choose you. Your spiritual path requires you to encounter your own dark side and what you have programmed yourself to avoid and to acknowledge your negative traits which inhibit the use of your full capacities and distort how you see things.
>
> Conocimiento deals with two or more dimensions. The goal is also to acquire knowledge and conocimiento, or lucid living. Lucid living means being conscious and fully aware of the fictitious nature of reality while performing one's daily tasks. It is a state of mental and emotional alertness that I call the *path of conocimiento* and I attempt to chart a map of consciousness, trace the journey of your spirit and soul. It's about mapping the shamanic journey on both planes, in the "real" world and in the separate reality, in both inner and outer paths. It means exploring consciously what is normally unconsciously. This results in attaining dual consciousness. We interact with these processes con "*conocimiento*," with consciousness. Conocimiento is about linking the pieces and mapping the journey of your life, your soul's journey. Rewriting a different way of perceiving, of knowing. The model of el mundo zurdo has expanded to the model of conocimiento by incorporating the soul and spirit with nepantla and consciousness/awareness acting as the bridge between political activism and spiritual activism.

This annotation is located on Anzaldúa's hard drive, in the "0. toc_ preface" subfolder: "chap annotations" (last saved April 13, 2004).

The chapter title changed very few times, from "Conocimientos, Now Let Us Shift: Inner Works and Public Acts" and "now let us shift . . . conocimientos . . . inner works and public acts" in October 2000 to "now let us shift . . . the path of conocimiento . . . inner work, public acts" by November. For *Light in the Dark*, Anzaldúa slightly modified the title to "now let us shift . . . conocimiento . . . inner work, public acts." Originally, the essay was to be only seven thousand words and was due in 2000. However (and not surprisingly), Anzaldúa did not meet the deadline or word count. As co-editors, we were able to negotiate an extension from Routledge and make space for her longer essay. I believe that this chapter best represents Anzaldúa's mature writing style because she was able take the time and word count to work through the essay until she achieved a fairly solid sense of satisfaction with it. Material for this chapter, including the most recent draft, is located on Anzaldúa's hard drive, in the folder "08h diss, biblio," subfolder "diss chapters," sub-subfolder "6. now let us shift." This sub-subfolder contains the following files: "add to cono" (last saved November 20, 2001); "cono 15" (last saved September 22, 2001); "cono 15-older" (last saved September 22, 2001); "now let us shift-proofed" (last saved June 20, 2002). Anzaldúa also saved ten more drafts of this essay in the folder "08de-drafts," subfolder "drafts-recent essays." The essay drafts are saved as "cono essay 5" (last saved November 11, 2000); "cono essay 6" (last saved November 22, 2000); "cono essay 7" (last saved December 27, 2000); "cono essay 8" (last saved January 18, 2001); "cono essay 9" (last saved February 1, 2001); "cono essay 10" (last saved May 17, 2001); "cono essay 11" (last saved June 18, 2001); "cono essay 12" (last saved July 13, 2001); "cono essay 13" (last saved August 8, 2001); and "cono essay 14" (last saved September 9, 2001).

Appendix 6 | Invitation and Call for Papers, Testimonios Volume

[The following e-mail is on file with the author. I thank Claire Joysmith for sending me the call for papers.]

From: Claire Joysmith
Date: Tue, 16 Oct 2001
To: Gloria Anzaldúa
Subject: Saludos de Claire y sobre testimonios Latinos

Gloria, I hope things are as good as they can be given the circumstances.

I send you light and good energy for these hard times. This is a time of violence and yet a time of love, too, a time for meeting one's own shadow and that of the human race for what it really is. I feel that what we do now counts even more than it ever did. Cada quien su granito de arena, but with good intentions. It's all we can do individually. The rest is so huge. I was just wondering what the new millennium was bringing and here it is. . . . This is like a purging fire to burn out, albeit with the blood of innocents, the mess we're in. . . . Maybe the new generations can start living for a new future. . . .

I'm sending you a call for testimonios, a project Clara Lomas and I are embarking on to gather feelings and perspectives on what has been happening. I really really hope you can take some time in your busy life to answer, even if very briefly. It is very important, I believe, at this moment, and also to gather all kinds of different voices for different audiences. There are people from many ways in life that have been invited to participate.

As to the deadline, it has been extended 'til after Día de Muertos, 2 de noviembre. I really hope que te vas a animar, mujer, and I appreciate your taking the time to read this and the form and to answer.

I have had you on my mind as I would love to participate in your and AnaLouise K's book, and have been in touch and responded. Pero tengo mucha chamba. . . . I'll try!

Te mando muchos abrazos y cordura en estos tiempos de locura desatada.
Claire

TESTIMONIOS LATINOS IN THE U.S.
11 SEPTEMBER–11 OCTOBER 2001

Compiled and edited by Claire Joysmith, Centro de Investigaciones Sobre América del Norte (CISAN), UNAM, Mexico, and Clara Lomas, Colorado College, U.S.

PROJECT DESCRIPTION
Given the current world events, y "para que no se lo lleve el viento," we are interested in documenting your views, experiences, emotions to these in the form of testimonios to share with Mexican-U.S. transnational audiences.

These testimonios can be expressed in the language(s) of your choice: English, Spanish, or bilingually. As part of this project, we plan to have these in both languages.

Given the pressure of rapidly changing events, we ask your response be limited to the events from September 11 to October 11, 2001, and that you respond by October 23, 2001. Please take time to answer this, even briefly, as this is a unique period historically and your input is of great value to this project. Your response to all these questions is, of course, optional.

FULL NAME:

OCCUPATION:

AFFILIATION:

AGE RANGE (20s, 30s, 40s, 50s, etc.):

CITY AND STATE:

ETHNIC, CULTURAL, LINGUISTIC OR OTHER INFORMATION YOU MIGHT WANT
TO ADD (i.e., Chicana/o, born on the border, second generation in the U.S.,
mother Mexican and father Mexican-American, English and Spanish spoken on
a daily basis, etc.):

QUESTIONS

1. What was your immediate reaction to the events of September 11 and what
   stories would you like to share regarding your experience at the time?

2. How have your feelings, views, and/or way of life changed (personally,
   politically, spiritually) from September 11 to October 11? Please refer to these
   in relation to various areas of your life and work.

3. What issues have opened up and/or changed for you (as regards gender,
   race, class, sexuality, etc.) within the context of this last month's events
   specifically as a Latino/a within the U.S.?

4. What are your perspectives on issues such as:
   · world peace, world war, "an eye for an eye" politics
   · the developing of peace politics and movements
   · cultural and racial differences within and outside the U.S.
   · individual, national and world security
   · the changing faces of justice, fear and forgiveness
   · prophetic and apocalyptic vistas
   · visual vs. verbal media impact
   · creative and aesthetic prospects and challenges
   · new thresholds for healing and spiritual practices

5. What are your views on the Mexican government's prior alliance with
   the U.S. and what impact do you consider recent events might have on
   Mexico-U.S. relations, (im)migration, border restrictions and related topics?

If you have something else you wish to share, such as further narratives or other insights you have not mentioned, please feel free to add this as well.

If you have any questions or comments, please send a separate email to Claire Joysmith and/or Clara Lomas.

Please forward to other Latinos/as you think might be interested in participating in these testimonios.

PLEASE FILL IN THE FOLLOWING:
WOULD YOU AGREE TO THE PUBLICATION OF YOUR ANSWERS IN A COMPLETE OR PARTIAL FORM?
YES _____ NO _____
PLEASE SIGN YOUR NAME IF YOU AGREE

_____

THANK YOU FOR SHARING YOUR TIME AND ENERGY.
OUR HOPE IS THAT THIS MAY BE OF BENEFIT TO OTHERS.

NOTES

Editor's Introduction. Re-envisioning Coyolxauhqui, Decolonizing Reality

1. I first used the term "metaphysics of interconnectedness" to describe Anzaldúa's metaphysics in AnaLouise Keating, "Risking the Personal: An Introduction," in Gloria E. Anzaldúa, *Interviews/Entrevistas*, ed. AnaLouise Keating (New York: Routledge, 2000), 1–15. I described it in more detail in AnaLouise Keating, "'I'm a citizen of the universe': Gloria Anzaldúa's Spiritual Activism as Catalyst for Social Change," *Feminist Studies* 34 (2008): 53–69. In this editor's introduction, I follow conventional philosophical distinctions between "metaphysics" and "ontology," defining the latter as a subfield of the former.

2. As I suggest later in my introduction, the more recent versions of Anzaldúa's book have an expanded emphasis on ontology not seen in the earlier versions. I bracket the prefix in "(trans)formation" to underscore the ambivalent, simultaneous shifts involving both creation and revision: the formation of alternative modes of existence and transitions/shifts between and among already-existing forms.

3. A few of the many titles are "Lloronas, mujeres que leen y escriben: Producing Writing, Knowledge, Cultures, and Identities"; "Lloronas—Women Who Wail: (Self)Representation and the Production of Writing, Knowledge, and Identity"; "Political Reimaginings: The Making of Identity, Spirituality, Reality"; and "Defying Borders, Enacting Nepantla: Rewriting Personal, Polemical, and Spiritual Identities." When I use the word "conversations," I'm referring to various interviews in which Anzaldúa discussed *Lloronas* and her theory of

conocimiento and to the many personal discussions she had with me and other writing comadres about the text. For additional information, see Gloria E. Anzaldúa, *Interviews/Entrevistas*, ed. AnaLouise Keating (New York: Routledge, 2000). Anzaldúa played with other titles, as well, and was very indecisive about which title would be best. In her most recent table of contents (last saved April 13, 2004, in the subfolder "0. toc_preface"), she listed three possibilities: "Light in the Dark: Luz en lo oscuro—Rewriting Identity, Spirituality, Reality"; "Enacting Nepantla: Rewriting Identity"; and "Political Reimaginings: The Making of Identity, Spirituality, Reality." For additional discussions of the dissertation/book drafts, see appendix 1 and appendix 5 in this volume.

4. I discuss most of these concepts later in this introduction and in the glossary. "Autohistoria" and "autohistoria-teoría" represent Anzaldúa's terms for polyvocal, transformational literary forms and methods that blend personal and cultural biography with memoir, fiction, history, myth, and other forms of storytelling. As Sonia Saldívar-Hull suggests, autohistoria represents "a new genre" that presents "history as a serpentine cycle rather than a linear narrative": Sonia Saldívar-Hull, "Critical Introduction," in Gloria Anzaldúa, *Borderlands/La Frontera: The New Mestiza*, 2d ed. San Francisco: Aunt Lute, 1999), 2. Similarly, autohistoria-teoría represents a new genre that engages with history in nonconventional ways. In a fax to Karima Ridgley dated October 20, 1998, Anzaldúa defines "authohistoria-teoría" as "a mixed genre which includes personal and theoretical essay, memoir and autobiography and that uses poetic and fictive elements": Gloria Evangelina Anzaldúa Papers, Benson Latin American Collection, University of Texas Libraries, University of Texas, Austin (hereafter, Anzaldúa Papers), box 133, folder 5. Both autohistoria and autohistoria-teoría foster individual and collective self-growth, sociopolitical resistance, and planetary transformation. While autohistoria focuses more closely on the author's life story and collective history, drawing from and at times fictionalizing it (seen, for example, in Anzaldúa's *Prieta* stories), autohistoria-teoría includes openly theoretical dimensions. I use the term "autohistoria-teoría" rather than "autohistoría," "auto-historia teoría," or any other variation because this is the term Anzaldúa used most often and most recently to describe her theory.

5. Given the changes in Anzaldúa's thought over the final decade of her life, it could be argued that she worked on several dissertations. And given the fact that she did not at any point submit versions of her book (or even proposal drafts of any individual chapters) to the faculty on her "dissertation" committees, it could be argued that Anzaldúa's book projects were dissertation in name only. Regardless, the version from the early 1990s focuses closely on La Llorona and the writing process, while the "final" version, *Light in the Dark*, has a more expansive focus.

6. I use the phrase "Prieta stories" to describe Anzaldúa's short-story cycle/novel-in-stories. Like *Light in the Dark*, Anzaldúa's Prieta stories underwent many revisions and title changes over the years. Anzaldúa began working on the stories (although with a differently named protagonist) in the 1970s and was still working on them at the time of her death. As her references to *Los ensueños de La Prieta* in the preface, chapter 2, and chapter 4 indicate, she was working on these stories simultaneously with *Light in the Dark*. For drafts of Anzaldúa's stories, see Anzaldúa Papers, box 73, folder 23, box 82, folders 1–6. Additional drafts are located on her hard drive in the folder "05i La Prieta," subfolder "naguala_nepantla." For Anzaldúa's discussions of the Prieta stories, see Anzaldúa's *Interviews/Entrevistas*. For a published example, see "Reading LP," in AnaLouise Keating, ed., *The Gloria Anzaldúa Reader* (Durham, NC: Duke University Press, 2009), 250–73.

7. Many examples of this aspect of Anzaldúa's writing process are in her extensive archives, the Anzaldúa Papers. For a discussion of these archives and their potential, see Bost, "Messy Archives and Materials that Matter," forthcoming in *PMLA* 130, no. 3 (2015). AnaLouise Keating, "Archival Alchemy and Allure: The Gloria Evangelina Anzaldúa Papers as Case Study," *Aztlán: A Journal of Chicano Studies* 35, no. 2 (2010): 159–71.

8. In the preface, Anzaldúa says that she borrows the term "daimon" from James Hillman. See chapter 2, note 2, for this discussion.

9. The drafts of two essays from the 1980s—"La Prieta" and "Speaking in Tongues"—offer an excellent illustration of how Anzaldúa moved material among several essays. See the discussion of this revision process in Betsy Dahms, "Shamanic Urgency and Two-Way Movement as Writing Style in the Works of Gloria Anzaldúa," *Letras Femeninas* 38, no. 2 (2012): 9–26. The drafts of "La Prieta" are in Anzaldúa Papers, box 14, folders 14–18. Drafts of "Speaking in Tongues" are in Anzaldúa Papers, box 14, folders 19–21, box 15, folders 1–3.

10. "Writing notas" was Anzaldúa's phrase for the collections of notes she curated for various projects.

11. In an unpublished early draft of what eventually became "Putting Coyolxauhqui Together: A Creative Process" (chapter 5 of this book), Anzaldúa summarized her writing process as a series of nine steps:

1. Dream, envision and conceptualize the total "story"; take notes; imaging sections/scenes, beginning, middle, and end; broad outline; freewrite
2. Research; take notes; key in everything; freewrite; print draft
3. Organize, add, delete sections (3 to 6 pre-drafts); freewrite
4. Gestate for several days
5. First draft, use imaging process to let the story develop on its own, occasionally looking at outline and notes; free write

6. Read through; revise; freewrite

7. Revision, revise, and rewrite (10–30 drafts). Too much detail confuses, bores. What does the reader need, how does she want to react? Write to the reader's expectations but also against her expectations. Comadres read the story

8. Gestate, lie fallow

9. Edit; rewrite; proofread; tidy up (two to four drafts); send out and go public. And to the marketplace.

12. Anzaldúa, *Interviews/Entrevistas*, 174.

13. Chapters 3 and 5 of this book illustrate Anzaldúa's post-publication revisions. For further discussion of these chapters and others, see appendix 5. Anzaldúa's extensive revision process, coupled with her perfectionist tendencies, opens additional possibilities for posthumous publications. I envision several additional volumes of Anzaldúa's previously unpublished work; these volumes include fiction, drama, autohistoria, philosophical essays, poetry, and interviews.

14. Gloria E. Anzaldúa and Hector A. Torres, "The Author Never Existed" (1990), in *Conversations with Contemporary Chicana and Chicano Authors*, ed. Hector A. Torres (Albuquerque: University of New Mexico Press, 2007), 122.

15. For a more detailed discussion of her reasons for leaving the doctoral program at the University of Texas, Austin, see Anzaldúa and Torres, "The Author Never Existed." For Anzaldúa's autohistoria-teoría of this event, see chapter 6 in this volume. It is worth noting that although Anzaldúa had not yet taken her qualifying exams, she had begun working on her dissertation, according to a journal entry dated December 13, 1975, in which she outlines her tentative chapters and writes, "I have two done and the short prose almost finished. I have the basic outline. I'm happy." The chapters were as follows:

1. Short fiction
2. Fantasy (Borges & Cortázar)
3. Fantasy short prose
4. Chicano lit
5. Surrealist
6. Lacan & Cortázar
7. Symbolism & Mysticism
8. Modern decadence
9. Meta-fiction
10. Aesthetics–Reality of art

This journal is located at the Benson Library.

16. "Sacred Vernacular—Female Deities," on file with the editor.

17. In an unpublished manuscript draft titled "SIC: Spiritual Identity Crisis: A Series of Vignettes," Anzaldúa includes an enigmatic statement indicating

that she also viewed her return to graduate school as an opportunity to challenge herself by practicing the genre of academic writing: "I've resisted academic language but then felt that there was a language I'd turn away from and that I should return to grad. school and learn that language[.]" This document, last saved August 27, 1999, is on Anzaldúa's hard drive in a subfolder titled "sic."

18. Anzaldúa had actually applied to UCSC's doctoral program in the History of Consciousness, but her application was denied. For her discussion of this event, see Anzaldúa and Torres, "The Author Never Existed."

19. Anzaldúa and Torres, "The Author Never Existed," 124.

20. Anzaldúa had two dissertation committees. In the 1990s, the committee was chaired by Helene Moglen and composed of Norma Alarcón, Donna Haraway, and José David Saldívar. Due to faculty departures, the 2000s committee was chaired by Moglen, with Haraway and Aída Hurtado as committee members. While writing this editor's introduction, I contacted all five of these faculty, who told me that they did not at any point see dissertation chapters, although all members of her committee in the 1990s recall her qualifying exam and discussions related to her ideas of the time. I am grateful to Professors Alarcón, Haraway, Hurtado, Moglen, and Saldívar for responding so quickly and generously to my queries about Anzaldúa's dissertation/book project.

21. See, e.g., Anzaldúa's statement near the end of chapter 2: "I propose a new perspective on imagining, and a new relationship to the imagination, to healing, and to shamanic spirituality." As an anonymous reviewer of this manuscript observed, "This language of 'I propose' seems very unlike Anzaldúa—not the style in which she advances ideas in her other published work." Perhaps Anzaldúa was here adopting an intentionally distinct scholarly tone. Consider also Anzaldúa's use of second person in chapter 5 and chapter 6. It could be useful to speculate on how these stylistic choices might have been influenced by her view of this manuscript as both a dissertation and a publishable book.

22. Ann E. Reuman, "Coming into Play: An Interview with Gloria Anzaldúa," MELUS 25, no. 2 (Summer 2000).

23. For a draft of Anzaldúa's dissertation proposal and projected table of contents (which she never submitted to her dissertation committee), see appendix 1.

24. This document is on Anzaldúa's hard drive in the folder "08h diss, biblio"; subfolder "4+for diss"; sub-subfolder "9. llorona." According to Anzaldúa's notes, she last revised it on March 9, 1999; it was last saved June 8, 2002. The document is in Anzaldúa Papers, box 93, folder 14.

25. According to Anzaldúa, Coyolxauhqui is pronounced "Ko-yol-sha-UH-kee." Coatlicue is pronounced "Kwat-LEE-kw-y."

26. Anzaldúa did not work on her Lloronas book chapter by chapter, drafting one chapter at a time. Instead, she worked on several chapters simultaneously. As she explained in an interview conducted in 1991 (at a time that she was working consistently on this project),

> In writing my dissertation [the committee] expected me to finish one chapter. And I said, "This is my process: I write all the chapters at the same time and bring them up through the second draft, the third draft all together. I don't have just one finished thing because I don't know where things are going to go." They don't understand that process because they plan a book: They perfect the introduction, they perfect the first chapter, the second chapter; they publish those. I don't work that way. All the pieces have to be on the table and I'm adding and subtracting pieces and I'm shifting them around. So there tends to be a lot of repetition in my work, I put the same thing in two or three chapters because ultimately I don't know where it's going to end up. (Anzaldúa, *Interviews/Entrevistas*, 175)

27. E-mail on file with the editor.

28. Because Anzaldúa was diagnosed with diabetes as an adult, scholars sometimes assume that she had type 2 diabetes. However, as I explain in "Working towards Wholeness," Anzaldúa was diagnosed with type 1 diabetes, which in many ways can be more life-altering. Unlike type 2 diabetes, which occurs when the body produces insulin but is unable to use it, type 1 diabetes occurs when the body stops producing insulin. Type 1 diabetes is an autoimmune-deficiency disease that happens when the body's autoimmune system no longer functions properly and begins killing off the cells in the pancreas that produce insulin. Type 2 diabetes can be prevented and managed through attention to exercise and diet. Type 1 diabetes, however, is caused by a combination of genetic and environmental factors, and treatment requires constant monitoring and medication. For additional information on diabetes, see Amelia María de la Luz Montes, "Glucose Logs: Anzaldúa and the Story of Blood," paper presented at El Mundo Zurdo: An International Conference on the Life and Work of Gloria Anzaldúa, San Antonio, November 2013, and "Why Diabetes Is Not Like Any Other Disease . . . And What You Can Do about It!" http://labloga.blogspot.com/2012/09/why-diabetes-is-not-like-any-other.html (accessed September 30, 2012). The following discussion of Anzaldúa's health is drawn from AnaLouise Keating, "'Working towards wholeness': Gloria Anzaldúa's Struggles to Live with Diabetes and Chronic Illness," in *The Cultural Mediations of Latina Health*, ed. Angie Chabram-Dernersesian and Adela de la Torres (Tucson: University of Arizona Press, 2008), 133–43; and the time I spent with Anzaldúa.

29. As she writes in chapter 6, "When first diagnosed with diabetes, your response was denial. This couldn't be happening, hadn't your body paid its dues? Why now, when you had the time and means to do good work. Digging in your heels you refused the reality—always your first line of defense to emotional pain. But the reality intruded: your body had betrayed you. You no longer had the agility to climb up to the roof to check the leak over the living room. Were you being punished for having been found wanting? No, it is you, not an external force, punishing yourself."

30. Although Anzaldúa mentions her struggles with diabetes in a few of the interviews collected in *Interviews/Entrevistas*, she offers the most intimate, extensive discussion of its impact on her writing and her psyche in the final two chapters of *Light in the Dark*. She also describes her relationship with diabetes in an unpublished manuscript, variously titled "SIC: Spiritual Identity Crisis" and "SIC: The Geography of Illness": Anzaldúa Papers, box 64, folder 22. For additional discussions, see Suzanne Bost, "Diabetes, Culture, and Food: Post-humanist Nutrition in the Gloria Anzaldúa Archive," in *Rethinking Chicana/o Literature through Food: Postnational Appetites*, ed. Nieves Pascual Soler and Meredith E. Abarca (New York: Palgrave Macmillan, 2014), 27–43; Montes, "Glucose Logs." Concerning her insomnia, Anzaldúa writes, "The bane of my life is insomnia, probably caused by mis-set internal clock which results in sleep-wake disorders. Again my circadian rhythms are disturbed—I have a conflict between my natural cycle and the sleep time I want to have. I have a shift work schedule—my sleeping times are never the same." This statement is in the file "Lloronas book: Rewriting Reality," subfolder "4+for diss." The document was last saved July 28, 2002, although it was probably written at least several years before that date.

31. Securing reasonably priced health insurance was a particularly difficult financial challenge for Anzaldúa because of her status as self-employed.

32. Here is the journal entry in its entirety:

Books
    Growing Up Working Class
    Prietita Tiene Un Amigo—Spanish version needs revision
    Entreguerras/entremundos—update table
    Lloronas, Woman Who Wails—prospectus for grants tidy—up table
Signs
    W(riting) Manos
    Theory By Chicanas
    De las otras/De los otros
    Nightface/Cara de noche
    Mestiza Consciousness

Projects—papers
  Five yrs of Income Tax
  Introduction—Dissenting Stories
  Q.E. [QUALIFYING EXAM]
Paper—Autohistorias
  I.D. for Liz Grosz
  The Loft Seminar—lesson plans
  Prospectus
Submissions for Publication
  Lesbian Love Stories II—Ms. Right
  Short Short—Irene Zahava "Puddles," A Tale, Ghost Trap, Dear P
  Mother/daughter—Irene Zahava Myself & (M)other
  Diane Freedman—Autobiographical Literary Criticism—Poet as Critic
  Betsy Warland—Lesbians Writing about their own writing Sept 30
  Shelley Fishkin—Silencio de me espacio
  Christian McEwen—Baring Witness [Baring] Oct. 31
  Gale Greene—Coppelia Kahn draft Dec 15 final end Jan
  Charles Tatum—"Dance of Death" Ghost Trap, Puddles
  Grand St. Magazine
Grant Proposals
  Guggenheim—Llorona
  FRA—Research in MX (José Saldívar–recom.)
  NEA—for the 6th time—Got it!
  Pergamnon—NWSA Grad. Sch. In [women's] Studies Feb 15
  Cottages at Hedgebrook July 10–Dec 10—deadline April 1/Jan 10–June 30—deadline Oct. 1

Note that Anzaldúa refers to her dissertation/book project in her list of "Grant Proposals." This entry is in Anzaldúa's journal dated February 5, 1990–May 21, 1994, Anzaldúa Papers.

33. This entry is in Anzaldúa's journal dated February 5, 1990–May 21, 1994, Anzaldúa Papers.

34. This mobile writing practice also contributed to Anzaldúa's almost constant sense of disappointment with her published work, which she never viewed as final or as finished. As she writes in her journal for August 1987, when she finished the article "En Rapport, In Opposition: Cobrando Cuentas a las Nuestras" for *Sinister Wisdom*, "I regret not having the time to hone it. I never get enough time. The deadlines are upon me before I know it." I noticed the same pattern during my work with Anzaldúa. She regularly criticized her "final" drafts and bemoaned the encroaching deadlines (which she typically renegotiated or ignored, in order to give more time to her various projects).

35. Anzaldúa wrote "now let us shift" for our edited collection *this bridge we call home*. We missed our submission deadline by an entire year because Anzaldúa would not stop revising her essay. This delay was possible only because Anzaldúa was co-editing the collection and Bill Germano, our editor at Routledge, respected Anzaldúa's work and was extremely patient. You can see Anzaldúa's many drafts of this chapter in Anzaldúa Papers, box 49, folders 2–14, box 50, folders 1–18, box 51, folders 1–12. For additional information on Anzaldúa's writing process, see chapter 5 in this volume and Anzaldúa Papers.

36. Las comadritas originally consisted of three other doctoral students—Irene Lara, Deb Vargas, and Yolanda Venegas. In early February 2002, Vargas withdrew from the dissertation group because of additional commitments. For additional information on las comadritas, see their e-mail communication in Anzaldúa Papers. For Anzaldúa's dissertation committees of the 1990s and 2000s, see note 20 in this editor's introduction. Neither dissertation committee saw or commented on any drafts of the dissertation. I base my summary of Anzaldúa's dissertation history on her e-mail communication, our conversations, and my communication with her committee members.

37. As Wilson explained to Anzaldúa, the dissertation fast track already existed. The department was not making an exception for her.

38. This short document is in the subfolder "old diss prospectus, biblio," in the dissertation folder on Anzaldúa's laptop. The document was last saved May 20, 2002, although Anzaldúa wrote it much earlier.

39. The previously published essays that Anzaldúa planned to revise and include were "To(o) Queer the Writer: Reading, Writing, and Identity"; "Border Arte: Nepantla, el lugar de la Frontera"; and "Putting Coyolxauhqui Together: A Creative Process." In September 2003, Anzaldúa decided to include only two of these three in the final version. She explained that she would not include "To(o) Queer the Writer," because it was "a much older piece & may be too different from the other chapters": e-mail on file with the editor.

40. Anzaldúa decided to include two of the essays she had been working on intermittently during the early 2000s: her "9/11 essay" and her "Geography of Selves" essay. These essays became chapter 1 and chapter 4, respectively. I discuss them in more detail later and offer additional background information in appendix 5. In an e-mail dated September 29, 2003, Anzaldúa suggests that she is close to finalizing the table of contents: "I'm thinking of using the 9/11 essay as a prologue as it alludes to most of the ideas found in the other chapters. if I do that I may want to have an epilogue, maybe just something a page long, like a poem or short prose piece, something that I've already written": e-mail communication, on file with the editor.

41. In fall 2003, Anzaldúa decided to include these last two projects in *Light in the Dark*, as the book's first and last chapters. For examples of Anzaldúa's

work during this time, see, e.g., Anzaldúa Papers, boxes 46–54, box 69, folders 15–17.

42. In the last years of her life, Anzaldúa was beset by numerous diabetes-related complications. For her description of these challenges, see appendix 2.

43. Anzaldúa's documentation was in disarray. Sometimes she used footnotes; sometimes she used endnotes. Sometimes she included page numbers; sometimes she did not. Sometimes she used a modified MLA style; other times, she used Chicago style or no particular documentation style at all. Often the bibliographical information was partial or even incorrect. One aspect of my work involved researching her sources to provide missing bibliographical details.

44. Anzaldúa used this phrase in an e-mail to me dated April 4, 2004.

45. Beginning with my 1991 interview with Anzaldúa, I had edited a number of her interviews; given her extensive feedback on drafts of her fiction, poetry, interviews, essays, and dissertation chapters; and worked with her as we co-edited this bridge we call home and the unpublished Bearing Witness, Reading Lives: Imagination, Creativity, and Cultural Change. After Anzaldúa's death, I edited The Gloria Anzaldúa Reader, a selection of her previously published and unpublished work in a range of genres. Although this extensive experience prepared me to edit Light in the Dark, Anzaldúa's dissertation project had some additional challenges. My work editing The Gloria Anzaldúa Reader included a large degree of flexibility as I sorted through Anzaldúa's unpublished material and selected the pieces to include, but editing Light in the Dark had more constraints. I could not simply swap out a chapter that seemed less polished with something else from Anzaldúa's extensive oeuvre. Light in the Dark's chapters and their organization had been predetermined by Anzaldúa herself.

46. For a useful discussion of Anzaldúa's theory of the Coyolxauhqui imperative, see Ricardo Vivancos Pérez, Radical Chicana Poetics (New York: Palgrave Macmillan, 2013).

47. Coyolxauhqui symbolizes multiple colonizations: the shift from egalitarian to patriarchal society, from the Mexica to the Aztec conquerors, from one world system to another. As Irene Lara notes, "According to feminist interpreters, this story marks a shift in Mexica history from a gynecentric to androcentric ordering of life and the simultaneous divestment of female power": Irene Lara, "Daughter of Coatlicue: An Interview with Gloria Anzaldúa," in EntreMundos/AmongWorlds: New Perspectives on Gloria Anzaldúa, ed. AnaLouise Keating (New York: Palgrave Macmillan, 2005), 41. See also Anzaldúa's comment, "Coyolxauhqui and putting herself, ourself, together is about healing the wounds, the work of striving for wholeness instead of being fragmented in little pieces": Lara, "Daughter of Coatlicue," 49.

48. Anzaldúa, quoted in Lara, "Daughter of Coatlicue," 44.

49. Curanderismo can be described as an indigenous Mexican healing practice, or shamanism, that relies on a mixture of rituals, belief, and specific practices. Anzaldúa often used the words "chamanismo" and "chamana" to challenge masculinist, eurocentric assumptions.

50. There is no single innovator for the term "spiritual activism." Anzaldúa and others began using it around the same time. For a discussion of Anzaldúa's spiritual activism, see Keating, "I'm a citizen of the universe." For a discussion of Anzaldúa's introduction of the term into feminist scholarship, see Karlyn Crowley, *Feminism's New Age: Gender, Appropriation, and the Afterlife of Essentialism* (Buffalo: State University of New York Press, 2011).

51. "Chican@" is used to signal all genders.

52. Anzaldúa's theory of new tribalism also represents a tongue-in-cheek rejoinder to those critics who viewed her theorization of identity in *Borderlands* as a romanticized appropriation of indigeneity. As she explains in the notes to chapter 4, "In 1991 I 'appropriated' and recycled the term 'new tribalism' from David Rieff who uses it to criticize . . . what he sees as my naive and nostalgic return to indigenous roots. . . . I take his criticism and go beyond . . . by taking the term 'new tribalism' to formulate other takes on identity particularly a more expanded and inclusive identity."

53. This quotation can be found in "Word Work File D 2950," last saved April 2, 2004.

54. I thank Betsy Dahms for reminding me of these connections.

55. See, e.g., Hernández, *Postnationalism in Chicana/o Literature and Culture* (Austin: University of Texas Press, 2009). Although Hernández focuses on Anzaldúa's twentieth-century work, she offers a useful analysis of some of Anzaldúa's postnationalist dimensions.

56. Anzaldúa explores her theories of "nos/otras," "nepantleras," and the "geography of self" in other unpublished writings, which I hope to edit for future publication. For previous discussions of these theories, see Anzaldúa, *Interviews/Entrevistas*, and her unpublished interviews in Anzaldúa Papers.

57. These notes are on Anzaldúa's hard drive, in the document "chap annotations," in the subfolder "o.toc_preface."

58. I put the prefix in "(non)completion" in parentheses to underscore Anzaldúa's drive to continue revising her work beyond deadlines and publication; even as she submitted the essay, she made plans to continue revising it. (And, as its inclusion in *Light in the Dark* indicates, she did indeed revise it after publication.)

59. For Anzaldúa, "imaginal" and "imaginary" are not synonymous. She follows James Hillman, who follows Henry Corbin, in using the term "imaginal" to refer to another aspect or dimension of reality with as much validity as the

conventional, visible world to which we generally refer using terms such as "reality." It would be fruitful to put Anzaldúa's theory of the imaginal in dialogue with recent work in transnational American studies: see, e.g., Laura Bieger et al., eds., *The Imaginary and Its Worlds: American Studies after the Transnational Turn* (Lebanon, NH: Dartmouth College Press, 2013).

60. As Anzaldúa states in her endnotes to the chapter, "This essay is sister to 'Putting Coyolxauhqui Together.'"

61. For useful discussions of conocimiento, see Kelli Zaytoun, "New Pathways towards Understanding Self-in-Relation: Anzaldúan (Re)Visions for Developmental Psychology," in Keating, *EntreMundos/AmongWorlds*, 147–59, and "Theorizing at the Borders: Considering Social Location in Rethinking Self and Psychological Development," NWSA *Journal* 18, no. 2 (2006): 52–72.

62. These notes are on Anzaldúa's hard drive, in the document "chap annotations," in the subfolder "o.toc_preface."

63. Anzaldúa saved these specific versions of her *Lloronas* table of contents and chapter outline from the 1990s in her twenty-first-century dissertation folder, in the subfolder "old diss prospectus, biblio." For additional information, see appendix 1.

64. For the history of Anzaldúa's composing and revision process for each chapter, see appendix 5.

65. When I discuss Anzaldúa's "outsider status," I am referring to her location as a woman of color working primarily outside the university, without conventional academic training in philosophy, who breaks conventional genre expectations and thus produces work that does not fit with typical assumptions about philosophical and theoretical discourse. As I explained in *Transformation Now!* Anzaldúa's work, like that of many other women of color, typically has been used to illustrate rather than to theorize.

66. See Sarah Ohmer, "Gloria E. Anzaldúa's Decolonizing Ritual de Conocimiento." *Confluencia* 26, no. 1 (2010): 141–53.

67. Ernesto Martínez, *On Making Sense: Queer Race Narratives of Intelligibility* (Stanford, CA: Stanford University Press, 2013).

68. I borrow the word "desconocimiento" from Anzaldúa, who coined the term and defines it as a type of (almost) willed ignorance, a partially chosen avoidance of knowing (conocimiento).

69. Mikko Tuhkanen, "Mestiza Metaphysics," in *Queer Times, Queer Becomings*, ed. E. L. McCallum and Mikko Tuhkanen (New York: State University of New York Press, 2011), 260. Sally Haslanger makes a similar point when she writes, "Academic feminists, for the most part, view metaphysics as a dubious intellectual project, certainly irrelevant and probably worse; and often the further charge is leveled that it has pernicious political implications as well": Sally Haslanger, "Feminism in Metaphysics: Negotiating the Natural," in *The Cam-*

bridge Companion to Feminism in Philosophy, ed. Miranda Fricker and Jennifer Hornsby (Cambridge: Cambridge University Press, 2000). For additional discussions of the limited attention paid to metaphysics and ontology, see "The Revival of Metaphysics in Continental Philosophy," in Graham Harman, *Towards Speculative Realism: Essays and Lectures* (Winchester, UK: Zero Books, 2010).

70. Tuhkanen, "Mestiza Metaphysics," 260.

71. See the analysis of the relational ontology in Anzaldúa's early poem, "Tihueque," in Robyn Henderson-Espinoza, "The Entanglement of Anzaldúan Materiality as Bodily Knowing: Matter, Meaning, and Interrelatedness." PhD diss., Iliff School of Theology, Denver, CO, 2015.

72. Speculative realism and object-oriented ontology are post-Kantian metaphysics, strands of twenty-first-century continental philosophy that decenter the human and shift the focus beyond epistemological concerns to include ontological issues—speculation about reality, as it were. Object-oriented ontology is a subset of speculative realism. For more on speculative realism, see Levi Bryant et al., *The Speculative Turn: Continental Materialism and Realism* (Melbourne: Re.press, 2011). For more on both speculative realism and object-oriented ontology, see Graham Harman, *Guerrilla Metaphysics: Phenomenology and the Carpentry of Things* (Chicago: Open Court, 2005); *Tool-Being: Heidegger and the Metaphysics of Objects* (Chicago: Open Court, 2002); and *Towards Speculative Realism*. Harman coined the term "object-oriented ontology" and defines it in *Tool-Being*; he has been one of its biggest proponents, along with Timothy Morton and Levi Bryant. Anzaldúa's object-oriented ontology preceded that of these figures. She was not in dialogue with them, although perhaps they should be in dialogue with her. I use the term "neo-materialism," rather than the more common "new materialisms," to distinguish recent trends in materialism from the earlier work by women-of-color theorists who have been producing intensely embodied, materialist theory for decades. I would, of course, include Anzaldúa in that category, with Norma Alarcón, Hortense Spillers, Sandy Soto, Emma Pérez, Paula Gunn Allen, and others. Rather than build on this important work, neo-materialists such as Clare Colbrook, Elizabeth Grosz, Susan Hekman, and Elizabeth Wilson often seem to view their approach as an almost entirely new "turn" in feminist or philosophical thought. Because these feminist neo-materialisms gained visibility after Anzaldúa's death, she did not put her work into dialogue with this scholarship; had she lived longer, she probably would have done so. One important connection between neo-materialisms and Anzaldúa is that Donna Haraway's work is generally put into this category and, as I mentioned earlier, Haraway taught at UCSC and was on Anzaldúa's dissertation committees (which indicates Anzaldúa's respect for Haraway's work, but because Haraway did not engage with Anzaldúa's dissertation/book project, we cannot presume any type of direct influence).

73. Harman, *Towards Speculative Realism*, 145.

74. Anthropocentrism centers human beings. While Anzaldúa generally focuses on human actions and human work in the world, she does not view humans as the center of the universe. Nor does she conflate reality with the ideas in our heads or with what we can know.

75. Stacy Alaimo and Susan Hekman, "Introduction: Emerging Models of Materiality in Feminist Theory," in *Material Feminisms*, ed. Stacy Alaimo and Susan Hekman (Bloomington: Indiana University Press, 2008), 9.

76. I use the word "material(izing)" to underscore language's ontological, agentic status and to distinguish Anzaldúa's aesthetics from mainstream poststructuralist approaches to language.

77. From the mid-1970s onward, Anzaldúa researched Nahuatl, Mayan, Celtic, Yoruban, and other indigenous philosophies and "shamanistic traditions," along with the I Ching, Tarot, Sabian Symbols, and other "alchemic" traditions and knowledge forms. For discussions of her wide-ranging research, see Anzaldúa, *Interviews/Entreviews*; Randy P. Conner, "Santa Nepantla: A Borderlands Sutra" (plenary speech), in *El Mundo Zurdo: Selected Works from the Meetings of the Society for the Study of Gloria Anzaldúa 2007 and 2009*, ed. Norma E. Cantú, Christina L. Guttiérrez, Norma Alarcón, and Rita E. Urquijo-Ruiz (San Francisco: Aunt Lute, 2010), 177–202; Amala Levine, "Champion of the Spirit: Anzaldúa's Critique of Rationalist Epistemology," in Keating, *EntreMundos/AmongWorlds*, 171–84. I understand that, by definition, esoteric traditions could be considered western. However, I view them as western discards because of their limited status in western academic contexts.

78. For additional analyses of Anzaldúa's shamanic imagery, see David Carrasco and Roberto Lint Sagarena, "The Religious Vision of Gloria Anzaldúa *Borderlands/La Frontera* as a Shamanic Space," in *Mexican American Religions: Spirituality, Activism, and Culture*, ed. Gastón Espinosa (Durham, NC: Duke University Press, 2008), 223–41; Dahms, "Shamanic Urgency and Two-Way Movement as Writing Style in the Works of Gloria Anzaldúa." I've borrowed and modified portions of this discussion from AnaLouise Keating, "Speculative Realism, Visionary Pragmatism, and Poet-Shamanic Aesthetics in Gloria Anzaldúa—and Beyond," *Women's Studies Quarterly* 40, nos. 3–4 (2012): 51–69.

79. This passage is from Anzaldúa's notes to chapter 2, last saved January 12, 2004, in the subfolder "2. flights of imagin."

80. This issue is further complicated by Anzaldúa's references to Carlos Castaneda and his pseudo-anthropological fiction. To be sure, Anzaldúa acknowledges the limitations of Castaneda's works, describing them in chapter 2 as "novels" that Castaneda "passed off as anthropological field notes." However, her respect for the imagination's epistemological and ontological functions prevents her from entirely rejecting Castaneda's work (because imagination,

according to Anzaldúa, gives us access to important truths—valid and useful information about reality). Josefina Saldaña-Portillo illustrates the critique of claims about indigenous identity made by Anzaldúa and other Chican@s; she argues that such claims represent a form of Mexican "indigenismo," a "state-sponsored policy" that "recuperat[es] and celebrat[es]" an indigenous past while simultaneously erasing contemporary Indian peoples and thus facilitating Mexican colonialism, including ownership of the land: Josefina Saldaña-Portillo, "Who's the Indian in Azatlán? Re-Writing Mestizaje, Indianism, and Chicanismo from the Lacandón," in *The Latin American Subaltern Studies Reader*, ed. Ileana Rodríguez (Durham, NC: Duke University Press, 2001), 408. For Anzaldúa's thoughtful engagement with Saldaña-Portillo's critique, see Gloria E. Anzaldúa, "Speaking across the Divide" (2003), in Keating, *The Gloria Anzaldúa Reader*, 282–94. As Anzaldúa notes, Saldaña-Portillo focuses too narrowly on a small section of *Borderlands* and overlooks the ways in which Anzaldúa's views changed in her later work. Sheila Contreras offers another extensive criticism of this colonizing gesture, arguing that Anzaldúa and other Chicana feminists developed an "indigenist feminism" that relied on a eurocentric "modern primitivism" that coopts and obscures the identities and needs of real-life indigenous peoples: Sheila Contreras, "Literary Primitivism and the New Mestiza," 56. As I suggest in this editor's introduction, I view these critiques of Anzaldúa as somewhat ungenerous and myopic. For additional discussions of this issue, see George Hartley, "Chican@ Indigeneity, the Nation-State, and Colonialist Identity Formations," in *Comparative Indigeneities of the Américas: Toward a Hemispheric Approach*, ed. M. Bianet Castellanos, Lourdes Gutiérrez Nájera, and Arturo J. Aldama (Tucson: University of Arizona Press, 2012), 53–66.

81. Lara, "Daughter of Coatlicue," 53.

82. Jeffrey J. Kripal, *Comparing Religions: Coming to Terms* (Malden, MA: Wiley-Blackwell, 2014).

83. Anzaldúa, *Interviews/Entrevistas*, 176.

84. For Anzaldúa's discussion of the volitional aspect in her theory of nepantleras, see esp. chapter 4 in this volume. For the autobiographical dimensions of the term's origins, see chapter 6.

85. See also Anzaldúa's discussion of the "nepantla brain" in chapter 4.

86. The phrase "liberatory space" is Emma Pérez's; see Pérez, "Gloria Anzaldúa." For more examples of typical interpretations, see the description of nepantla as a state of mind analogous to the Coatlicue state in Alicia Gaspar de Alba, "Crop Circles in the Cornfield: Remembering Gloria E. Anzaldúa (1942–2004)," *American Quarterly* 56, no. 3 (2004): iv–vii, and the reference to nepantla as a "cultural and psychological location" in Laura E. Pérez, "Spirit Glyphs: Re-imagining Art and Artist in the Work of Chicana Tlamatinime," *Modern Fiction*

Studies 44, no. 1 (1998): 51. Scholars who focus on "now let us shift," Anzaldúa's essay version of chapter 6 in this volume, have offered the most expansive analyses of nepantla thus far. As Norma Alarcón notes, "In this essay, the concept-metaphor of Nepantla receives a broader and larger characterization and definition than ever before in the Anzaldúan corpus": Norma Alarcón, "Anzaldúan Textualities: A Hermeneutic of the Self and the Coyolxauhqui Imperative," in *El Mundo Zurdo 3: Selected Works from the 2012 Meeting of the Society for the Study of Gloria Anzaldúa*, ed. Larissa M. Mercado-López, Sonia Saldívar-Hull, and Antonia Castañeda (San Francisco: Aunt Lute, 2013), 199. See also the description of nepantla as "identity-related, but also an epistemology, as well as a creative faculty," in Sarah Ohmer, "Gloria E. Anzaldúa's Decolonizing Ritual de Conocimiento," *Confluencia* 26, no. 1 (2010), and as "the precarious but only possible home for a nepantlera subjectivity" in Martina Koegeler-Abdi, "Shifting Subjectivities: Mestizas, Nepantleras, and Gloria Anzaldúa's Legacy," MELUS 38, no. 2 (2013): 71.

87. José David Saldívar, "Unsettling Race, Coloniality, and Caste: Anzaldúa's *Borderlands/La Frontera*, Martinez's *Parrot in the Oven*, and Roy's *God of Small Things*," *Cultural Studies* 21, nos. 2–3 (2007): 350.

Preface. Gestures of the Body

1. Epistemology, the theory of knowledge, studies the means of cognition.

2. "Daimon" is a term from the ancient Greeks. James Hillman calls psychic figures "daimons," while the Catholic Church calls them "demons." According to James Hillman, Carl Jung discovered "psychic reality," claiming that it is peopled by poetic, dramatic fictions, "powers with voice, body, motion, and mind, fully felt but wholly imaginary. This is psychic reality, and it comes in the shape of daimons. By means of these daimonic realities, Jung confirmed the autonomy of the soul": James Hillman, *Healing Fictions* (Dallas, TX: Spring, 1983), 56. For Hillman, "Both daimon and unconscious are modes of imagining, modes of writing fictions": Hillman, *Healing Fictions*, 69.

3. Musings of the sort put forth by post-Jungian archetypal or "imaginal psychologists" such as James Hillman and Thomas Moore.

4. *Editor's note:* "Espanto" is one of the stories Anzaldúa was developing for her novel-in-stories, titled (among other things), *Los ensueños de la Prieta*. See Anzaldúa Papers, box 74, folder 6, for a version of this story.

5. Margaret R. Somers and Gloria D. Gibson, "Reclaiming the 'Epistemological Other': Narrative and the Social Constitution of Identity," in *Social Theory and the Politics of Identity*, ed. Craig Calhoun (Cambridge, MA: Blackwell, 1994), 58–59.

Chapter 1. Let us be the healing of the wound

Gracias a mis writing comadres Carmen Morones, AnaLouise Keating, Kit Quan, Yolanda Venegas, and Irene Lara for commenting on this essay and Andrew Baum for digging up population statistics.

1. After the first hijacked plane crashed into the World Trade Center, the U.S. closed the Mexican border and then the Canadian border to reinforce national identity, giving the anti-immigration advocates ammunition. "There are proposals to hire 20,000 more Border Patrol agents and 10,000 military troops for the border. What's ironic is that the terrorists that blew up the buildings entered the country legally with passports and visas, through the Canadian border, not the Mexican border," said Roberto Martinez, American Friends Service Committee, U.S.-Mexico Border Program, San Diego, CA, quoted in *ColorLines*, December 2001, 4.

2. See endnote 5.

3. Not only did the United States pull out of the United Nations World Conference against Racism in Durgan, South Africa, but President Bush withdrew the United States (the world's largest emitter of carbon dioxide) from negotiations of the Kyoto Protocol, in which 178 nations met to address critical environmental problems, confront global climate change, reduce carbon dioxide emissions, and set worldwide standards. Bush's energy proposals continue to subsidize fossil fuel industries. Newspaper editorials nationwide denounced the arrogance of his administration, which is in denial about the damage we're doing to the environment and is not willing to share responsibility for finding solutions: Jane H. Meigs, "Sailing Towards a Sustainable Shore," *Symposium* (Winter 2002).

4. *Editor's note:* Barbara Lee's speech can be found in Alexander et al., *Sing, Whisper, Shout, Pray: Feminist Visions for a Just World* (San Francisco: Edgework Books, 2003).

5. According to Kathryn Sikkink, The bombs killed more than 100,000 people (according to others, the total is 200,000), most of them civilians: Kathryn Sikkink, "A Human Rights Approach to Sept. 11," Social Science Research Council website, http://essays.ssrc.org/sept11/essays/sikkink.htm. For a series of short essays written by social scientists specifically in response to 9/11, see http://essays.ssrc.org/sept11/archive.

6. According to the mainstream media, many were facing potential starvation before. The U.S. employed rhetoric of concern for civilians. Commenting on an earlier draft of this chapter, AnaLouise Keating wrote, "While it's possible that they really do view civilians simply as collateral damage, they took unprecedented care (as compared to previous US violence) to appear to try not to harm them."

7. Prior to 9/11, the U.S. had given $43 million to the Taliban. Not everyone was shocked by the U.S. actions. According to Luis Rubio, general director of the Research Center for Development (CIDAC) in Mexico City, "What separates the United States from all previous major powers in history is that it is the least territorial and the most idealistic of them all. Americans see themselves as a benign power and are often embarrassed by the use of power, and much more so of force; hardly the behavior that was the trademark of the Greek, Roman, British or Soviet empires in their times. In stark contrast with those hegemons, Americans like to be loved as they project their power. There's no question Americans have an uphill selling job to do." "Terrorism and Freedom: An Outside View," Social Science Research Council website, published in 2011. http://essays.ssrc.org/10yearsafter911/terrorism-and-freedom-an-outside-view/.

8. The mainstream media does not document this view.

9. Sunera Thobani, "War Frenzy," in an e-mail from Yael Ben-zvi, sent October 21, 2001. I thank Michelle Zamora for forwarding it to me.

10. Neil Smith, "Global Executioner: Scales of Terror," Social Science Research Council website, http://essays.ssrc.org/sept11/essays/nsmith.htm. President Bush and Vice-President Dick Cheney have backgrounds in the oil business. According to Kim Sengupta and Andre Gumbel, Asia has almost 40 percent of the world's gas reserves, and the natural gas reserves in Afghanistan are the world's second largest after the Persian Gulf. "New U.S. Envoy to Kabul Lobbied for Taliban Oil Rights," The Independent (January 20, 2002).

11. Women and children are the majority of those killed and wounded in armed conflicts worldwide and 80 percent of the refugees.

12. The U.S. mainstream media also refuses to show images of the victims of the bombing in Afghanistan. For less mainstream media, see The Nation's website at http://www.thenation.com; and Farai Chideya's website at http://www.popandpolitics.com.

13. For information on your constitutional rights, see the National Lawyers Guild website at http://www.nlg.org and the American Civil Liberties Union website at http://www.aclu.org.

14. Poverty in the U.S. forces those with no job prospects into the Army, which is now 60 percent people of color.

15. According to the U.S. Labor Department, the number of unemployed surged to 8.2 million in November: UAW Solidarity, January–February 2002. According to the UAW Region Five Report, the drop in travel hit hotels, travel agencies, airlines, and restaurants hard. The number of workers forced to work part time (because that is all they could get) rose by 274,000, to 4.5 million. Joblessness also hit minorities and teens harder than other groups: "Job Losses Related to Attacks Continue Rise," UAW Region Five Report December 2001, 22. Mean-

while, House Republicans shoved through a bill that contained more than $25 billion in rebates to corporations for taxes they had paid all the way back to 1986. This bill rewarded GOP campaign contributors, 55 percent going to the wealthiest 1 percent of taxpayers: "Jumpstarting the Economy," AUW *Solidarity*, January–February 2002.

16. The United States is the third most populous country in the world, with 275 million of the world's 6 billion people.

17. "Nepantleras" is my term for mediators of in-between spaces. *Editor's note:* Anzaldúa discusses nepantleras in more detail in chapters 4 and 6.

18. For more on nepantla, conocimiento, desconocimiento, and spiritual activism, see chapter 6 in this volume.

19. According to the *Power of Peace* newsletter, January 11, 2002, http://peacebreath.com, one-tenth of 1 percent (.1%) unified by a single cause can change the consciousness of the world. This statistic has been recorded by prophets and sages of times past and recently by the research of David R. Hawkins. In his book *Power versus Force*, he synthesizes years of research by assigning vibrational energy values to different attributes. Fear is measured at 200; love, at 500; peace, at 600. He has shown that one person at level 500 (love) can counterbalance 750,000 people of a lower vibration. One person at level 700 can raise the consciousness of 70 million people.

20. Many posts to activists' listservs offer guidance. Other listservs, like the Women's Spiritual Network, offer spiritual approaches to activism.

Chapter 2. Flights of the Imagination

1. "Spirit" is an English term from the Latin that has been imposed on other cultures.

2. "Shamanism" is an invention of western anthropologists. The word "shaman" originated with the Tungus tribe of Siberia. A shaman is "one who sees in the dark" and has the ability to see "with the strong eye," or to travel to the hidden spirit worlds to find information and to perform acts that will heal a person or the community. The precursor to neo-shamanism is Mircea Eliade: see Mircea Eliade, *Shamanism: Archaic Techniques of Ecstasy* (1951), trans. W. R. Trask (Princeton, NJ: Princeton University Press, 1964). Shamanism or its Spanish equivalent, "chamanería," is a system of healing based on spiritual practices that is more than forty thousand years old and has survived through the ages. The Spanish word for shaman is *chamán; chamanes* is the plural. Another is *hechicero* (sorcerer). The Spanish terms are as secondhand as the English terms. Indigenous tribes had different names for chamanes. In this book, I choose to use the feminine gender "chamana" rather than the Spanish masculine or the English term.

Editor's note: In her notes for this chapter, Anzaldúa writes:

Is consciousness synonymous with spirit? "State of consciousness" means the totality of a person's thinking, feeling, and sensing at any given moment. Consciousness refers to that part of our being that shamans would have called spirit. Trees, rocks, rivers and animals have consciousness. Consciousness is a 15–20 billion-year cosmic process (according to living systems theory). Consciousness is the aspect of reality that is within a person, an interior feeling awareness that underlies all experience. [It] is an organism's awareness of its own self and surroundings. In *Primal Awareness*, Don Trent Jacobs describes consciousness as a "knowingness, that, once discovered, brings the world into harmony. It is the spark of life that pervades all things and, although we are often unaware of it, we can join with it. This discovery of consciousness or joining with it occurs when, during certain states of concentration, we activate our inherent ability to cooperate on nonverbal levels with energies that surround us. Of all the lessons we might learn from the primal view of life, this is perhaps the most vital." (Don Trent Jacobs, *Primal Awareness* [Rochester, VT: Inner Traditions, 1998], 138.

These notes are in Anzaldúa's computer subfolder for chapter 2, "2. flights of imagin," in the file "notes-flights of imaginal," last saved January 12, 2004.

3. *Editor's note:* Anzaldúa's notes for this chapter also include the following definition of conocimiento:

Conocimiento is a politics of embodied spirituality, el legado espiritual. Spirit is the common life force within humans and all beings. A spiritual belief of the self is that it is sacred and interconnected with all things in the world. This knowledge or belief empowers. In constructing our spiritualities, we struggle to valorize our worldviews, views that the dominant cultures imagine as other, as coming from ignorance. We struggle to decolonize spiritual beliefs. We struggle to heal cultural "sustos," resulting from the trauma of colonial abuses, trauma which fragments our psyches, pitching us into states of nepantla. "What is even more significant is that subjective or psychological phenomena are now increasingly seen as having epistemological and even practical functions. Fantasy is no longer felt to be a private and compensatory reaction against public situations, but rather a way of reading those situations, of thinking and mapping them, of intervening in them, albeit in a very different form from the abstract reflections of traditional philosophy or politics." (Fredric Jameson, "On Negt and Kluge," *October* 46 [Fall 1988]: 159).

These notes are in her computer subfolder for chapter two "2. flights of ima-gin, in the file "notes-flights of imaginal," last saved on January 12, 2004.

4. Joy Harjo, "A Postcolonial Tale," 18, *The Woman Who Fell from the Sky*, 18–19 (New York: W. W. Norton, 1994).

5. James Hillman, *The Dream and the Underworld* (New York: William Morrow, 1979), 46.

6. Hillman, *The Dream and the Underworld*, 142–43.

7. Cesar Macazaga Ordoño, *Diccionario de la lengua Nahuatl* (Mexico City: Editorial Innovación, 1979).

8. See "La salamandra called axolotl," in my novel in stories *Los ensueños de la Prieta. Editor's note*: Versions of this story can be found in the Anzaldúa Papers, box 78, folders 1, 2, 3.

9. Rosan A. Jordan, "The Vaginal Serpent and Other Themes from Mexican-American Women's Lore," in *Women's Folklore, Women's Culture*, ed. Rosan A. Jordan and Susan J. Kalčik (Philadelphia: University of Pennsylvania Press, 1985), 44.

10. *Los Ensueños de La Prieta* has two werejaguar stories ("De reojo" and "The Mouth of the Werejaguar"), which also deal with ensueños and other realities; one werelizard story ("El vigilio de la lagartija"); and naguales, snakes, and la Llorona in many of the others. In these fictions and others, I explore the same themes found in this nonfiction book.

11. When I'm giving talks that deal with this topic, I draw Serpent Woman as a coiled snake with a woman's head; for an image of Llorona with a horse's head, see Frank Romero's painting *La Llorona*.

12. Imaginal perception. "Imaginal" is a term derived from Henry Corbin, a scholar of Islamic mysticism, and later used by James Hillman: see Corbin, "Mundus Imaginalis, or the Imaginary and the Imaginal" (1964), in *Swedenborg and Esoteric Islam*, trans. Leonard Fox (West Chester, PA: Swedenborg Foundation, 1995); James Hillman, *The Myth of Analysis: Three Essays in Archetypal Psychology* (Evanston, IL: Northwestern University Press, 1972). The term blurs the distinction between the *real* as factual and the *imaginal* as another kind of real, a fictive real. As I discuss later in this chapter, reality cannot be linked exclusively to physical phenomena perceived through the senses nor to that represented by the rational intellect. Corbin articulates a world between these two, a median and mediating place, the "mundus imaginalis" (the world of images). (*Editor's note*: For more on Anzaldúa's interest in Corbin, see the section draft "Acts of reading, writing, storytelling, and self-making" in appendix 3.)

13. "Healing spirituality" is a psycho-spiritual movement, a kind of neo-shamanism, activated by Carlos Castaneda's Don Juan novels (which he passed off as anthropological field notes).

14. In nagualism (the Toltec belief in an animal double who can roam at night and cause sickness), the nagual is your animal counterpart. The shaman is also called "nagual." In *Tales of Power*, Don Juan describes another kind of nagual, explaining that the nagual is not mind, soul, thoughts, state of grace, heaven, pure intellect, psyche, energy, vital force immortality, life principle, God, or even nothingness but that it can be understood as "power" and that it gives rise to creativity: Carlos Castaneda, *Tales of Power* (New York: Simon and Schuster, 1974), 118–46. El nahual or la naguala are endowed with the power to transform themselves into animal forms. "Nahualli" is the Nahuatl word for nahual, a hispanicized term for "brujo" or "bruja" in pre-Hispanic times and throughout the sixteenth century and seventeenth century: Daniel G. Brinton, *Nagualism: A Study of Native American Folk-lore and History* (Philadelphia: Mac-Calla, 1894).

15. Hillman, *The Dream and the Underworld*, 150.

16. James Hillman, "Going Bugs," *Spring* (1988): 40–72.

17. Hillman, *The Dream and the Underworld*, 148.

18. *Editor's note:* As indicated in her most recent draft of this chapter ("essay flights of imaginal 2," last saved April 4, 2004), Anzaldúa planned to include a section here that was tentatively titled "Soul and image work: distinguishing soul from spirit." For her very short draft of this section, see appendix 3.

19. *Editor's note:* In her outline from April 2004 (at the top of "essay flights of imaginal 2"), Anzaldúa inserted "[notas 1-3]," indicating that she would develop a section titled "The underworld" and insert it here. However, she has no notes or draft for the section in her files.

20. Daniel C. Noel, *The Soul of Shamanism: Western Fantasies, Imaginal Realities* (New York: Continuum, 1997), 153.

21. Keep in mind that the word "spirit," an English term from the Latin, has been imposed by English speakers on other cultures.

22. For a description of these terms, including nepantleras, see chapter 6 in this volume.

23. Castaneda invented the terms "ordinary reality" and "nonordinary reality."

24. Carlos Castaneda, *Journey to Ixtlan* (Harmondsworth, UK: Penguin, 1974), 299–300.

25. See Arnold Mindell, *Working with the Dreaming Body* (Boston: Routledge and Kegan Paul, 1985).

26. Noel, *The Soul of Shamanism*.

27. C. G. Jung, *Letters: Volume 1, 1906–1950*, ed. Gerhard Adler and Aniela Jaffe, trans. R.F.C. Hull, Bollingen Series XCV:1 (Princeton, NJ: Princeton University Press, 1973), 460.

28. Robert Bosnak, *A Little Course in Dreams* (Boston: Shambhala, 1986), 44.

29. C. G. Jung, *Collected Works*, vol. 7, ed. H. Read, M. Fordham, G. Adler, and W. McGuire, trans. R.F.C. Hull, Bollingen Series 20 (Princeton, NJ: Princeton University Press, 1971), para. 354. *Editor's note:* According to her most recent draft, "essay flights of imaginal 2," last saved April 4, 2004, Anzaldúa planned to follow this section with a section titled "Acts of reading, writing, storytelling, and self-making." For her notes to this section, see appendix 3.

30. *Editor's note:* In "essay flights of imaginal 2," last saved April 4, 2004, Anzaldúa inserted "[notas 1-3]," indicating that she planned to add material from her writing notas and expand this section.

31. Edith Turner, "The Reality of Spirits," *ReVision* 15, no. 1 (1992): 31.

32. "Imaginals" is a plural noun coined in Turner, "The Reality of Spirits," 31.

33. Mary Watkins, *Waking Dreams* (1976), 3d ed. (Dallas, TX: Spring, 1984), 6–7.

34. *Editor's note:* See Gloria Anzaldúa, "Foreword to *Cassell's Encyclopedia of Queer Myth, Symbol and Spirit: Gay, Lesbian, Bisexual and Transgender Lore*" (1996), in *The Gloria Anzaldúa Reader*, ed. AnaLouise Keating (Durham, NC: Duke University Press, 2009), 229–31. At this point in "essay flights of imaginal 2," last saved April 4, 2004, Anzaldúa inserted the following: "Why all people lump spirituality with new age—my position, stance." This statement indicates that she planned to explain in more detail her definition of spirituality, distinguishing it from conventional "New Age" understandings.

35. See Claude Lévi-Strauss, "The Effectiveness of Symbolism," in *Structural Anthropology* (New York: Basic Books, 1963), 186–205, esp. 193.

36. *Editor's note:* As indicated in "essay flights of imaginal 2," last saved April 4, 2004, Anzaldúa planned to follow this section with a section titled "Glifo de la lengua: serpent's tongue." For her notes to this section, see appendix 3.

37. Art and imaginal psychology both pay close attention to the image and work through the imagination. There's also a tie between shamanism and art (see, e.g., Andreas Lommel, *The Beginnings of Art* [New York: McGraw-Hill, 1967]) and between art and medicine (see Shaun McNiff, *Art as Medicine: Creating a Therapy of the Imagination* [Boston: Shambhala, 1992]). Chamanes have been called the first psychoanalysts and the first artists.

38. Quoted in Jeffrey Green, "An Interview with Stanley Plumly," *Writer's Chronicle*, December 2000, 23. *Editor's note:* Anzaldúa included notes for a section titled "Creating Reality": see appendix 3.

39. Ralph Strauch, *The Reality Illusion: How You Make the World Your Experience* (1983) (Barrytown, NY: Station Hill Press, 1989), 2.

40. *Editor's note:* In "essay flights of imaginal 2," last saved April 4, 2004, Anzaldúa had additional notes for this section, indicating that she planned to expand it: see appendix 3.

41. See Castaneda, *Journey to Ixtlan*, 26, 35, 40, 43, 53, 60, 89, 213; *Tales of Power*, 232–33, 236; *The Eagle's Gift* (New York: Simon and Schuster, 1982), 130, 137, 234–36.

42. *Editor's note:* In "essay flights of imaginal 2," last saved April 4, 2004, Anzaldúa also included these notes: "The empiricist asserts the importance of sense experience, rather than pure reflection or contemplation, for acquiring knowledge about the world, but the thinking subject was at the center of this epistemological system. Empirical reaction posits a world that we can know objectively, which exists independently of our thoughts. According to the empirical perspective, language's primary function is to describe reality and represent the world. The empiricist George Berkeley asserted that we do not need the concept that there is only thought and that thought constitutes reality. This leads to the idea that the material world will be transcended by information."

43. Carolyn Myss, *Why People Don't Heal and How They Can* (New York: Random House, 1998).

Chapter 3. Border Arte

1. See also Amalia Mesa-Bains, "El Mundo Femenino: Chicana Artists of the Movement—A Commentary on Development and Production," in CARA, *Chicano Art: Resistance and Affirmation*, ed. Richard Griswold Del Castillo, Teresa McKenna, and Yvonne Yarbro-Bejarano (Los Angeles: Wight Art Gallery, University of California, 1991), 131–40.

2. See Gloria E. Anzaldúa, *Borderlands/La Frontera: The New Mestiza* (San Francisco: Aunt Lute, 1985).

3. The exhibition discussed in this piece moved to seven sites, beginning in San Diego.

4. *Editor's note:* Anzaldúa includes pronunciation guides to these two figures, suggesting that Coatlicue be pronounced "Co-at-LEE-Kwa" and Coyolxauhqui be pronounced "Ko-yol-sha-UH-kee."

5. See the untitled essay by Luz María and Ellen J. Stekert's in the art catalogue *Santa Barraza*, March 8–April 11, 1992, La Raza/Galeria Posada, Sacramento, CA.

6. Barraza, quoted in Jennifer Heath, "Women Artists of Color Share World of Struggle," *Sunday Camera*, March 8, 1992, 9C.

7. *Editor's note:* In her notes on this chapter dated May 31, 2002, Anzaldúa glosses "use" as "put the images in the service of art-making."

8. See Carmen Lomas Garza's beautifully illustrated bilingual children's book *Family Pictures/Cuadros de familia* (San Francisco: Children's Book Press, 1990). Garza had three pieces in the exhibition "La Frontera/The Border: Art

about the Mexico/United States Border Experience," Museum of Contemporary Art and el Centro Cultural de la Raza, San Diego.

9. The Maya huipil is a large rectangular weaving with a slit for the head that is worn as a blouse. It describes the Maya cosmos, portraying the world as a diamond. The four sides of the diamond represent the boundaries of space and time; the smaller diamonds at each corner, the cardinal points. The weaver maps the heavens and underworld.

10. Dianna Williamson, personal communication, June 1992.

11. Roberta H. Markman and Peter T. Markman, eds., *Masks of the Spirit: Image and Metaphor in Mesoamerica* (Berkeley: University of California Press, 1989).

12. See Carlos Castaneda, *The Eagle's Gift* (New York: Simon and Schuster, 1982), *The Fire from Within* (London: Transworld, 1984), *Journey to Ixtlan* (Harmondsworth, UK: Penguin, 1974), *The Power of Silence* (New York: Simon and Schuster, 1987), *The Second Ring of Power* (New York: Simon and Schuster, 1979), and *Tales of Power* (New York: Simon and Schuster, 1974).

13. Brundage, *The Fifth Sun*, 83.

14. Wendy Rose and Ward Churchill object to the rip-off of their spirituality by self-acclaimed "white shamans": see Wendy Rose, "The Great Pretenders: Further Reflections on White Shamanism," in *The State of Native America*, ed. M. Annette Jaimes (Boston: South End, 1992), 403–21; Ward Churchill, "Spiritual Hucksterism: The Rise of Plastic Medicine Men," in *Fantasies of the Master Race*, ed. M. Annette Jaimes (Monroe, ME: Common Courage, 1992), 215–28.

15. Vine Deloria Jr., "Foreword/American Fantasy," in *The Pretend Indians: Images of Native Americans in the Movies*, ed. Gretchen M. Bataille and Charles L. P. Silet (Ames: Iowa State University Press, 1980).

16. See also Ken Eagle Feather, *A Toltec Path: A User's Guide to the Teachings of Don Juan Matus, Carlos Castaneda, and Other Toltec Seers* (Norfolk, VA: Hampton Roads, 1995), and *Traveling with Power* (Norfolk, VA: Hampton Roads, 1992).

17. Another Mexican, Victor Sanchez, also conducts workshops in Mexico: see Victor Sanchez, *The Teachings of Don Carlos*, trans. Robert Nelson (Santa Fe, NM: Bear, 1995).

18. See Jorge Luis Borges, *Ficciones* (1944), trans. Emceé Editores (New York: Grove, 1962).

19. Hall's exact assertion is, "We have an internalization of fixed space learned early in life. One's orientation in space is tied to survival and sanity. To be disoriented in space is to be psychotic": Edward T. Hall and Mildred Reed Hall, "The Sounds of Silence," I *Conformity and Conflict: Readings in Cultural Anthropology*, ed. Jams P. Spradley and David W. McCurdy (Boston: Little, Brown, & Co., 1987).

20. The exhibition was part of Festival Internacional de la Raza 92. The artworks were produced in the Silkscreen Studios of Self Help Graphics, Los

Angeles, and in the Studios of Strike Editions in Austin. Self Help Graphics and the Galería sin Fronteras in Austin organized the exhibition.

21. *Editor's note:* Here Anzadúa has a boldfaced note to herself: "**[describe Dos Mundos and show how it deals with images of la frontera].**"

22. As I discussed in *Borderlands/La Frontera*, I use mestizaje to talk about the process of mixing cultures.

23. For a discussion of Chicano posters, almanacs, calendars, and cartoons that join "images and texts to depict community issues as well as historical and cultural themes," metaphorically link Chicano struggles for self-determination with the Mexican revolution, and establish "a cultural and visual continuum across borders," see Tomás Ybarra-Fausto, "Grafica/Urban Iconography," in *Chicano Expressions: A New View in American Art* (New York: INTAR Latin American Gallery, 1986), 21–24.

24. Among the alternative galleries and art centers that combat assimilation are the Guadalupe Cultural Arts Center in San Antonio, Mexic-Arte Museum and Galería sin Fronteras in Austin, and the Mission Cultural Center in San Francisco.

25. Irene Lara after reading this essay, commented that the bat reminded her of the chupacabra phenomena. When I asked her whether she'd seen the *X-Files* episode about the chupacabra, she said she had. This is an example of how cultural myth is commodified and becomes part of popular culture.

26. *Editor's note:* In her draft dated May 31, 2002, Anzaldúa has a note to herself and her writing comadres here asking whether she should include more on this topic.

27. *Editor's note:* Here Anzaldúa writes, "More recently I discovered my Mayan signs" and then inserts this question in boldface: "**[elaborate on this earlier?].**"

28. See Guy Brett, *Transcontinental: An Investigation of Reality* (London: Verso, 1990). The book, which accompanied the exhibition at Ikon Gallery in Birmingham and Cornerhouse, Manchester, explores the work of nine Latin American artists: Waltercio Caldas, Juan Davila, Eugenio Dittborn, Roberto Evangelista, Victor Grippo, Jac Leirner, Cildo Meireles, Tunga, and Regina Vater.

29. See *Ex profeso, recuento de afinidades colectiva plástica contemporánea: Imágenes: gay-lésbicas-eróticas*, put together by Círculo Cultural Gay in Mexico City and exhibited at Museo Universitario del Chope during la Semana Cultural Gay de 1989, June 14–23.

Chapter 4. Geographies of Selves

Editor's note: As indicated earlier, this chapter went through many iterations. Anzaldúa's penultimate draft for the chapter, last saved March 23, 2003, contains a different version of the essay's opening sections, which had subsections titled "Raza studies today"; "The ground from which I speak"; "Re-imagining identities"; "Which 'I' are you?"; "Identity is a composition of a composites"; "A field of 'subpersonalities'"; "Identity is a social position"; "The role of imagination in identity formation"; "Virtual identities, pretend selves"; and "Decolonizing identity." For a version of this alternative opening, see appendix 4.

Epigraph: "Amor es" poema escrita por la cubana Dulce Maria Loynaz. I thank Ruth Behar for introducing me to this poet.

Epigraph: Robbie Robertson, "Making a Noise," *Classic Masters*, compact disc, Capitol Records, 2002. Anzaldúa often listened to Robbie Robertson's music during the last years of her life, writing to me on January 2, 2004, "i've been listening nonstop to my new Robbie Robertson (Mohawk/Jewish) CD *Music for the Native Americans*. i almost wore out the other CD of his that i have, *Classic Masters*. i really like his music."

1. In Pedro Almodóvar's film *Todo sobre mi madre*, winner of the 2000 Oscar for Best Foreign Language Film, we witness cultures' refusal to accept gender fluidity and transgendering.

2. "Race" is a social fabrication. Henceforth, I will forgo the quotation marks, not because they imply a racial certainty, but for stylistic reasons: to avoid continuously distracting the reader.

3. *Editor's note:* Anzaldúa describes her Guadalupe tree in chapter 2 of this volume.

4. "Milagro" means miracle; "milagritos" are little miracles. Illness, disease, misfortune are the result of invasion of the body by an invisible force. Exvotos (a Latin term meaning "from a vow") contain and neutralize the agents of disease and misfortune. At Denison University, I gave a talk titled, "Nepantleras: Healing the Wounds—Spiritual, Intellectual, and Activist Acts of Bridge Building." I focused on the idea of connecting through wounds, and I suggested that experiencing pain may serve as a bridge. I wore a milagro necklace and pair of milagro earrings that a friend had made for me. Holding a tiny milagro corncob, I talked about my mother making promesas (vows) to la Virgen de San Juan when my brother was missing in action in Vietnam. Women's Studies provided their students with cards containing quotes from my works. Attached to each card was un milagrito. [*Editor's note:* Anzaldúa spoke at Denison University on October 30, 2003.]

5. In Mexican indigenous mythology (Nahuas), el árbol de la vida is in Tamoanchan (paraíso mítico y lugar de origen de los dioses), situated above the thirteen heavens: see Yolotl González Torres, *Diccionario de mitología y religión de Mesoamérica* (Mexico City: Ediciones Larousse, 1995). The world tree, "axis mundi," is tripartite. The underworld world, represented by the roots, exists below the surface of the earth; it is the realm of Earth energies, animal spirits, the dead

who have not moved on to the next level of existence. The middle world, symbolized by the trunk, is the physical plane where we live our ordinary lives; it is the realms of the planet and outer reaches of the universe. The upper world, represented by the branches, is above the sky; it is the world of noncorporeal energies, spirits who are gods and goddesses, spirits of the dead who have progressed beyond the land of the dead. The three worlds are the same place and are interconnected and overlapping. The tree of life is found in many cultures. In the Jewish Kabbala, it has seven levels and is called the Sephirot. A central Mayan belief involves "the cosmic tree," the belief in the Earth's ability to renew itself: humans and the Earth are partners, and humans must continually renew their relationship with the Earth.

6. In 1991, I "appropriated" and recycled the term "new tribalism" from David Rieff, who uses it to criticize me for being "a professional Aztec" and for what he sees as my naïve and nostalgic return to indigenous roots: see David Rieff, "Professional Aztecs and Popular Culture," *New Perspectives Quarterly* 8, no. 2 (Winter 1991): 42–46. He takes me to task for my "romantic vision" in *Borderlands/La Frontera*, claiming that Americans should think a little less about race and a little more about class. I take his criticism and go beyond by acknowledging that shift in power, by taking the term "new tribalism" to formulate other takes on identity, particularly a more expanded and inclusive identity. Grace: you probably don't remember, but I met you at the University of California, Los Angeles, on February 12, 1991. Thanks for giving me this article.

7. Physics will no longer be a metaphor or model for reality. An ecosystem can be used to describe a social system. It is through a systems approach to living organisms that we will learn about life.

8. This discussion summarizes and expands the personal journey I narrate in Gloria E. Anzaldúa, *Borderlands/La Frontera: The New Mestiza* (San Francisco: Aunt Lute, 1985), and "now let us shift . . . the path of conocimiento . . . inner work, public acts," in *this bridge we call home: radical visions for transformation*, ed. Gloria E. Anzaldúa and AnaLouise Keating (New York: Routledge, 2002), 540–78.

9. For a discussion of how the Coyolxauhqui imperative functions in creative processes, see chapter 5 in this volume.

10. I thank Randy Conner for telling me (in his critique of this paper on October 24, 2003) about the rhizome structural model used by Gilles Deleuze and Félix Guattari.

11. When I discuss geographies of selves during my talks, I use several glifos (drawn images, hieroglyphics) to depict this theory. One drawing is a woman's body veined like the map of a country (figure 4.1); another is a woman's body lying on the equator.

12. I'm reminded of Ray Bradbury's science fiction novel *The Illustrated Man* (New York, Bantam, 1976).

13. *Editor's note:* In her copious notes to this chapter, Anzaldúa writes that "the mestiza/o is a person who inhabits many worlds and cultures and transgresses boundaries."

14. For more on desconocimiento, see Gloria E. Anzaldúa, *Interviews/Entrevistas*, ed. AnaLouise Keating (New York: Routledge, 2000), and chapter 6 in this volume.

15. Corn is miraculous. Plant one grain of corn on good land and you get eight hundred grains. For one grain of wheat, you get four; for rice, you get forty to fifty grains: John H. Grose, *A Voyage to the East Indies, with Observations of Various Parts There*, vol. 1 (London: Hooper and Morley, 1757), 33.

16. *Editor's note:* For Anzaldúa's theory of the "way station," see *Interviews/Entrevistas.*

17. *Editor's note:* Anzaldúa considered developing this discussion further and wrote the following in her notes:

> In this narrative, "Other" refers to those of El Mundo Zurdo: women, people of color, inhabitants of the so-called Third World, lesbians, gays, and the "disabled"—that is, all groups traditionally denied economic and political power. Because we've made social/political inroads, the "other"/la otra has assumed characteristics of the subject and has taken on some of that privilege. For example, those people of color who share power are included in the dialogue slash, whereas todas las "otras" of earlier decades/generations were denied voice or could not speak the rhetoric because they never made it to graduate school. The concept of nos/otras moves us beyond a counter-discourse and its cultural displacement into a more complex stance and a more dynamic dialogue between people on both sides of the slash. Many who have previously been forced to represent the position of "otras" may have moved up one or two class rungs, shifted into the intellectual, artistic, and middle or upper classes. When viewed from a nos/otras position assimilation is no longer a disconnection from ethnic culture and community, it is more of a mediation of contradictory experiences. We are both subject and object, conquered and conqueror. Nos/otras moves us beyond a counter-discourse. Internal tensions, differences, and splits can be bridged by nos/otras as can external ones such as academy/community, academics/activists splits, Latinos in the US and Latinos in Latin American countries. The traditional assigning of "nos" to the good guys and "otras" to the bad guys doesn't work (and has never worked). Though the divide has always been racialized to favor "whites," at one time or another we all have been on both sides of the divide.

18. Our brain has the processing power of a hundred billion personal computers joined together.

19. For my definition of la naguala, see chapter 6, note 3.

20. *Editor's note:* Here Anzaldúa instructed herself to include an "ex[ample] from my life."

21. Leonard Cohen, ife.fe.selon *The Future*, Compact Disc, Columbia, New York, 1992.

22. Jean Houston, *Possible Human, Possible World*, videocassette, Thinking Allowed Productions, 1992.

23. *Editor's note:* According to her notes, Anzaldúa planned to add a series of concrete examples, such as the following: "A transgendered, half Korean, half Mexican who has changed class and sexual orientation no longer perceives these categories as they did before the changes."

24. For an examination of historical trauma, see Edén E. Torres, *Chicana without Apology: The New Chicana Cultural Studies* (New York: Routledge, 2004).

25. For a discussion of melancholic responses to racial grief, see Anne Anlin Cheng, *The Melancholy of Race: Psychoanalysis, Assimilation, and Hidden Grief* (Oxford: Oxford University Press, 2001). Cheng posits racial identity as a melancholic formation and offers intervention through psychoanalysis.

26. *Editor's note:* Anzaldúa uses "conocimiento" in two related ways: (1) as individual insights; (2) as an entire theory of embodied knowing. As she wrote in an earlier draft of this chapter:

> Part of our agenda is to heal the wounds, to repair the damage that certain groups have done to other groups. El daño that people have done to others in their own group; that men have done to women and women to men, and that both have done to children. Ours is a healing agenda. Each of us, and ourselves as a group, needs to figure out exactly how we're going to go about doing the inner/outer work of healing and removing and rewriting negative inscriptions. The chief premise of this epistemological model (world view, philosophy) is the root word conocer, to know, and its connection with activism. To be in conocimiento with someone or some group is to pool resources, share knowledge, and do the work of repairing the wounds. I call this the Coyolxauhqui imperative—the imperative includes fighting against fragmentation, and once fragmented, of pulling the pieces of the self, of the soul, together.

Anzaldúa offers the most extensive discussion of her theory of conocimiento in chapter 6 in this volume.

27. Anzaldúa's journals are located with the Anzaldúa Papers.

28. See Caroline Myss, *Why People Don't Heal and How They Can* (New York: Random House, 1998).

29. Aung San Suu Kyi, "Freedom from Fear," Acceptance speech for the 1990 Sakharov Prize for Freedom of Thought, July 1991.

Chapter 5. *Putting Coyolxauhqui Together*

1. *Editor's note:* The phrase "tribe of writing" seems very intentional, although it might sound counterintuitive at first. Irene Lara (whose revision comments Anzaldúa respected) suggested that she change "writing" to "writers," and Anzaldúa chose not to adopt this recommendation. I wonder whether she was constructing an affinity-based identity that exceeds the human and focuses more on the action than the person.

2. *Editor's note:* Anzaldúa's writing process involved multiple pre-drafts and multiple drafts. In her notes for this chapter, she indicated that she generally created three to six pre-drafts.

3. *Editor's note:* A sample of Anzaldúa's writer's prayers is in AnaLouise Keating, ed., *The Gloria Anzaldúa Reader* (Durham, NC: Duke University Press, 2009).

4. *Editor's note:* See, e.g., draft ten (titled "Embodying the Story: How I Write"), in which Anzaldúa used the following four headings and fifteen subheadings:

> The call
> Dreaming the bones of la historia:
> > Walking the story con ojos de aguila
> > Sacando vueltas, skirting around the work—prewriting rituals
> > Who is doing the writing, for whom and to whom?
> > Making the bones—note taking, free writing, and drafting
> > Animating the bones, the work of naguala
> Assembling the story:
> > Tracking la historia, reading the signs
> > Raising the skeleton and shaping la historia
> > Re-membering the bones, putting Coyolxauhqui together
> > Nepantla: navigating the worlds
> Revising the story:
> > The shadow side of writing
> > Dealing with desconocimientos and changing behavior
> > Reenvisioning, remapping, and revising la historia
> > Emotional fallout in questioning conventions
> > Dancing the story—the flash of reconocimiento
> > Al fin

By draft twelve (titled "Working the Story: Como escribes/How You Write"), Anzaldúa had deleted the subheadings and had only the following headings: "The call"; "Dreaming the bones"; "Walking the story con ojos de aguila";

"Embodying: the work of naguala"; "Tracking the story"; "Re-membering the bones, putting Coyolxauhqui together"; "Nepantla: moving between the worlds"; "Animating the bones"; "Disillusioned"; "Block: the shadow side of writing"; "Conocimiento"; and "Dancing the story."

5. Clarice Lispector, "Since One Feels Obliged to Write . . . ," in *Lives on the Line: The Testimony of Contemporary Latin American Authors*, ed. Doris Meyer, trans. Giovanni Pontiero (Berkeley: University of California Press, 1988), 36.

6. *Editor's note:* Readers might notice that Anzaldúa previously referred to a deadline "less than two weeks away." Anzaldúa often missed such deadlines; indeed, missing deadlines seems to have been a regular part of her writing process.

7. *Editor's note:* Anzaldúa used first person for her previous drafts of this chapter.

8. *Editor's note:* In draft ten, Anzaldúa included the following paragraph:

> The most virulent virus, depression, lays siege on my body. This depression is one of a long chain set in motion long ago by setbacks and traumas I've long forgotten but which left scars that hardened into self-imposed limitations—unconscious beliefs about myself. These beliefs run my life. The internal monologue goes like this: You don't have the skills, English is your second language, after all; the project is too complex, you'll never make it as perfect as you want. Stop indulging in procrastination, cabrona. Clack, clack, too chicken of what the writing might reveal. Keep this up and you won't meet your deadline.

9. *Editor's note:* In draft twelve, Anzaldúa inserted the following statement: "(yes, you got an extension)."

10. Kenneth Atchity, *A Writer's Time* (New York: W. W. Norton, 1986), 13.

11. *Editor's note:* In her copious writing notas (but not notes specifically for this chapter), Anzaldúa has the following:

> People who use their intuition and imagination are boats. The land is the rational mode of reasoning; the ocean is the unconsciousness (the imaginal world, the underworld); and the shore is the interface or border that connects the two. The boat is moored to the land, the pier. It goes out into the sea, returns to land, goes back and forth between the two worlds. [footnote: I borrowed the shore metaphor from Kenneth Atchity, *A Writer's Time*, and extended it to fit my ideas.] As a writer I traffic back and forth between the two worlds, switching from one mode of consciousness to the other and I live in the interface between the two. To me the imaginal one is as "real" as the external one.

Chapter 6. now let us shift

Quiero darle las gracias a mis "comadres in writing" por sus comentarios: a Carmen Morones, Randy Conner, Irene Reti, Liliana Wilson, Kit Quan, and most especially AnaLouise Keating for her numerous, generous readings, right-on suggestions, and co-creation of this essay—les agradesco por animarme cuando me desanimaba. Thanks also to Bonnie Bentson and my graduate students in the Public Intellectuals Program at Florida Atlantic University. This essay is sister to "Putting Coyolxauhqui Together."

Epigraph: Ming-Dao Deng Ming-Deo, 365 *Dao Daily Meditations* (New York: Harperone, 1992), 48.

1. "Conocimiento" derives from *cognoscera*, a Latin verb that means "to know;" it's the Spanish word for knowledge and skill. I call conocimiento that aspect of consciousness urging you to act on the knowledge gained.

2. "Nepantla" es una palabra indígena for an in-between space, el lugar entremedio, un lugar/no lugar. I have expanded this word to include certain workings of consciousness.

3. "Naguala" is the feminine form of nagual, the Mexican indigenous capacity some people (such as shamans) have of shape shifting—becoming an animal, place, or thing by inhabiting that thing or by shifting into the perspective of their animal companion. I have extended the term to include an aspect of the self that is unknown to the conscious self. Nagualismo is a Mexican spiritual knowledge system in which the practitioner searches for spirit signs. I call the maker of spirit signs "la naguala," a creative, more dreamlike consciousness able to make broader associations and connections than waking consciousness.

4. Xochiquetzal is the Aztec goddess of love, del amor; her name means "Flor Preciosa, Precious Flower" or, more literally, "Pluma de Flor," and her cult descended from los toltecas. Tomoanchan is one of the levels of heaven (paradise), according to Aztec mythology.

5. According to the neurologist Antonio R. Damasio, consciousness is the sense of self in the act of knowing. The inner sense is based on images of feelings; without imaging you can't have feelings, you can't have consciousness. Antonio Damasio, *The Feeling of What Happens: Body and Emotion in the Making of Consciousness* (New York: Harcourt, 1999).

6. La Llorona is a ghost woman with long black hair and dressed in white who appears at night, sometimes near bodies of water, sometimes at crossroads, calling with loud and terrifying wails for her lost children. She has her origins in various pre-Hispanic deities: Cihuacoatl, Xtabai, Xonaxi Quecuila, and Auicanime. See Gloria E. Anzaldúa, *Prietita and the Ghost Woman/Prietita y la Llorona* (San Francisco: Children's Book Press, 1995).

7. Toltec nagualism's idea of "seeing" beyond the apparent reality of the mundane world and into the spiritual was described to Carlos Castaneda by Don Juan.

8. The seven planes of reality are the physical, emotional, mental, Buddhic, atmic, monadic, and cosmic. Carolyn Myss, medical intuitive, suggests that the seven chakras correspond to the seven Christian sacraments and the sefirot of the Kabbala: *Advanced Energy Anatomy*, Sounds True Audio Cassette, Boulder, CO, 2001.

9. I wrote about this incident in one of the Prieta stories, "The Crack between the Worlds." *Editor's note:* Anzaldúa also titled this story "La Barranca"; see Anzaldúa Papers, box 66, folder 25.

10. Don Miguel Ruiz, *The Four Agreements: A Practical Guide to Personal Freedom* (San Rafael, CA: Amber Allen, 1997); Charles T. Tart, *Waking Up: Overcoming the Obstacles to Human Potential* (Boston: Shambhala: 1986).

11. Susto, fright sickness, attributed to being frightened out of one's soul. Indigenous people in the Americas believed in the physicality of the soul. The Mexica believed that a person had multiple souls that could be verified through the senses: these include the soul that animates the body and confers individual personality, aptitudes, abilities, and desires; the soul as breath; and the soul as an invisible shadowy double: Jill Leslie McKeever Furst, *The Natural History of the Soul in Ancient Mexico* (New Haven, CT: Yale University Press, 1997).

12. AnaLouise Keating, in one of her many generous readings of different drafts of this essay, made this comment about the mind/body split: "In various places throughout, you insist that you can't solve the cartesian mind/body split. yes & no. what you write *does* offer a solution—a solution that's difficult to live out in our lives, but the vision of spirit is the solution. it's finding pathways to manifest that vision in our lives (bodies) which is so damn tricky."

13. Una lechuza is a human owl, or naguala, usually una viejita who shape shifts into an owl.

14. "Autohistoria" is a term I use to describe the genre of writing about one's personal and collective history using fictive elements, a sort of fictionalized autobiography or memoir; an autohistoria-teoría is a personal essay that theorizes.

15. I describe this experience in my Prieta story "Canción de cascabel/Song of the Rattlesnake." *Editor's note:* A version of this story can be found in Anzaldúa Papers, box 68, folder 2.

16. As I explained in chapter 4, I've borrowed the term from David Rieff, who states that Americans should think a little less about race and a little more about class. Calling me "a professional Aztec," he takes me to task for my "romantic vision": see David Rieff, "Professional Aztecs and Popular Culture," *New Perspectives Quarterly* 8, no. 2 (Winter 1991): 42–46. I wish he'd attempted a more sensitive analysis of Chicano culture.

17. Richard Tarnas, "The Great Initiation," in *Noetic Sciences Review* 47 (1998), 24–33.

18. Margaret Read, "Two Goats on the Bridge," in *Peace Tales: World Folktales to Talk About* (North Haven, CT: Linnet Books, 1992).

19. I borrow the term "connectionist" from the "connectionist nets," the neural net consisting of billions of neurons in the human cortex. Connections are made in all states of consciousness, the broadest in artistic reverie and in dreaming, not in focused logical waking thought. The power of the imaginary must be used in conflict resolution.

20. See my discussion of the yoga of the body in Gloria E. Anzaldúa, *Interviews/Entrevistas*, ed. AnaLouise Keating (New York: Routledge, 2000), 97. As I explain in the interview, "'Yoga' means union of body with mind and spirit": Anzaldúa, *Interviews/Entrevistas*, 99.

21. See Keyes, *Emotions and the Enneagram*, especially the discussion of reframing.

22. The Latin term *respectus* comes from a verb that means "to turn around to look back." It is the root of the word "respect." You wonder whether the word "perspective" shares this etymology.

23. AnaLouise Keating, *Women Reading Women Writing: Self-Invention in Paula Gunn Allen, Gloria Anzaldúa and Audre Lorde* (Philadelphia: Temple University Press, 1996), 75–81.

24. According to a comment AnaLouise made while critiquing this essay.

25. Jean Houston, *The Search for the Beloved: Journeys in Sacred Psychology* (Los Angeles: Jeremy P. Tarcher, 1987), 105–6.

26. The cognitive scientist and mathematician David Chalmers makes a similar point, claiming that consciousness is not confined to the individual brain and body or even to the present moment: David Chalmers, "The Puzzles of Conscious Experience" (*Scientific American*, vol. 273, December 1995), 62–68.

27. Rupert Sheldrake, *Dogs That Know When Their Owners Are Coming Home and Other Unexplained Powers of Animals* (New York: Three Rivers, 2000), 311.

28. The charging of the sun is an ancient Mayan ritual.

29. Lhasa de Sela's (Mexican American/Jewish) "El desierto," in *La Llorona*, Atlantic, CD, 1998.

Appendix 4: Alternative Opening

1. Roberto Assagioli, *Psychosynthesis: A Manual of Principles and Techniques* (New York: Viking, 1965), 67.

2. Editor's note: Anzaldúa had a note here to herself and her writing comadres asking whether she should move this section elsewhere in the manuscript.

GLOSSARY

[These brief glosses on some of Anzaldúa's most important terms and topics do not do justice to the theories themselves. Check the index to locate her discussions on these items. An earlier version of this glossary is in *The Gloria Anzaldúa Reader*. I have updated the entries, as necessary, to reflect my current understanding of the terms].

árbol de la vida: An identity-related theory, first introduced in *Interviews/ Entrevistas* and further developed in *Light in the Dark*. Using metaphors of roots and grafting, Anzaldúa emphasizes the potentially relational, flexible aspects to identity formation and change.

autohistoria: Anzaldúa coined this term, as well as the term "autohistoria-teoría," to describe women-of-color interventions into and transformations of traditional western autobiographical forms. Deeply infused with the search for personal and cultural meaning, or what Anzaldúa describes as "putting Coyolxauhqui together," both autohistoria and autohistoria-teoría are informed by reflective self-awareness employed in the service of social-justice work. Autohistoria focuses on the personal life story, but as the auto-historian tells her own life story, she simultaneously tells the life stories of others.

autohistoria-teoría: Theory developed by Anzaldúa to describe a relational form of autobiographical writing that includes both life story and self-reflection on this storytelling process. Writers of autohistoria-teoría blend their cultural and personal biographies with memoir, history, storytelling, myth, and other forms of theorizing. By so doing, they create interwoven individual and collective identities. Personal experiences—revised and in other ways redrawn—become a lens with which to reread and rewrite existing cultural stories. Through this lens, Anzaldúa and other autohistoria-teorístas expose the limitations in the existing paradigms and create new stories of healing, self-growth, cultural critique, and individual and collective transformation. Anzaldúa described *Borderlands/La Frontera* as an example of one form autohistoria-teoría can take; *Light in the Dark* illustrates another.

borderlands: When Anzaldúa writes this term with a lowercase "b," it refers to the region on both sides of the Texas-Mexico border.

Borderlands: For Anzaldúa, *Borderlands*, with a capital "B," represents a concept that draws from yet goes beyond the geopolitical Texas-Mexico borderlands to encompass psychic, sexual, and spiritual Borderlands. These B/borderlands— in both their geographical and metaphorical meanings—represent intensely painful yet also potentially transformational spaces where opposites converge, conflict, and transform.

cenote: Cenotes are sinkholes that connect to underground water. Anzaldúa borrows this concept from Mayan sacrificial practices and Jungian psychology, using it in her epistemology and aesthetics, where it represents "an underground well of shamanic images," intuitive types of information and knowledge, our connections with various realms, and so on.

Coatlicue: An autochthonous earth god/dess. According to Aztec mythic history, Coatlicue (Kwat-LEE-kway), whose name means "Serpent Skirts," is the earth goddess of life and death and mother of the gods. As Anzaldúa explains in the fourth chapter of *Borderlands*, Coatlicue has a horrific appearance, with a skirt of serpents and a necklace of human skulls. According to some versions of the story, after being impregnated by a ball of feathers, Coatlicue was killed by her daughter Coyolxauhqui and her other children.

Coatlicue state: An important element in Anzaldúa's epistemology; she coined this term to represent the resistance to new knowledge and other psychic states triggered by intense inner struggle, which can entail the juxtaposition and the transmutation of contrary forces, as well as paralysis and depression. Anzaldúa associates the Coatlicue state with a variety of situations, including depression, creativity, and writing blocks. These psychic conflicts are analogous to those she experiences as a Chicana; she explains that the opposing Mexican, Indian, and Anglo worldviews she has internalized lead to self-division, cultural confusion, and shame.

conocimiento: A Spanish word for "knowledge" or "consciousness," Anzaldúa uses this term to represent a key component of her post-*Borderlands* onto-epistemology. With conocimiento, she elaborates on the potentially transformative elements of her earlier theories of mestiza consciousness and la facultad. Like mestiza consciousness, conocimiento represents a nonbinary, connectionist mode of thinking; like la facultad, conocimiento often unfolds within oppressive contexts and entails a deepening of perception. With conocimiento, Anzaldúa underscores and develops the imaginal, spiritual-activist, and radically inclusionary possibilities implicit in these earlier theories.

conocimientos: While "conocimiento" refers to the theory in general (see above), "conocimientos" refers to specific insights acquired through the process of conocimiento. This distinction is an important one, according to Anzaldúa.

Coyolxauhqui: According to Aztec mythic history, Coyolxauhqui (Ko-yol-sha-UH-kee), also called "la diosa de la luna" (goddess of the moon), was Coatlicue's oldest daughter. After her mother was impregnated by a ball of feathers, Coyolxauhqui encouraged her four hundred brothers and sisters to kill Coatlicue. As they attacked their mother, the fetus Huitzilopochtli sprang fully grown and armed from Coatlicue, tore Coyolxauhqui into more than a thousand pieces, flung her head into the sky and her body down the sacred mountain, and killed his siblings. Coyolxauhqui became increasingly important to Anzaldúa throughout the years.

Coyolxauhqui imperative: Drawing from the story of Coyolxauhqui, Anzaldúa developed this theory to describe a complex healing process, an inner compulsion or desire to move from fragmentation to complex wholeness. As she explains in "Speaking across the Divide," "The path of the artist, the creative impulse, what I call the Coyolxauhqui imperative, is basically an attempt to heal the wounds. It's a search for inner completeness." Anzaldúa often associated this imperative with cultural trauma and other individual and collective woundings, as well as her desire to write. She folds her theories of the Coyolxauhqui process (which she describes in chapter 2 as "a sort of shamanic initiatory dismemberment that gives suffering a spiritual and soulful value") into the Coyolxauhqui imperative.

El Mundo Zurdo: One of Anzaldúa's earliest, least discussed concepts, El Mundo Zurdo (The Lefthand World) has various ethical, epistemological, and aesthetic definitions. Most generally, El Mundo Zurdo represents relational difference. Applied to alliances, it indicates communities based on commonalities, visionary locations where people from diverse backgrounds with diverse needs and concerns coexist and work together to bring about revolutionary change. In the late 1970s, Anzaldúa initiated a reading series and writing workshops called "El Mundo Surdo." These readings and workshops, while grounded in women-of-color perspectives, were diverse and open to progressive people of any identity.

Geographies of selves/geography of self: An identity-related theory that underscores the potentially relational, multiplicitous, hybrid nature of identity, as well as our porous boundaries. As Anzaldúa writes in her chapter annotations, "The geography of our identity is vast, has many nations. Where you end and the world begins is not easy to distinguish. Like a river flooding its bank, cutting a new channel that winds in a new direction, we escape our skin, our present identity and forge a new one." Anzaldúa associates this theory with her theories of the new tribalism and árbol de la vida.

Guadalupe: Also known as "La Virgen de Guadalupe," she appeared to Juan Diego in 1531 with a message. Generally viewed as a more recent version of the indigenous goddess Tonantzin, Guadalupe represents a synthesis of multiple traditions. In *Borderlands/La Frontera* Anzaldúa describes her as "the single most potent religious, political, and cultural image of the Chicano/mexicano."

Huitzilopochtli: An Aztec sun god and god of war. He sprang, fully developed and armed, from his mother, Coatlicue, and dismembered his sister Coyolxauhqui (see above).

La Chingada: Literally translated to English as "the fucked one," this term is often associated with Malinche, the indigenous woman given to Hernán Cortés upon his arrival on the continent and, as such, the symbolic mother of the Mexican people.

la facultad: Anzaldúa's term for an intuitive form of knowledge that includes but goes beyond logical thought and empirical analysis. As she explains in *Borderlands/La Frontera*, it is "the capacity to see in surface phenomena the meaning of deeper realities, to see the deep structure below the surface. It is an instant 'sensing,' a quick perception arrived at without conscious reasoning[;] .... an acute awareness mediated by the part of the psyche that does not speak, that communicates in images and symbols which are the faces of feelings." While la facultad is most often developed by those who have been disempowered (or as Anzaldúa puts it, "pushed out of the tribe for being different"), it is latent in everyone.

La Llorona: Sometimes referred to as the "Weeping Woman," Llorona is a central figure in Mexican, Mexican American, and Chicano/a folklore, as well as an important presence in Anzaldúa's work. There are many different versions of the story, but in most versions Llorona is the ghost of a beautiful young woman, seduced and abandoned by a man, who kills her children (usually by drowning). She is destined to wander forever, crying for her lost children.

mestiza consciousness: One of Anzaldúa's best-known concepts, this "consciousness of the Borderlands" is a holistic, both/and way of thinking and acting that includes a transformational tolerance for contradiction and ambivalence.

mestizaje: The Spanish word for "mixture," mestizaje, in Anzaldúa's work, generally refers to transformed combinations.

naguala: The Nahuatl word for shapeshifter, Anzaldúa uses this term in a variety of ways, including shapeshifter, shaman, guardian spirit, epistemological faculty, inspiration, and inner guide. She associates it with the creative process, magical thinking, and various types of shapeshifting.

nagualismo: Variously defined as a "Mesoamerican magic supernaturalism," a Toltec worldview, shamanism, world traveling, an alternative, folk epistemology, and (especially) shapeshifting. Anzaldúa associates nagualismo with "spirituality, spiritual activism, mestiza consciousness, and the role of nepantla and nepantleras" (chapter 2).

nepantla: A Nahuatl word meaning "in-between space." Anzaldúa used this term (and it uses her) to develop her post-*Borderlands* theory of process, liminality, and potential change that builds on her theories of the Borderlands and the Coatlicue state. For Anzaldúa, nepantla represents temporal, spatial, psychic, and intellectual point(s) of crisis (among other things). Nepantla occurs during the many transitional stages of life and can describe issues and concerns related to identity, aesthetics, epistemology, and/or ontology.

nepantleras: A term Anzaldúa coined to describe a unique type of mediator, those who have survived (and been transformed by) their encounters with/in nepantla. Nepantleras are threshold people, living within and among multiple worlds; through painful negotiations, they develop what Anzaldúa describes as "perspective[s] from the cracks." They use these transformed perspectives to invent holistic, relational theories and tactics that enable them to reconceive or in other ways transform the various worlds in which they exist.

new mestiza: Anzaldúa's theory of the "new mestiza" represents an innovative expansion of previous biologically-based definitions of mestizaje. For Anzaldúa, "new mestizas" are people who inhabit multiple worlds because of their gender, sexuality, color, class, bodies, personality, spiritual beliefs, and/or other life experiences. This theory offers a new concept of personhood that synergistically combines apparently contradictory Euro-American and indigenous traditions. Anzaldúa further develops her theory of the new mestiza into an epistemology and ethics she calls "mestiza consciousness" (see above).

new tribalism: Anzaldúa develops this theory in dialogue with criticisms of *Borderlands/La Frontera*, challenging readers who viewed her concept of mestizaje as narrow nationalism or essentializing. With her theory of a planetary new tribalism, she attempts to develop an affinity-based approach to alliance-making and identity formation, offering provocative alternatives to both assimilation and separatism.

nos/otras: A theory of intersubjectivity Anzaldúa developed in her post-*Borderlands* writings. "Nosotras," the Spanish word for the feminine "we," indicates a type of group identity or consciousness. By partially dividing "nosotras" into two, Anzaldúa affirms this collective yet also acknowledges the sense of divisiveness so often felt in contemporary life (*nos* implies *us*, while *otras* implies *others*). Joined together, nos+otras holds the promise of healing: We contain the others; the others contain us. Significantly, nos/otras does not represent sameness; the differences among "us" still exist, but they function dialogically, generating previously unrecognized commonalities and connections. Anzaldúa's theory of nos/otras offers an alternative to binary self-other constellations, a philosophy and praxis that enables us to acknowledge, bridge, and sometimes transform the distances between self and other.

spiritual activism: Although Anzaldúa did not coin this term, she used it to describe her visionary, experientially-based epistemology and ethics, as well as an aspect of her theory of conocimiento. At the epistemological level, spiritual activism posits a metaphysics of interconnectedness and employs non-binary modes of thinking. At the ethical level, spiritual activism requires concrete actions designed to intervene in and transform existing social conditions. Spiritual activism is spirituality for social change, spirituality that recognizes the many differences among us, yet insists on our commonalities and uses these commonalities as catalysts for transformation.

susto(s): Anzaldúa describes susto as a Mexican "indigenous belief" (see Anzaldúa, *The Gloria Anzaldúa Reader*, 79), which she uses to represent soul loss—individual/collective trauma, fragmentation, and other wounds caused by sexism, homophobia, "racism, and other acts of violation." As she explains in her chapter annotations, "During or after the original trauma we lose parts of our souls as an immediate strategy to minimize the pain. This keeps you from being with your whole soul." She associates susto with the Coyolxauhqui imperative, desconocimientos, nepantla, and the shadow beast.

Yemayá: According to Yoruban beliefs, Yemayá is the orisha (goddess) associated with the oceans and other waters.

BIBLIOGRAPHY

Alaimo, Stacy, and Susan Hekman. "Introduction: Emerging Models of Materiality in Feminist Theory." In *Material Feminisms*, ed. Stacy Alaimo and Susan Hekman, 1–19. Bloomington: Indiana University Press, 2008.

Alarcón, Norma. "Anzaldúan Textualities: A Hermeneutic of the Self and the Coyolxauhqui Imperative." In *El Mundo Zurdo 3: Selected Works from the 2012 Meeting of the Society for the Study of Gloria Anzaldúa*, ed. Larissa M. Mercado-López, Sonia Saldívar-Hull, and Antonia Castañeda, 189–206. San Francisco: Aunt Lute, 2013.

Alexander, M. Jacqui, Lisa Albrecht, Sharon Day, Mab Segrest, ed. *Sing, Whisper, Shout, Pray! Feminist Visions for a Just World*. San Francisco: Edgework Books, 2003.

Anzaldúa, Gloria E. *Borderlands/La Frontera: The New Mestiza*. San Francisco: Aunt Lute, 1985.

———. "Foreword to *Cassell's Encyclopedia of Queer Myth, Symbol and Spirit: Gay, Lesbian, Bisexual and Transgender Lore*" (1996). In *The Gloria Anzaldúa Reader*, ed. AnaLouise Keating, 229–31. Durham, NC: Duke University Press, 2009.

———. *The Gloria Anzaldúa Reader*, ed. AnaLouise Keating. Durham, NC: Duke University Press, 2009.

———. "Haciendo caras, una entrada." In *Making Face, Making Soul/Haciendo Caras: Creative and Critical Perspectives by Women of Color*, ed. Gloria Anzaldúa, xv–xxviii. San Francisco: Aunt Lute Foundation, 1990.

———. *Interviews/Entrevistas*, ed. AnaLouise Keating. New York: Routledge, 2000.

———. "now let us shift . . . the path of conocimiento . . . inner work, public acts." In *this bridge we call home: radical visions for transformation*, ed. Gloria E. Anzaldúa and AnaLouise Keating, 540–78. New York: Routledge, 2002.

———. *Prietita and the Ghost Woman/Prietita y la Llorona*. Ill. Maya Christina Gonzalez. San Francisco: Children's Book Press, 1995.

———. "Speaking across the Divide" (2003). In *The Gloria Anzaldúa Reader*, ed. AnaLouise Keating, 282–94. Durham, NC: Duke University Press, 2009.

———. "Speaking in Tongues: A Letter to Third World Women Writers" (1981). In *The Gloria Anzaldúa Reader*, ed. AnaLouise Keating, 26–35. Durham, NC: Duke University Press, 2009.

———. "Tihueque" (1974). In *The Gloria Anzaldúa Reader*, ed. AnaLouise Keating, 19. Durham, NC: Duke University Press, 2009.

Anzaldúa, Gloria E., and AnaLouise Keating, eds. *this bridge we call home: radical visions for transformation*. New York: Routledge, 2002.

Anzaldúa, Gloria E., and Hector A. Torres. "The Author Never Existed" (1990). In *Conversations with Contemporary Chicana and Chicano Authors*, ed. Hector A. Torres, 115–45. Albuquerque: University of New Mexico Press, 2007.

Assagioli, Roberto. *Psychosynthesis: A Manual of Principles and Techniques*. New York: Viking, 1965.

Aung San Suu Kyi. "Freedom from Fear." Acceptance speech for the 1990 Sakharov Prize for Freedom of Thought, July 1991.

Atchity, Kenneth. *A Writer's Time*. New York: W. W. Norton, 1986.

Ballard, J. G. *Crash* (1973), French edition. Paris: Calmann-Lévy, 1974.

Barad, Karen. *Meeting the Universe Halfway: Quantum Physics and the Entanglement of Matter and Meaning*. Durham, NC: Duke University Press, 2007.

Bieger, Laura, Ramón Saldívar, and Johannes Voelz, eds. *The Imaginary and Its Worlds: American Studies after the Transnational Turn*. Lebanon, NH: Dartmouth College Press, 2013.

Borges, Jorge Luis. *Ficciones* (1944), trans. Emceé Editores. New York: Grove, 1962.

Bosnak, Robert. *A Little Course in Dreams*. Boston: Shambhala, 1986.

Bost, Suzanne. "Diabetes, Culture, and Food: Posthumanist Nutrition in the Gloria Anzaldúa Archive." In *Rethinking Chicana/o Literature through Food: Postnational Appetites*, ed. Nieves Pascual Soler and Meredith E. Abarca, 27–43. New York: Palgrave Macmillan, 2014.

———. *Encarnación: Illness and Body Politics in Chicana Literature*. New York: Fordham University Press, 2010.

———. "Messy Archives and Materials That Matter: Making Knowledge with the Gloria Evangelina Anzaldúa Papers. *PMLA* 130, no. 3 (May 2015).

Bradbury, Ray. *The Illustrated Man*. New York, Bantam, 1976.

Brett, Guy. *Transcontinental: An Investigation of Reality*. London: Verso, 1990.

Brinton, Daniel G. *Nagualism: A Study of Native American Folk-lore and History*. Philadelphia: MacCalla, 1894.

Brundage, Burr Cartwright. *The Fifth Sun: Aztec Gods, Aztec World*. Austin: University of Texas Press, 1979.

Bryant, Levi, Nick Srnicek, and Graham Harman, eds. *The Speculative Turn: Continental Materialism and Realism*. Melbourne: Re.press, 2011.

Carrasco, David, and Roberto Lint Sagarena. "The Religious Vision of Gloria Anzaldúa: *Borderlands/La Frontera* as a Shamanic Space." In *Mexican American Religions: Spirituality, Activism, and Culture*, ed. Gastón Espinosa, 223–41. Durham, NC: Duke University Press, 2008.

Castaneda, Carlos. *The Art of Dreaming*. New York: HarperCollins, 1993.

———. *The Eagle's Gift*. New York: Simon and Schuster, 1982.

———. *The Fire from Within*. London: Transworld, 1984.

———. *Journey to Ixtlan*. Harmondsworth, UK: Penguin, 1974.

———. *The Power of Silence*. New York: Simon and Schuster, 1987.

———. *The Second Ring of Power*. New York: Simon and Schuster, 1979.

———. *Tales of Power*. New York: Simon and Schuster, 1974.

Chalmers, David J. "The Puzzles of Conscious Experience." *Scientific American*, vol. 273, December 1995, 62–68.

Cheng, Anne Anlin. *The Melancholy of Race: Psychoanalysis, Assimilation, and Hidden Grief*. Oxford: Oxford University Press, 2001.

Churchill, Ward. "Spiritual Hucksterism: The Rise of Plastic Medicine Men." In *Fantasies of the Master Race*, ed. M. Annette Jaimes, 215–28. Monroe, ME: Common Courage, 1992.

Cohen, Leonard. "Anthem." On *The Future*. Compact Disc, Columbia, New York, 1992.

Colebrook, Clare. "On Not Becoming Man: The Materialist Politics of Unactualized Potential." In *Material Feminisms*, ed. Stacy Alaimo and Susan Heckman, 52–84. Bloomington: Indiana University Press, 2008.

Conner, Randy P. "Santa Nepantla: A Borderlands Sutra" (Plenary Speech). In *El Mundo Zurdo: Selected Works from the Meetings of the Society for the Study of Gloria Anzaldúa 2007 and 2009*, ed. Norma E. Cantú, Christina L. Guttiérrez, Norma Alarcón, and Rita E. Urquijo-Ruiz, 177–202. San Francisco: Aunt Lute, 2010.

Contreras, Sheila Marie. "Literary Primitivism and the New Mestiza." *Interdisciplinary Literary Studies* 8, no. 1 (Fall 2006): 49–71.

Coole, Diana, and Samantha Frost. "Introduction." In *New Materialisms: Ontology, Agency, and Politics*, ed. Diana Coole and Samantha Frost. Durham, NC: Duke University Press, 2010.

Corbin, Henry. "Mundus Imaginalis, or the Imaginary and the Imaginal" (1964). In *Swedenborg and Esoteric Islam*, trans. Leonard Fox. West Chester, PA: Swedenborg Foundation, 1995.

Crowley, Karlyn. *Feminism's New Age: Gender, Appropriation, and the Afterlife of Essentialism*. Buffalo: State University of New York Press, 2011.

Dahms, Betsy. "Shamanic Urgency and Two-Way Movement as Writing Style in the Works of Gloria Anzaldúa." *Letras Femeninas* 38, no. 2 (2012): 9–26.

Damasio, Antonio. *The Feeling of What Happens: Body and Emotion in the Making of Consciousness*. New York: Harcourt, 1999.

Darder, Antonia, and Rudolfo D. Torres, eds. *The Latino Studies Reader: Culture, Economy and Society*. Malden, MA: Blackwell, 1998.

Deleuze, Gilles, and Félix Guattari. "Introduction: Rhizome." In *A Thousand Plateaus: Capitalism and Schizophrenia*, trans. Brian Massumi, 3–25. Minneapolis: University of Minnesota Press, 1987.

———. *Rhizôme*. Paris: Minuit, 1976.

Deloria Jr., Vine. "Foreword/American Fantasy." In *The Pretend Indian: Images of Native Americans in the Movies*, ed. Gretchen M. Bataille and Charles L. P. Silet, ix–xvi. Ames: Iowa State University Press, 1980.

Deng Ming-Deo, *365 Dao Daily Meditations*. New York: Harperone, 1992.

Eagle Feather, Ken. *A Toltec Path: A User's Guide to the Teachings of Don Juan Matus, Carlos Castaneda, and Other Toltec Seers*. Norfolk, VA: Hampton Roads, 1995.

———. *Traveling with Power*. Norfolk, VA: Hampton Roads, 1992.

Eliade, Mircea. *Shamanism: Archaic Techniques of Ecstasy* (1951), trans. W. R. Trask. Princeton, NJ: Princeton University Press, 1964.

Furst, Jill Leslie McKeever. *The Natural History of the Soul in Ancient Mexico*. New Haven, CT: Yale University Press, 1997.

Gaspar de Alba, Alicia. "Crop Circles in the Cornfield: Remembering Gloria E. Anzaldúa (1942–2004)." *American Quarterly* 56, no. 3 (2004): iv–vii.

Greene, Jeffrey. "An Interview with Stanley Plumly." *Writer's Chronicle*, December 2000.

Grose, John H. *A Voyage to the East Indies, with Observations of Various Parts There*, vol. 1. London: Hooper and Morley, 1757.

Grosz, Elizabeth. "Darwin and Feminism: Preliminary Investigations for a Possible Alliance." In *Material Feminisms*, ed. Stacy Alaimo and Susan Heckman, 237–64. Bloomington: Indiana University Press, 2008.

Halifax, Joan. *Shamanic Voices: A Survey of Visionary Voices*. New York: E.P. Dutton, 1979.

———. *Shaman: The Wounded Healer*. New York: Thames and Hudson, 1988.

Hall, Edward T., and Mildred Reed Hall. "The Sounds of Silence." In *Conformity and Conflict: Readings in Cultural Anthropology*, ed. James P. Spradley and David W. McCurdy. Boston: Little, Brown, 1987.

Hall, Stuart. "Gramsci's Relevance for the Study of Race and Ethnicity." In *Stuart Hall: Critical Dialogues in Cultural Studies*, ed. David Morley and Kuan-Hsing Chen, 411–41. New York: Routledge, 1996.

Harjo, Joy. "A Postcolonial Tale." In *The Woman Who Fell from the Sky*, 18–19. New York: W. W. Norton, 1994.

Harman, Graham. *Guerrilla Metaphysics: Phenomenology and the Carpentry of Things*. Chicago: Open Court, 2005.

———. *Tool-Being: Heidegger and the Metaphysics of Objects*. Chicago: Open Court, 2002.

———. *Towards Speculative Realism: Essays and Lectures*. Winchester, UK: Zero Books, 2010.

Harner, Michael. *The Way of the Shaman: A Guide to Power and Healing* (1980). New York: Bantam, 1982.

Hartley, George. "Chican@ Indigeneity, the Nation-State, and Colonialist Identity Formations." In *Comparative Indigeneities of the Américas: Toward a Hemispheric Approach*, ed. M. Bianet Castellanos, Lourdes Gutiérrez Nájera, and Arturo J. Aldama, 53–66. Tucson: University of Arizona Press, 2012.

Haslanger, Sally. "Feminism in Metaphysics: Negotiating the Natural." In *The Cambridge Companion to Feminism in Philosophy*, ed. Miranda Fricker and Jennifer Hornsby, 107–26. Cambridge: Cambridge University Press, 2000.

Hawkins, David R. *Power versus Force: The Hidden Determinants of Human Behavior* (1995), rev. ed. Carlsbad, CA: Hay House, 2002.

Heath, Jennifer. "Women Artists of Color Share World of Struggle." *Sunday Camera*, March 8, 1992, 9C.

Hekman, Susan. "Constructing the Ballast: An Ontology for Feminism." In *Material Feminisms*, ed. Stacy Alaimo and Susan Hekman, 85–119. Bloomington: Indiana University Press, 2008.

Henderson-Espinoza, Robyn. "The Entanglement of Anzaldúan Materiality as Bodily Knowing: Matter, Meaning, and Interrelatedness." PhD diss., Iliff School of Theology, Denver, 2015.

Hernández, Ellie D. *Postnationalism in Chicana/o Literature and Culture*. Austin: University of Texas Press, 2009.

Hillman, James. *The Dream and the Underworld*. New York: William Morrow, 1979.

———. "Going Bugs." *Spring* (1988): 40–72.

———. *Healing Fictions*. Dallas, TX: Spring, 1983.

———. *The Myth of Analysis: Three Essays in Archetypal Psychology*. Evanston, IL: Northwestern University Press, 1972.

———. "Peaks and Vales: The Soul/Spirit Distinction as Basis for the Differences between Psychotherapy and Spiritual Discipline." In *Puer Papers*, ed. James Hillman et al., 54–74. Dallas, TX: Spring, 1974.

Hogan, Linda. *Dwellings: A Spiritual History of the Living World*. New York: Simon and Schuster, 1995.

Houston, Jean. "Cyber Consciousness." *Yes! Magazine*, Spring 2000.

———. *Possible Human, Possible World.* Videocassette. Thinking Allowed Productions, 1992.

———. *The Search for the Beloved: Journeys in Sacred Psychology.* Los Angeles: Jeremy P. Tarcher, 1987.

Hurtado, Aída. *Voicing Chicana Feminisms: Young Women Speak Out on Sexuality and Identity.* New York: New York University Press, 2003.

Ingram, Sandra. *Soul Retrieval: Mending the Fragmented Self.* New York: HarperCollins, 1991.

Jacobs, Don Trent. *Primal Awareness.* Rochester, VT: Inner Traditions, 1998.

Jacobson, Matthew Frye. *Whiteness of a Different Color: European Immigrants and the Alchemy of Race.* Cambridge, MA: Harvard University Press, 1998.

Jameson, Fredric. "On Negt and Kluge." *October* 46 (Fall 1988): 151–77.

JanMohamed, Abdul R. "The Economy of Manichean Allegory: The Function of Racial Difference in Colonialist Literature." *Critical Inquiry* 12 (1985): 59–87.

Jordan, Rosan A. "The Vaginal Serpent and Other Themes from Mexican-American Women's Lore." In *Women's Folklore, Women's Culture,* ed. Rosan A. Jordan and Susan J. Kalčik, 26–44. Philadelphia: University of Pennsylvania Press, 1985.

Jung, C. G. *Collected Works,* vol. 7, ed. H. Read, M. Fordham, G. Adler, and W. McGuire, trans. R.F.C. Hull, Bollingen Series 20. Princeton, NJ: Princeton University Press, 1971.

———. *Letters: Volume 1, 1906–1950,* ed. Gerhard Adler and Aniela Jaffe, trans. R.F.C. Hull, Bollingen Series XCV: 1. Princeton, NJ: Princeton University Press, 1973.

Keating, AnaLouise. "Archival Alchemy and Allure: The Gloria Evangelina Anzaldúa Papers as Case Study." *Aztlán: A Journal of Chicano Studies* 35, no. 2 (2010): 159–71.

———. "'I'm a citizen of the universe': Gloria Anzaldúa's Spiritual Activism as Catalyst for Social Change." *Feminist Studies* 34 (2008): 53–69.

———. "Risking the Personal: An Introduction." In Gloria E. Anzaldúa, *Interviews/Entrevistas,* ed. AnaLouise Keating, 1–15. New York: Routledge, 2000.

———. "Speculative Realism, Visionary Pragmatism, and Poet-Shamanic Aesthetics in Gloria Anzaldúa—and Beyond." *Women's Studies Quarterly* 40, nos. 3–4 (2012): 51–69.

———. *Transformation Now! Toward a Post-Oppositional Politics of Change.* Urbana: University of Illinois Press, 2013.

———. *Women Reading Women Writing: Self-Invention in Paula Gunn Allen, Gloria Anzaldúa and Audre Lorde.* Philadelphia: Temple University Press, 1996.

———. "'Working towards wholeness': Gloria Anzaldúa's Struggles to Live with Diabetes and Chronic Illness." In *The Cultural Mediations of Latina Health,* ed.

Angie Chabram-Dernersesian and Adela de la Torres, 133–43. Tucson: University of Arizona Press, 2008.

Keyes, Margaret Frings. *Emotions and the Enneagram: Working through Your Shadow Life Script*. Muir Beach, CA: Molysdatur, 1992.

Koegeler-Abdi, Martina. "Shifting Subjectivities: Mestizas, Nepantleras, and Gloria Anzaldúa's Legacy." MELUS 38, no. 2 (2013): 71–88.

Kripal, Jeffrey J. *Comparing Religions: Coming to Terms*. Malden, MA: Wiley-Blackwell, 2014.

Lara, Irene. "Daughter of Coatlicue: An Interview with Gloria Anzaldúa." In *EntreMundos/AmongWorlds: New Perspectives on Gloria Anzaldúa*, ed. AnaLouise Keating, 41–55. New York: Palgrave Macmillan, 2005.

Lee, Barbara. 2001. *Sojourner*, October 2001, 5.

Levine, Amala. "Champion of the Spirit: Anzaldúa's Critique of Rationalist Epistemology." In *EntreMundos/AmongWorlds: New Perspectives on Gloria Anzaldúa*, ed. AnaLouise Keating, 171–84. New York: Palgrave Macmillan, 2005.

Lévi-Strauss, Claude. "The Effectiveness of Symbols." In *Structural Anthropology*, 186–205. New York: Basic Books, 1963.

———. *Structural Anthropology*. New York: Basic Books, 1963.

Lispector, Clarice. "Since One Feels Obliged to Write . . ." In *Lives on the Line: The Testimony of Contemporary Latin American Authors*, ed. Doris Meyer, trans. Giovanni Pontiero. Berkeley: University of California Press, 1988.

Lomas Garza, Carmen. *Family Pictures/Cuadros de familia*. San Francisco: Children's Book Press, 1990.

Lommel, Andreas. *The Beginnings of Art*. New York: McGraw-Hill, 1967.

Markman, Roberta H., and Peter T. Markman, eds. *Masks of the Spirit: Image and Metaphor in Mesoamerica*. Berkeley: University of California Press, 1989.

Martínez, Ernesto. *On Making Sense: Queer Race Narratives of Intelligibility* (Stanford, CA: Stanford University Press, 2013.

McNiff, Shaun. *Art as Medicine: Creating a Therapy of the Imagination*. Boston: Shambhala, 1992.

Meigs, Jane H. "Sailing Towards a Sustainable Shore." *Symposium: The Journal of the Millbrook Symposium* (Winter 2002).

Mesa-Bains, Amalia. "El Mundo Femenino: Chicana Artists of the Movement—A Commentary on Development and Production." In CARA, *Chicano Art: Resistance and Affirmation*, ed. Richard Griswold Del Castillo, Teresa McKenna, and Yvonne Yarbro-Bejarano, 131–40. Los Angeles: Wight Art Gallery, University of California, 1991.

Mignolo, Walter D. *The Darker Side of the Renaissance: Literacy, Territoriality, and Colonization*. Ann Arbor: University of Michigan Press, 1995.

———. *Local Histories/Global Designs: Coloniality, Subaltern Knowledges, and Border Thinking*. Durham, NC: Duke University Press, 2000.

Mindell, Arnold. *Working with the Dreaming Body*. Boston: Routledge and Kegan Paul, 1985.

Montes, Amelia María de la Luz. "Glucose Logs: Anzaldúa and the Story of Blood." Paper presented at El Mundo Zurdo: An International Conference on the Life and Work of Gloria Anzaldúa, San Antonio, November 2013.

———. "Why Diabetes Is Not Like Any Other Disease . . . And What You Can Do about It!." http://labloga.blogspot.com/2012/09/why-diabetes-is-not-like-any-other.html. Accessed September 30, 2012.

Moore, Thomas. *Care of the Soul: A Guide for Cultivating Depth and Sacredness in Everyday Life*. New York: HarperCollins, 1992.

———. *The Re-Enchantment of Everyday Life*. New York: HarperCollins, 1996.

———. *The Soul of Sex: Cultivating Life as an Act of Love*. New York: HarperCollins, 1998.

———. *The Soul's Religion: Cultivating a Profoundly Spiritual Way of Life*. Audiobook Cassette, New York: HarperCollins, 2002.

Myss, Caroline. *Advanced Energy Anatomy*. Sounds True Audio Cassette, Boulder, CO, 2001.

———. *Why People Don't Heal and How They Can*. New York: Random House, 1998.

Noel, Daniel C. *The Soul of Shamanism: Western Fantasies, Imaginal Realities*. New York: Continuum, 1997.

Ohmer, Sarah. "Gloria E. Anzaldúa's Decolonizing Ritual de Conocimiento." *Confluencia* 26, no. 1 (2010): 141–53.

Omi, Michael, and Harold Winant. *Racial Formations in the United States: From the 1960s to the 1980s*. London: Routledge, 1986.

Ordoño, Cesar Macazaga. *Diccionario de la lengua nahuatl*. Mexico City: Editorial Innovación, 1979.

Palmer, Helen. *Enneagram: The Placement of Attention*. Credence Cassettes, 1994.

Pérez, Emma. "Gloria Anzaldúa: La Gran Nueva Mestiza Theorist, Writer, Activist-Scholar." NWSA *Journal* 17, no. 2 (2005): 1–10.

Pérez, Laura E. "Spirit Glyphs: Reimagining Art and Artist in the Work of Chicana Tlamatinime." *Modern Fiction Studies* 44, no. 1 (1998): 36–76.

Read, Margaret. "Two Goats on the Bridge." In *Peace Tales: World Folktales to Talk About*. North Haven, CT: Linnet Books, 1992.

Reuman, Ann E. 1995. "Coming into Play: An Interview with Gloria Anzaldúa." MELUS 25, no. 2 (Summer 2000): 3–45.

Rieff, David. "Professional Aztecs and Popular Culture." *New Perspectives Quarterly* 8, no. 2 (Winter 1991): 42–46.

Rose, Wendy. "For My People." In *Bone Dance: New and Selected Poems, 1965–1993*. Tucson: University of Arizona Press, 1994.

———. "The Great Pretenders: Further Reflections on White Shamanism." In *The State of Native America*, ed. M. Annette Jaimes, 403–21. Boston: South End, 1992.

Ruiz, Don Miguel. *The Four Agreements: A Practical Guide to Personal Freedom*. San Rafael, CA: Amber Allen, 1997.

Ryan, Marian. "An Interview with Andrea Barrett." *Writer's Chronicle*, vol. 32, no. 3, December 1999, 4–9.

Saldaña-Portillo, Josefina. "Who's the Indian in Azatlán? Re-Writing Mestizaje, Indianism, and Chicanismo from the Lacandón." In *The Latin American Subaltern Studies Reader*, ed. Ileana Rodríguez, 402–23. Durham, NC: Duke University Press, 2001.

Saldívar-Hull, Sonia. "Critical Introduction." In Gloria Anzaldúa, *Borderlands/La Frontera: The New Mestiza*, 2d ed. San Francisco: Aunt Lute, 1999.

Saldívar, José David. "Unsettling Race, Coloniality, and Caste: Anzaldúa's *Borderlands/La Frontera*, Martinez's *Parrot in the Oven*, and Roy's *God of Small Things*." *Cultural Studies* 21, nos. 2–3 (2007): 339–67.

Sanchez, Victor. *The Teachings of Don Carlos*, trans. Robert Nelson. Santa Fe, NM: Bear, 1995.

Sheldrake, Rupert. *Dogs That Know When Their Owners Are Coming Home and Other Unexplained Powers of Animals*. New York: Three Rivers, 2000.

Somers, Margaret R., and Gloria D. Gibson. 1994. "Reclaiming the 'Epistemological Other': Narrative and the Social Constitution of Identity." In *Social Theory and the Politics of Identity*, ed. Craig Calhoun, 58–59. Cambridge: Blackwell, 1994.

Strauch, Ralph. *The Reality Illusion: How You Make the World Your Experience* (1983). Barrytown, NY: Station Hill Press, 1989.

Tarnas, Richard. "The Great Initiation," in *Noetic Sciences Review* 47 (1998), 24–33,

Tart, Charles T. *Waking Up: Overcoming the Obstacles to Human Potential*. Boston: Shambhala, 1986.

Thobani, Sunera. "You Cannot Slaughter People into Submission." *Sojourner* (November 2001).

Torres, Edén E. *Chicana without Apology: The New Chicana Cultural Studies*. New York: Routledge, 2004.

Torres, Yolotl González. *Diccionario de mitología y religión de Mesoamérica*. Mexico City: Ediciones Larousse, 1995.

Tuhkanen, Mikko. "Mestiza Metaphysics." In *Queer Times, Queer Becomings*, ed. E. L. McCallum and Mikko Tuhkanen, 259–94. New York: State University of New York Press, 2011.

Turner, Edith. "The Reality of Spirits." *ReVision* 15, no. 1 (1992): 28–32.

Turner, Victor. *The Ritual Process: Structure and Anti-Structure*. Chicago: University of Chicago Press, 1969.

van Gennep, Arnold. *The Rites of Passage*, trans. Monika B. Vizedom and Gabrielle L. Caffee. Chicago: University of Chicago Press, 1961.

Vivancos Pérez, Ricardo. *Radical Chicana Poetics*. New York: Palgrave Macmillan, 2013.

Watkins, Mary. *Waking Dreams* (1976), 3rd ed. Dallas: Spring, 1984.

Wilson, Elizabeth A. "Organic Empathy: Feminism, Psychopharmaceuticals, and the Embodiment of Depression." In *Material Feminisms*, ed. Stacy Alaimo and Susan Hekman, 373–99. Bloomington: Indiana University Press, 2008.

Ybarra-Fausto, Tomás. "Grafica/Urban Iconography." In *Chicano Expressions: A New View in American Art*, 21–24. New York: INTAR Latin American Gallery, 1986.

Zaytoun, Kelli. "New Pathways towards Understanding Self-in-Relation: Anzaldúan (Re)Visions for Developmental Psychology." In *EntreMundos/Among Worlds: New Perspectives on Gloria E. Anzaldúa*, ed. AnaLouise Keating, 147–59. New York: Palgrave Macmillan, 2005.

———. "Theorizing at the Borders: Considering Social Location in Rethinking Self and Psychological Development." *NWSA Journal* 18, no. 2 (2006): 52–72.

INDEX

Anzaldúa, Gloria (*continued*)
xxxvi–xxxvii, 59–60, 66, 141, 182,
183–84; social justice vision, xxx;
speaking engagements ("gigs"),
76, 154, 167; theory, xxviii; writing
block(s), xi. *See also under individual titles. See also* diabetes; writing
process
appropriation, 48, 50; Anglos' 53; in
art, xxv, 58
árbol de la vida, 5, 23–25, 67, 68, 94,
140–41, 231n5, 241
archetypal experience, 5
archetype(s), xxvii, 55; cultural, 88;
Jungian, 28; mythic, 33. *See also*
cenote, el
arrebatamiento, 16, 24, 35. *See also*
conocimiento
arrebato, 9, 121–22, 124–26. *See also*
conocimiento
art, 7, 54, 63, 115, 178; Chicana/o, 59;
embodied, xxi; as medicine, 10;
healing, 92; as spiritual discipline,
40–41; transformational, xxiv, 10.
See also artist(s); border arte
artist(s), 50, 60, 62, 166, 168; border, 58, 59, 60; Chicana/o, 47, 62;
Chicana/Latina, 51–52, 56; as
chamana, 39–41; as healers, xxxii;
and nepantla, 57; subjugated,
xxiv; vocation, 10
artist-activist, x, 82
Asia, 12
Assagioli, Roberto, 186
assimilation, xxv, xxxii, 53, 79,
233n17. *See also* new tribalism
astrology, 120
Atchity, Kenneth, 115
Aung San Suu Kyi, 92
autobiography. *See* autohistoria(s);
autohistoria-teoría(s); genre

autohistoria(s), x, xxiii, 4, 142–43, 147,
177; and border art, 62; defined,
6, 206n4, 238n14, 241; ethnic, 169.
See also autohistoria-teoría(s);
fiction
autohistoria-teoría(s), x, xxiii, xxvii,
xxix, xxxiv, 168; defined, 6, 206n4,
238n14, 241–42; as method, 3. *See
also* autohistoria(s); *Borderlands/
La Frontera*
awareness, 178, 186, 198; of self, 43.
See also conocimiento; perception
axis mundi, 25
axolotl, 26, 225n8
Aztec(s), 48, 53, 92; culture, 57. *See
also* indigenous

Baca, Judy, 59
bacteria, 43
Barajas, Rafael, 64
Barraza, Santa, xxv, 50–51, 52, 53
bearing witness, 10, 21
beliefs, 119, 150
binary thinking, xxxvi, 82, 142.
See also binaries; Cartesian split;
oppositionality
bin Laden, Osama,13, 16
binaries, 79; us/them, 77, 81. *See also*
binary thinking; oppositionality
biology, 66, 138–39
bisexual, 56, 81
body, 120, 132, 134–35, 138, 140, 142,
143, 151, 155, 156, 165; and creativity, 40; dreaming, 34; energetic, 128; as ground of thought,
5; knowledge, 24, 100, 115;
physical, 89; trans-temporal, 135;
and soul, 184. *See also* Coatlicue
state; diabetes; epistemology;
health; mind/body split; nepantla;
spirit(s); writing

bodymindsoul, 24, 133. *See also* body; spirit(s)

border: Mexico-U.S., 54, 63, 221n3; as mobile, 48

border arte, 44, 62; defined, xxiv. *See also* border artists

border artists, xxiv, 53

borderland(s), xxxiv, 57, 64, 242; theory of, xxv. See also *Borderlands/La Frontera*, border(s)

Borderlands/La Frontera: The New Mestiza, xi, xiv, xxiii, xxix, xxxiii, xxxiv, 219n80, 232n6, 244; as autohistoria-teoría, 242

border thinking, xxix, xxxvi

Borges, Jorge Luis, 57

Bost, Suzanne, 162, 207n7, 211n30

Bradbury, Ray, 233n12

bridge(s), 137, 147. *See also* nepantla; nepantlera(s); threshold

British literature, xxiv

Buddhism, 81

Bush, George W., 11, 12, 13, 14, 15, 16, 221n3, 222n10

Canada, 59, 132

capitalism, 118

Cartesian split, 135, 142, 238n12

Castaneda, Carlos, 32, 34, 55, 218n80, 225n13. *See also* Don Juan

Castellanos, Rosario, 103, 126

categories, 119. *See also* identities

Catholic Church, 30, 220

cenote, el, xxvi, 4, 36, 55–56, 57, 99, 108; of collective wisdom, 20; defined, xxv, 24, 66, 98, 242; inner, 58; multicultural, 88; and writing, 104, 177

chakras, 123, 138, 238n8

chamana, la, 155–56, 223n2; journeying, 25–26

chamanería, 37. *See also* shamanism

change, 86, 89, 137, 156, 159

chaos theory, 101, 103

Chicana(s), 76, 136, 183; literature, 166, 169

Chicana/o: artists, 48; intersections with Native Americans, 51, 53, 54; theory, 168, 169 writers, 7, 49

Chicana/mestiza, 3, 49–50, 166

Christianity, 120. *See also* Catholic Church

Cihuacoatl, 96, 121, 166

citizens: planetary, xxxvi, 168, 205n1; world, 22, 81, 85, 141. *See also* planetary citizenship

class, 73, 86, 135, 186; and knowledge production, 167. *See also* identity

Coatlicue, xv, xxi, 124, 242. *See also* Coatlicue state; Coyolxauhqui; serpent(s)

Coatlicue state, xxxiv, 123, 128–34, 142, 150, 219n86, 242. *See also* conocimiento

codices, 51, 59, 60

Cohen, Leonard, 84, 161

collaboration, 93

colonialism, xxxii, 48, 87, 166; and knowledge production, 167; mental, 182; U.S., xxiii. *See also*, Native Americans; neocolonialism; United States

colonization, 65, 119, 168; of the Americas, 54. *See also* United States

coming out, 56

commonalities, 20, 81, 154. *See also* El Mundo Zurdo; nepantlera(s); nos/otras; spiritual activism

common ground, 123, 144, 149

communication, 75, 93

compassion, 16, 19–20, 22, 92, 150, 181

complicity, xxiii, 21, 60, 82–83, 144,
    182; United States, 10, 11, 16
conflict, 83, 88, 144, 154, 239n19
connectionist thinking, 83, 149, 150,
    239n19, 243
Conner, Randy, 104, 106, 161, 162,
    218n77, 232n10, 237
conocimiento, x; xxxv, 40, 66, 137,
    153, 168; defined, xxvii, 18–19, 119,
    224n3, 234n26, 237n1, 243; path of
    xxiii, 46, 118–21, 142, 198; seven
    stages, 121–24; as spiritual prac-
    tice, 154; to be in, 91. See also
    arrebato; desconocimientos;
    nepantla; spiritual activism
conocimientos, x, 20, 92
consciousness, 44–45, 55, 134, 165,
    184, 224n2; awakening, 117; body,
    132; and chamanas, 24; colo-
    nized, 169; cosmic, 24, 35, 154;
    embodying, 105; hybrid, 79; and
    identity, 168, 186; kinesthetic, 129;
    negative, 22; ordinary, 7; rational,
    103; shifts, 139; transformed, 24;
    universal, 43. See also arrebato;
    conocimiento; desconocimien-
    tos; dreaming; dreams; mestiza
    consciousness
consumerism, 15, 118, 178
contemplation, 19, 92, 178
Contreras, Sheila, 219n80
conversion, 123, 134–38. See also
    conocimiento
corazón, 16, 153
Corbin, Henry, 177, 215–16n59,
    225n12
corn, 74, 107, 117, 233n15
Corpi, Lucha 130
cosmovisión, 118
Coyolxauhqui, xv, xxi; xxii, 8, 14,
    49, 51, 107, 124, 125, 128, 243;

fragmented, 17, 67–68; as healing
    image, 10, 143; as imaginal figure,
    7; modern-day, 139; the moon, 1,
    9, 103, 133, 178; and night, 172; as
    symbol, 19–20, 49, 50, 133, 214n47;
    tiempos de, 21; and writing, 108,
    109, 116. See also conocimiento;
    Coyolxauhqui consciousness;
    Coyolxahhqui imperative
Coyolxauhqui consciousness, xxi,
    135, 142
Coyolxauhqui imperative, xxi, xiii,
    xxvi, xxxv, 19–20, 22, 92, 214n46,
    232n9, 234n26, 246; defined, 1–2,
    243. See also writing
Coyolxauhqui process, xxiv, xxv,
    xxvi, 29, 74, 86–89, 189. See also
    writing
cracks between the worlds, 44, 71–73,
    93, 108,
creation, 40
creative process, x, xxxiv, 39–41, 96,
    100, 115
creativity, 2, 19, 40–41, 44, 83, 108, 140,
    149; and colonialism, 168. See also
    art; imagination; naguala; writing
crisis, 6, 17, 122, 245. See also Coat-
    licue state; identity; nepantla;
    transitions; trauma(s)
cultural trance, xxxvi
curandera(s), 29–39. See also cha-
    mana; curanderisimo; healing;
    shamanism; wound(s)
curanderisimo, xxiv, xxxiii, 44,
    215n49. See also curandera;
    shamanism
cyborg, 141

Dahms, Betsy, 162, 207n9, 215n54
daimon, 27, 131, 207n8, 220n2.
    See also nagual

20–21. See also Coyolxauhqui; curandera; spiritual activism; wound(s)

heart, 22, 27, 54; intellect, 117, 120; and story, 106, 109

heterosexual(s), 56, 57

Henderson-Espinoza, Robyn, 161, 217n71

Hillman, James, xxxiii, 2, 28, 29, 176–77, 207n8, 215–16n59, 220n2, 220n3, 225n12

Hiroshima, 12

history, 66. See autohistoria; colonialism; past; United States

Hogan, Linda, 178

homosexuality. See gay men; lesbian(s); queer(s)

hope, 125, 141, 142, 155. See also conocimiento; nepantleras; spiritual activism; transformation

hopelessness, 38, 123

Houston, Jean 153–54

Huitzilopochtli, xxi, 49, 107, 124, 244

Hurtado, Aída, 162

hyperrationality, 135. See also knowledge

I Ching, 120, 151, 218n77

idear, 2–3

identity, 2, 36, 64, 76, 89, 138, 165, 167–67, 182; categories, 66; crisis, 57, 61, 86, 118, 147; decolonized, 189; defined, 185; dismantling, 84; inclusive, 73; labels, 59, 77; loss, 179; multiple, xxxvii, 184, 185–86; mythic components, 166; narratives, 7, 140, 182–83; as process, 69, 71; racial, 83; rewriting, 75–76, 86–87; sexual, 135; shifts, xiii, 3, 82. See also identity politics; indig-enous; mestizaje; nepantla; new tribalism; nos/otras; way station

identity formation/construction, xxi, 3, 74, 166, 187. See also árbol de la vida; autohistoria-teoría; mestiza; new tribalism

identity politics, ix, 84. See also political correctness

illness, 133–34; chronic illness, 115; defined, xxxii. See also diabetes

image(s), 5–6, 35, 89–90, 98–100, 136, 177; and art-making, 4, 177; consciousness, 36; as daimonic forces, 28; healing, 29; and language, 49. See also imaginal; imagination; metaphor(s)

imaginal, xxvi, xxxi, 34, 38, 98, 215–16n59, 243; animal, 27; awareness, 4, 108; defined, 225n12; figures, xxx; identities, 36–37; intelligence, 36; in nagualismo, 7; states, 122; world, 236n11. See also image(s); mundus imaginalis

imaginary, the, 178, 215n59, 220n2, 225n12, 239n19

imagination, xi, xxiv, xxxiii, 2, 23, 26, 36–37, 90, 139, 165, 169, 236n11; and el cenote, 56, 58, 177; collective, 16; defined, 35; embodied, x; human, 98; and identity, 185, 186, 188–89; intellectual faculty, xxiii; and knowledge production, xxxiv, 218–19n80; and ontology, xxxiii; and reality, 35; and soul, 29; and transformation, 20, 44, 178. See also cenote, el; naguala; shaman aesthetics; soul

immigrant, 57, 67

inclusivity. See commonalities; new tribalism; nos/otras; spiritual activism

nagualismo, xxiv, 32, 102, 127–28,
226n14, 237n3, 245; Toltec, 44,
238n7
nahual. *See* naguala
nationalism, x, xxiii, 7, 68, 75; United
States, 11. *See also* new tribalism;
Raza
nationality, 66, 73
Native American(s), 53; appropriation of, 55; genocide, 15, 132. *See
also* Chicana/o; indigenous
Native American Studies, 181
Natural Bridges (Santa Cruz), 107
nature, xxxi, 38, 66, 77, 100, 140, 168;
designs, 101; ensouled, 117, 137,
141–42
near-death experiences, 34, 134
neocolonialism, xxiv, 12, 16, 169
neomaterialism, x, 217n72
neoshamanism, 225n13
nepantla, x, xiii, xxvi, xxvii, 35, 44,
55, 64, 90, 109, 122, 150, 168, 198,
246; agentic, xxxiv–xxxv; body,
34; brain, 82; as bridge, 28–29; and
el cenote, 98; and change, 86–87,
119; and creativity, 21, 62, 107–8;
as consciousness, xxvi, 114; dangers, 58; defined, 2, 17, 56, 237n2,
245; and identity, 186; and mestizas, 71–72; multiple, 2; people, 57;
perspective, 82; threshold, 133. *See
also* conocimiento
nepantlera(s), x, xxvi, xxvii, 44, 81–83,
94, 148, 156, 215n56; activism, 84;
artists/activists, 17; and conflict,
83, 148–49, 150–51, 155; defined,
xxxv–xxxvi, 245; and identity, 85,
93; and path of conocimiento,
126–28. *See also* new mestiza
nepantla body, xxiv
New Age, xxiv, 39, 227n34

new materialisms, xxx
new mestiza, xxvii, xxxvi, 71, 152, 245
new tribalism, x, xxxv, xxxvi, 7,
67–68, 85, 94, 140–41, 151–52, 156,
215n52; defined, xxv–xxvi, 232n6,
245–46. *See also* identity; Raza;
solidarity
New York City, 68–69
night, 103, 108–9, 170
9/11, xix, xxiii, 202; and susto,
9–10; U.S. response, 10–18
nos/otras, x, xxxv, 63, 76–77, 78,
79–81, 92–93, 141, 151, 152, 154,
215n56; and creativity, 168; defined, xxv–xxvii, 233n17, 246; imperative, 85; and self-identity, 185.
See also commonalities; identity;
spiritual activism
numerology, 120

object-oriented ontology, x, xxx, xxxi,
217n72
ocean, 66, 67, 95, 96, 98, 110, 155–56;
ensoulment, 101, 142; grieving, 10.
See also Yemayá
offering, 98, 117–18, 137
Ohmer, Sarah, xxix, 220n86
olla, la, 90–91, 100. *See also* creativity
Olmos, Edward James, 50, 53, 63
onto-epistemology, xxiii, 243
ontology, x, 205n1; 205n2; decolonizing, xxxiii; realism, xxix; transformational, xxix, xxxi. *See also*
decolonization; language; metaphysics of interconnectedness;
onto-epistemology; writing
oppositionality, 11, 126–27, 146–47,
233n17. *See also* identity;
nepantlera(s)
oppression, 154, 181. *See also* racism
Outer Limits, The, 103

pain, xiv, 9, 32, 45, 50, 68, 103, 132, 133–34; body, 138; as bridge, 231n4; emotional, 129, 131

"paisano is a bird of good omen, El," 66

Palestine, 13

patlache, xxxvii, 128, 141, 168

peace, 14, 19, 22, 149

people of color, 10, 57, 233n17; intellectuals, 167. See also women of color

perception, 41, 45, 238n7; doubled, 28, 45, 125, 127–28; hyperempathic, 104; shifts in, 16, 118, 131; whole body, 24. See also Coatlicue state; conocimiento; nepantla; "seeing through"

Pérez, Emma, 219n86

Pérez, Lourdes, 102

phenomenology, xv

philosophy: continental, xxx; and poetry, 168; western, xxix. See also poet

physical, xxx, 104; world, xxxi

physics, 232n7

planetary citizenship, xxxvi, 5, 20, 76, 149. See also citizen; spiritual activism

planets, 43

plants, 33, 117

Plumly, Stanley, 41

poet, 41, 59, 94, 103, 130; philosopher, 168, 169, 212

poetics, 6, 103, 108, 206n4, 214n46

poetry, 4, 41, 59, 94, 103, 109, 196, 208n13, 214n45

postcolonial subject, 165, 168

postnationalism, xxvi, 215n55

poststructuralism, xxxi

prayer, 90, 94, 141, 149, 154, 156–57, 173, 178; writer's, 102

"Prieta, La," 207n9

Prieta stories, x, 206n4, 207n6, 238n9, 238n15. See also autohistoria; autohistoria-teoría; Ensueños de la Prieta, Los

privilege(s), 60, 62, 73, 82, 169; Anzaldúa's, 3, 56. See also whiteness

process(es): spiritual, 5–6. See also writing

"Putting Coyolxauhqui Together," xxi, 138–43

psyche, 36, 39, 176

psychic: worlds, xxx. See also Mundo Zurdo, El; New Age

psychology, 138–39; archetypal, 55; of the image, 2, 227n37; western, 34, 38

Quan, Kit 161, 172, 221, 237

queer(s), 56, 57, 81, 128, 136, 198; body, 182. See also gay men; patlache; tortillera(s)

Quincentennial, 49

race, 7, 73, 82, 86, 119, 127, 135, 145, 156, 186; and knowledge production, 167. See also identity; mestizaje; new mestiza

race studies, 7

racial profiling, 14

racism, xxiii, xxxii, 1, 39, 65, 87, 143; white women's, 145. See also neoconservatives

rage, xxiii. See also anger

Raza, 68, 71, 73–74, 75, 84, 94, 183, 185, 188; narratives, 74. See also Chicana/o

Raza studies, xxv, 7, 84, 180, 181–82

reader(s), xi, 41–42, 95, 96, 110, 182; response theory, 166; as voyeur, 169. See also reading